the economics companion

Palgrave Student Companions are a one-stop reference resource providing essential information for students about the subject – and the course – they've chosen to study.

Friendly and authoritative, *Palgrave Student Companions* support the student throughout their degree. They encourage the reader to think about study skills alongside the subject matter of their course, offer guidance on module and career choices, and act as an invaluable source book and reference that they can return to time and again.

Palgrave Student Companions – your course starts here . . .

Published
The Economics Companion
The English Language and Linguistics Companion
The English Literature Companion
The Health Studies Companion
The MBA Companion
The Nursing Companion
The Politics Companion
The Psychology Companion
The Social Work Companion

Forthcoming
The Anthropology Companion
The History Companion
The Law Companion
The Media Studies Companion
The Sociology Companion
The Theatre, Drama and Performance Companion

www.palgravestudentcompanions.com

the **economics** companion

graham mallard

your course ... one source

palgrave
macmillan

© Graham Mallard 2012

All rights reserved. No reproduction, copy or transmission of this
publication may be made without written permission.

No portion of this publication may be reproduced, copied or transmitted
save with written permission or in accordance with the provisions of the
Copyright, Designs and Patents Act 1988, or under the terms of any licence
permitting limited copying issued by the Copyright Licensing Agency,
Saffron House, 6-10 Kirby Street, London EC1N 8TS.

Any person who does any unauthorized act in relation to this publication
may be liable to criminal prosecution and civil claims for damages.

The author has asserted his right to be identified
as the author of this work in accordance with the Copyright,
Designs and Patents Act 1988.

First published 2012 by
PALGRAVE MACMILLAN

Palgrave Macmillan in the UK is an imprint of Macmillan Publishers Limited,
registered in England, company number 785998, of Houndmills,
Basingstoke, Hampshire RG21 6XS.

Palgrave Macmillan in the US is a division of St Martin's Press LLC,
175 Fifth Avenue, New York, NY 10010.

Palgrave Macmillan is the global academic imprint of the above companies
and has companies and representatives throughout the world.
Palgrave® and Macmillan® are registered trademarks in the United States,
the United Kingdom, Europe and other countries.

ISBN : 978–0–230–23569–4

This book is printed on paper suitable for recycling and made from fully
managed and sustained forest sources. Logging, pulping and manufacturing
processes are expected to conform to the environmental regulations of the
country of origin.

A catalogue record for this book is available from the British Library.

A catalog record for this book is available from the Library of Congress.

10   9   8   7   6   5   4   3   2   1
21   20   19   18   17   16   15   14   13   12

Printed and bound in China

brief contents

list of figures and tables   xi
list of boxes   xv
acknowledgements   xvii
foreword   xviii
introduction   xx

1   what it's all about and how to study it   1

1   what is economics?   3

2   why study economics?   17

3   what to expect from your economics course   24

4   studying economics successfully   30

2   introducing smaller-scale analysis: the microeconomic world   55

5   what consumers buy   57

6   how much producers make and sell   87

7   when consumers and producers interact   108

8   when the interaction goes wrong   133

3   introducing larger-scale analysis: the macroeconomic world   151

9   the size of the economy   153

10   demand and supply but on a bigger scale   187

11   unemployment, money and inflation   200

12   the economy in its international setting   229

4 how it has all come about   241

13 the evolution of economics   243

14 the masters of the subject   252

5 where else to look   267

15 recommended resources   269

    index   273

contents

list of figures and tables   xi
list of boxes   xv
acknowledgements   xvii
foreword   xviii
introduction   xx

1   what it's all about and how to study it   1

1   what is economics?   3
1.1 the study of the allocation of limited resources?   3
1.2 the dismal science?   6
1.3 the study of money?   8
1.4 a way of thinking?   8
1.5 a branch of maths?   11
1.6 what is economics, then?   12
1.7 economics as a diverse social science   14
1.8 summary   15

2   why study economics?   17
2.1 understanding the wider world   17
2.2 other transferable skills   18
2.3 employment opportunities   19
2.4 summary   23

3   what to expect from your economics course   24
3.1 typical structure and content   24
3.2 selecting your course and modules   27
3.3 summary   29

4   studying economics successfully   30
4.1 tackling all the reading   30
4.2 tackling theoretical analysis: the diagrams and maths   37
4.3 tackling statistics   49
4.4 thinking critically   51
4.5 summary   54

2   introducing smaller-scale analysis: the microeconomic
    world   55

5   **what consumers buy**   **57**
    5.1 the products consumers would like to buy   57
    5.2 the products consumers can afford to buy   64
    5.3 the products consumers actually buy   66
    5.4 consumer demand   67
    5.5 determinants of demand   71
    5.6 elasticity of demand   77
    5.7 criticisms of the standard model   80
    5.8 summary   85

6   **how much producers make and sell**   **87**
    6.1 production costs   88
    6.2 revenue   94
    6.3 how much output producers make and sell   96
    6.4 supply   98
    6.5 criticisms of the standard model of producer behaviour 104
    6.6 summary   107

7   **when consumers and producers interact**   **108**
    7.1 market demand and supply analysis   109
    7.2 market welfare   112
    7.3 perfect competition   117
    7.4 pure monopoly   121
    7.5 monopolistic competition   126
    7.6 oligopoly   128
    7.7 summary   132

8   **when the interaction goes wrong**   **133**
    8.1 market power   134
    8.2 merit and demerit goods   136
    8.3 externalities   143
    8.4 summary   149

3   introducing larger-scale analysis: the macroeconomic
    world   151

9   **the size of the economy**   **153**
    9.1 a two-economy circular flow   153
    9.2 economic size and standard of living   160
    9.3 international comparisons of GDP   164
    9.4 determination of output in the long run: the classical
         model   165

9.5	determination of output in the short run: the Keynesian model	175
9.6	summary	186
10	**demand and supply but on a bigger scale**	**187**
10.1	aggregate demand	188
10.2	aggregate supply	190
10.3	the complete model	193
10.4	the IS-LM and AD-AS models compared	195
10.5	summary	199
11	**unemployment, money and inflation**	**200**
11.1	unemployment	200
11.2	money	210
11.3	inflation	216
11.4	inflation, unemployment and expectations	222
11.5	summary	228
12	**the economy in its international setting**	**229**
12.1	why economies trade	229
12.2	the trade balance and the national accounts identity	231
12.3	the nominal exchange rate	232
12.4	the real exchange rate and the trade balance	234
12.5	purchasing power parity	236
12.6	summary	239
4	**how it has all come about**	**241**
13	**the evolution of economics**	**243**
13.1	the development of economic thought	243
13.2	classical economics	243
13.3	neoclassical economics	246
13.4	Keynes's revolution	248
13.5	neoclassical economics – but with serious maths	249
13.6	a new chapter?	250
13.7	summary	251
14	**the masters of the subject**	**252**
14.1	Smith (1723–1790)	252
14.2	Ricardo (1772–1823)	253
14.3	Malthus (1766–1834)	254
14.4	Marx (1818–1883)	255
14.5	Marshall (1842–1924)	256
14.6	Keynes (1883–1946)	257
14.7	The Cambridge Circus	258

14.8 Hicks (1904–1989)   260
14.9 Friedman (1912–2006)   261
14.10 Simon (1916–2001)   262
14.11 Arrow (1921–)   263
14.12 Lucas (1937–)   264
14.13 Acemoğlu (1967–)   265
14.14 Saez (1972–)   265

5   where else to look   267
15   recommended resources   269
15.1 books   269
15.2 useful websites   271
15.3 interesting journal articles   272

index   273

list of figures and tables

figures

1.1	Some of the many applications of economics	9
1.2	Some of the many economic schools of thought	10
2.1a	Destinations of UK and EU graduates from the University of Bath in 2005: economics, and economics and politics, against all graduates	20
2.1b	Destinations of UK and EU graduates from the University of Bath in 2006: economics, and economics and politics, against all graduates	20
2.2	Destinations of UK and EU graduates of economics, and economics and politics	21
3.1	Economics degree programme at the University of Edinburgh	24
3.2	Economics degree programme at the University of Helsinki	25
3.3	Economics degree programme at the University of Bath	26
4.1	Preparing your reading	33
4.2	Example of diagrammatical analysis	41
5.1	Consumption bundles	59
5.2a	A well-behaved indifference curve	60
5.2b	A well-behaved indifference map	60
5.3	Why indifference curves should not cross	61
5.4	The budget line	65
5.5a	The budget line and increased income	65
5.5b	A change in the price of X	65
5.6	The consumption decision	66
5.7a	Price offer curve	67
5.7b	Demand curve	67
5.8a	Income offer curve for a normal product	69
5.8b	Engel curve for a normal product	69
5.9	Substitution and income effects	72

5.10	Outward shift in demand	75
B5.4	Linear inverse demand curve	76
6.1	The short run average cost curve	91
6.2	Short and long run average cost curves	92
6.3	Average and marginal cost curves in the short and long run	94
6.4	Profit maximisation	97
6.5a	Producer making normal profit	98
6.5b	Producer making sub-normal profit	98
6.6	Marginal cost and supply curves	100
6.7	Outward shift in supply	102
B6.2	Linear inverse supply curve	104
7.1	The spectrum of competition	108
7.2	Market equilibrium	109
7.3a	Equilibrium and a shift in demand	110
7.3b	Equilibrium and a shift in supply	110
7.4	Market welfare	113
B7.2	Consumer surplus	115
B7.3	Producer surplus	116
7.5a	A perfectly competitive market	119
7.5b	A perfectly competitive producer	119
7.6a	A perfectly competitive market adjusting to equilibrium	120
7.6b	A perfectly competitive producer adjusting to equilibrium	120
7.7a	Pure monopoly	123
7.7b	Pure monopoly and perfect competition	123
7.8a	First-degree price discrimination	126
7.8b	Second-degree price discrimination	126
7.8c	Third-degree price discrimination	126
7.9a	A producer in monopolistic competition	128
7.9b	Monopolistic competition and perfect competition compared	128
7.10a	A producer under oligopoly	130
7.10b	Oligopoly and perfect competition compared	130
7.11	Hotelling's location model with two producers	131
8.1a	Merit good	137
8.1b	Demerit good	137
8.2a	Indirect taxation	138
8.2b	Subsidisation	138
8.3a	Production quota	141
8.3b	Price ceiling	141
8.4	External cost	145

8.5	External benefit	145
8.6	Edgeworth box analysis of missing markets	147
9.1	A two-economy circular flow of income and expenditure	154
9.2a	Unambiguous Lorenz curve analysis	162
9.2b	Ambiguous Lorenz curve analysis	162
9.3a	Consumption function	167
9.3b	Investment function	167
9.4	The output market	172
9.5	The market for loanable funds	173
9.6	The Keynesian Cross	178
9.7a	The Keynesian Cross again	178
9.7b	The investment function again	178
9.7c	The IS curve	179
9.8	Analysing the IS curve	179
9.9a	Money market	181
9.9b	LM curve	181
9.10	Analysing the LM curve	182
9.11a	IS-LM analysis when LM changes	183
9.11b	IS-LM analysis when IS changes	183
9.12	IS-LM analysis	185
10.1a	Price level changes	188
10.1b	LM curve	188
10.2a	Price level changes	189
10.2b	Aggregate demand	189
10.3	The short run aggregate supply curve	192
10.4	Increased government spending in the AD-AS model	194
10.5	Monetary tightening in the AD-AS model	195
10.6a	Reduction in government spending in the IS-LM model	196
10.6b	Reduction in government spending in the AD-AS model	196
B10.1	The business cycle	197
11.1	A production possibility frontier	200
11.2	The classical model of unemployment	202
11.3	Sticky wages in the Classical model of unemployment	203
11.4	Unemployment hysteresis	209
11.5	Cost-push inflation and monetary accommodation	220
11.6	Demand-pull inflation and monetary validation	221
11.7a	The original Phillips curve relationship	223
11.7b	The conventional Phillips curve	223
11.8	AD, AS and the Phillips curve	224
11.9	Expectations-augmented Phillips curve analysis and NAIRU	224

11.10a The level effects of an inflationary gap   226
11.10b The inflationary effects of an inflationary gap   226

12.1a   Increased demand for a currency and its nominal
        exchange rate   234
12.1b   Increased supply of a currency and its nominal
        exchange rate   234

13.1   Very brief timeline of economic thought   244

tables

4.1   Useful economics shorthand (omitting standard mathematical
        symbols that are also useful in economics note-taking)   35
4.2   Definitions of common mathematical symbols   48

9.1   Theoretical marginal propensities   157

12.1   The benefits of trade   230

list of boxes

4.1	Prominence and consumer search	37
4.2	An example of diagrammatical analysis	41
4.3	An example of mathematical analysis	44
4.4	Econometrics in action: income differences across countries	50
5.1	Functions	63
5.2	Marginal utility	63
5.3	Constrained optimisation	69
5.4	Linear demand curves, and normal and inverse demands	76
5.5	Behavioural economics, *Paul Dolan (Imperial College, University of London) and Robert Metcalfe (University of Oxford)*	84
6.1	The relationship between a linear average revenue curve and the associated marginal revenue curve	96
6.2	Linear supply curves, and normal and inverse supplies	103
7.1	Market equilibrium	111
7.2	Consumer surplus	114
8.1	Public economics, *Phil Jones (University of Bath)*,	142
8.2	Environmental economics, *Anil Markandya (University of Bath)*	148
9.1	Public choice, *Toke Aidt (University of Cambridge)*,	159
9.2	Development economics, *Oliver Morrissey (University of Nottingham)*	163
9.3	More on consumption functions	167
9.4	The shameful treatment of Lorie Tarshis	176
10.1	Business cycles and stabilisers	197
11.1	Labour economics, *John Sessions (University of Bath)*	209
11.2	A brief and descriptive history of money	210
11.3	Inflation and interest rates	216

11.4   Money, banking and finance, *Bruce Morley (University of Bath)*   227

14.1   The first female economist   255

acknowledgements

I would like to thank the following people:

> Paul Dolan, Robert Metcalfe, Phil Jones, Anil Markandya, Toke Aidt, Oliver Morrissey, John Sessions and Bruce Morley for the boxes outlining specific areas of economics they have contributed to this book;

> Stephen Glaister, Kate Barker, Arran Lawson, Tom Gallagher, Chris Pinner, Matt Nottingham, Maria Tubbs, Richard Bailey, Venetia Bell, Steven Arnold, Kaazim Hussain, Alexis Pavlou, Dennis Owusu-Sem, Dennis Hammond and Simon Fowell for their comments and points-of-view that appear in this book;

> Chris Martin for his very kind foreword and helpful suggestions;

> Jayne Hacker at the Careers Advisory Service of the University of Bath for permission to use data from the university's leavers' destination survey in Chapter 2;

> Jaime Marshall, Aléta Bezuidenhout and five anonymous reviewers for their extremely helpful suggestions, advice, encouragement and support;

> Elizabeth Stone for all her suggestions and advice during the editing stage, which improved the book tremendously;

> All my family and friends for their encouragement and support throughout the writing process; and, most importantly of all,

> Fay, Oculi and Omni for all their love, patience and encouragement that I couldn't have done without whilst writing this book.

foreword

This is an excellent book, the best introduction to studying economics that I know. It manages to do two different things very well. The first part of the book is a guide to studying economics at university, explaining what economics is, discussing why it is such an interesting subject to study, outlining what university courses look like and how to study the subject most effectively. The second part of the book is an outline of modern economic theory that manages to be clear, concise and wonderfully free of jargon.

I am not surprised that Graham has written such a good book. He has a creative and curious approach to all areas of economics: this has helped him become a superb teacher. He is unusual in having taught economics in both a school and a university. That has given him insights into what students are taught and how they learn at both levels, a perspective that other textbook writers do not have. He has carefully thought through those aspects of economics that students typically find difficult and has come up with innovative ways to explain them.

Part 1 is the most distinctive part of the book. Chapter 1 outlines the subject, showing what economics is (and what it is not). Chapter 2 explains why it is such a rewarding subject to study. Anyone considering studying economics at university should study Chapter 3 carefully. It explores what economics degrees look like, why they are structured as they are and how degree courses differ. This is invaluable in preparing potential students for what is to come and is a useful guide for deciding between different economics degrees. Chapter 4 is a clear and well-thought-out guide on how to study economics effectively. Reflecting Graham's experience of teaching economics at both school and university, this is the best guide to studying economics I have seen.

Parts 2 and 3 of the book explain the core of economic theory. There are many other books that also do this, but the explanations in this book combine clarity and insight with a complete lack of jargon and a refreshing and often novel approach. Chapters 5–8, on how consumers and firms behave, how they interact and how their interactions can create problems, are models of how to put complex ideas across simply and concisely. Chapters 9–12 cover the 'big picture' issues of national income, unemployment, inflation, interest rates and exchange rates, also in a clear and concise way. I have taught these topics for many years, but I still found some novel insights in the way Graham describes these fascinating topics.

Part 4 provides context to modern economic ideas by discussing the development of economic thinking and the work of pioneers in the subject. This part of the book makes it clear that there are few novel problems or fundamental ideas in economics, showing that economists cannot neglect the earlier ideas of those who shaped the subject we know today.

In summary, this is an excellent book. It is the best of its type that I know. I hope you enjoy reading it as much as I did.

Chris Martin
Professor of Economics
University of Bath, March 2011

introduction

the world of economics

The first economics book I picked up was a glossy GCSE textbook brimming with simple diagrams and photographs of stock-exchange traders trying to make their fortunes. Flicking through that book, and glimpsing just a few of the many areas of everyday life into which economics extends, captivated my interest and imagination, and marked the start of my exploration of the world of economics. Ever since, and despite the inevitable highs and lows of any pursuit, my intrigue and interest have continued to deepen. This is partly due to simple curiosity and an enjoyment from 'doing economics', but also because of my conviction that the world of economics is fundamental to the real world, that the work of economists affects the everyday lives of us all, and that economics holds the solutions to many of the world's most serious problems.

For example, economists across the world are trying to identify the least costly strategies to offset the effects of climate change; they are analysing how to reduce the threat of terrorism through the use of economic incentives; they are developing ways of improving the lives of those in the poorest countries of the world; and they are furthering their understanding of why financial crises occur, why they sometimes spread around the globe, and how their appalling effects can be controlled. Economic theories have been used to justify invasions and wars; they have led to revolutions and massacres, sustained the ever-increasing affluence of some countries, whilst leading to the impoverishment of others; and they have shaped the ways countries interact with one another. The influence of the world of economics and those who study it cannot be unjustifiably exaggerated: economists can, and do, help mould the very foundations upon which society is built, and by which it will either stand or fall.

But what do I mean when I refer to the world of economics? I mean the simplified view of the world that economists have had to develop in order to study reality. The complexity of the real world is indescribable. There are innumerable decisions being made at any one time, and countless people interacting with one another in a vast number of different situations. Faced with such complexity, economists have had to create their own world that includes only the most important features of reality. This is a world of groups such as consumers and producers, and in which their decisions are necessarily simplified.

It's by studying this simpler world that lessons about reality can be learned: lessons that enhance our understanding of the world in which we live, and that lead to ways in which it can be improved. This is the world of economics that this book will help you explore.

As I sit at my desk writing this introduction, it's apparent that this is by far the most exciting time to be studying economics in living memory, and the excitement is going to last for many years to come. The recent global financial crisis, which is a recurring theme throughout this book, has shaken not only the real world but the world of economics as well, and it's as yet unclear how much of its structure will remain after all the repercussions have subsided.

The crisis is causing suffering for a multitude of individuals – particularly through unemployment and poverty – and the cost of its effects on society as a whole is simply too great to be measured. Not since the Great Depression of the 1930s has the developed world experienced such economic destitution. However, similar to the 1930s depression, it has also illustrated the limits to our understanding of the world and our ability to control such damaging effects. The world of economics has been found wanting; but this creates a very exciting opportunity. In response to the 1930s depression the world of economics and the policies promoted by economists underwent dramatic changes, and the world of economics is changing again in response to the recent crisis. The ultimate form this change will take is still being determined, but it's likely that economics will look very different in a few years time. It is an exciting thought that we may have a much more accurate and complete understanding of the world in which we live, and a much more effective ability to shape it for the good of everyone, as a result of the situation we're in today.

about this book

An entire lifetime of uninterrupted study would be vastly insufficient to acquire a full understanding of economics – a problem continually worsened by the relentless advance of the subject – and so to present such an understanding is certainly not the purpose of this book. Rather, this book is intended to be a guide for you as you start your exploration of the world of economics, perhaps in the form of an undergraduate course in the subject or out of simple curiosity.

In Part 1, I share my understanding of what economics actually is (a question that by no means has an obvious answer), what studying economics involves, the reasons for exploring economics, and my experiences of how economics courses should be tackled in order to minimise stress, wasted time and frustration, and to maximise success and enjoyment. I wish I had been aware of the tips presented in Chapter 4 when I entered my undergraduate lecture halls for the first time.

In Parts 2 and 3, I present chapters devoted to each of the primary strands of the subject, guiding you through the principal theories and ideas covered in the first year of most undergraduate courses. The purpose of these chapters is to make this material accessible, to provide you with a more intuitive way of understanding it all, and to introduce you to many of the surrounding controversies. These chapters aim to supplement and enhance your textbook, but will certainly not replace it. As such, detailed lists of the best learning resources that I've come across for each of these topics are provided in Part 5.

Finally, in Part 4, you will find a brief narrative of how economics has developed as a subject, and of the lives and contributions of the most influential economic thinkers. Only by understanding where economic ideas and theories have come from and how they've evolved can we fully understand the ideas and theories themselves.

Throughout the book there are definitions of the key terms you should know, identifying how they relate to other areas of the subject; boxes of interesting examples, stories and controversies that bring the subject to life; and introductions to the important mathematical ideas and techniques required to successfully complete the first year of an undergraduate course.

It must be stressed that although this book is an aid to undergraduate success, to get the most from it requires work. The material contained here needs to be:

1 **Studied**: read carefully and condensed into your own notes.

2 **Digested**: thought about over time.

3 **Questioned**: it needs to be tested by comparing it with your own experiences and knowledge of the world, enabling you to form a critical opinion of it – never accept what's written simply because it's in print.

It's only by doing these three things that you can fully understand the material presented here and be successful in your study. However, this book will only take you so far: to truly and comprehensively understand the subject requires applying the studying-digesting-questioning process to other books and sources of information about economics as well. There's only a limited amount that can be covered in any given book, and different authors have different opinions, different styles of writing and different ways of explaining economic concepts. The more widely you can apply this process, the deeper your understanding will become.

Studying any subject requires dedication and hard work, and economics is no exception. The tips provided in Chapter 4 will certainly help you do this, but there will still be times when the going is tough. For me this came in the second year of my undergraduate course, a time I found particularly testing because of the difficulty I had in getting to grips with the required mathematical techniques. Thanks largely to the support of my family and my Director of Studies, Toke Aidt, I decided to press on with the subject and I've never looked back: I've even mastered the maths! From my experience, studying economics is undoubtedly worth the effort. It's enjoyable and extremely rewarding. It will give you an everyday understanding of the world, help you develop a range of transferable study skills, and will open up a multitude of possible and interesting employment opportunities. I hope this book provides you with the essentials needed to study economics, as well as a taste of the enthusiasm and interest that I have for this vital subject.

If you're embarking on your first economics course, good luck and enjoy! The pursuit of economic understanding is a fantastically exciting one, and there's been no better time to begin it than now.

Graham Mallard
September, 2011

what it's all about and how to study it

1

In this first part we examine:

1   What economics actually is – which isn't as simple to answer as you would perhaps think (Chapter 1).

2   Why taking a degree course in economics is a good idea (Chapter 2).

3   What you should expect from an economics degree course if you decide to embark on one (Chapter 3).

4   Tips about how you should study economics at undergraduate level if you're to minimise your stress and frustration, and maximise your success and enjoyment (Chapter 4).

1 what is economics?

There's no obvious, undisputed answer to the question what economics actually is. In fact, students are often awarded the highest possible grades in their under-graduate degrees without ever being able to give a convincing answer to this question. In this chapter an array of possible answers is presented, but, as the chapter concludes, none of these alone suffices: a multi-faceted answer is required.

1.1 the study of the allocation of limited resources?

The GCSE textbook I mention in the Introduction boldly pronounced – probably at the top of page 1 – that economics is the study of how to allocate scarce resources. This is the most common definition of economics and was first proposed in the following, perhaps unnecessarily complicated, passage by Lionel Robbins in 1932:

[Economics is] the science which studies human behaviour as a relationship between ends and scarce means which have alternative uses.

The textbook went on to define the **basic economic problem** as the situation in which there's a limited amount of resources – of the four **factors of production** – but an unlimited volume of human needs (those things necessary for life: food, water, shelter, clothing and warmth) and wants (everything humans desire that aren't necessary to sustain life).

Key term: factors of production

The factors of production are the four general inputs essential to every production process:

(1) **Land** – natural resources such as water, oil and sand.
(2) **Labour** – human time and effort.
(3) **Capital** – man-made inputs into production such as machinery, buildings and components.
(4) **Entrepreneurship** – the risk-taking involved in organising the other three factors into a production process.

The basic economic problem leads to three practical questions:

(a) **What should a society produce for its population?** A choice inevitably has to be made as it's impossible to satisfy all the wants and needs of a population. Public health services, such as the National Health Service (NHS) in the UK, face this problem on a daily basis. The NHS employs a whole team of economics graduates to ensure that its limited budget is spent on providing the procedures and medicines representing the best value for money – a choice that can appear callous, but one that's absolutely necessary. The converse of this question is now extremely important as well: what should societies stop producing? Many developed countries today find themselves in huge amounts of debt, having spent beyond their means during the good times since the mid-1990s and having had to spend large amounts in trying to get themselves out of the recession caused by the recent financial crisis. Most are announcing harsh public spending cuts, but this necessarily means they have to cut back on their production, which raises the question what to cut back on. Responses to this question have caused social unrest such as strikes and protests in some countries.

(b) **How should society produce its output?** There are many modes of production and different ways of combining the available factors of production to produce most products, and so a choice needs to be made about which to use. Some of these are more financially costly than others, thereby restricting the number of items that can be produced, some are more harmful to human health or to the environment, and others lead to less equitable divisions of the resulting wealth.

(c) **For whom should the produce be made?** It's impossible to satisfy the wants and needs of every individual, and so a choice needs to be made about whom to satisfy. Should every individual be partly satisfied or should some be fully satisfied at the expense of others?

These choices are made in all economies, usually without much thought being given to them. They also lead to the extremely important notion of **economic efficiency**, which is a measure by which these decisions can be theoretically judged. There are two aspects to this:

❶ **Productive efficiency**. This measures the extent to which output is produced at the lowest feasible average cost. Only when an economy is productively efficient is it not wasting resources unnecessarily, and is producing the most from its limited factors of production.

❷ **Allocative efficiency**. This measures the degree to which an economy is using its resources to produce the products most valued by its population, and the degree to which it's distributing those products to maximise total welfare – also called **utility** – in the economy.

Key term: utility

The term utility is used by economists to refer to welfare or satisfaction. Saying that product A affords more utility to a consumer than product B means the consumer is better-off – enjoys more satisfaction or is happier – from consuming product A than ⬎

product B. Economists working at the end of the nineteenth century thought it would eventually be possible to measure utility in units they called utils, but this objective has now been discarded as unnecessary, if not impossible. Utility is referred to throughout this book, but is used interchangeably with satisfaction and welfare – as it is by most economists.

Only when there's both productive and allocative efficiency is there economic, or Pareto efficiency – the situation in which it's impossible to give one individual or group greater utility without reducing that of another. This is a purely theoretical concept but one that's of the utmost importance in economic analysis.

Key term: economic or Pareto efficiency

Pareto efficiency refers to how effectively an economy uses its resources. Only when an economy is both productively and allocatively efficient is it Pareto efficient, meaning it maximises its total utility. This term is named after the nineteenth–twentieth-century Italian economist Vilfredo Pareto, and is very important in our analysis of markets in Chapter 7.

The three questions raised by the basic economic problem are certainly real and are the focus of a considerable amount of economic analysis. Historically, there have been two general ways of answering them. Some governments have taken decisions completely into their own hands. Examples include the **centrally planned economies** of Stalin's Russia (his five-year plans that you may have come across in history courses) and the Licence Raj in India (a system during the second half of the twentieth century in which businesses had to obtain licences to operate). Others have relinquished as much responsibility as possible to the **free market**, in which the population determines the solutions amongst itself. No economy exists that relinquishes all its decision-making power to free markets – as already alluded to, public health services involve some degree of central planning, as do state-provided schools and emergency services – but the overwhelming trend during the twentieth century was for economies to move further in that direction.

The view that economics is the study of scarcity is prevalent across those working in the subject. However, as shown throughout this book, there are different schools of thought within economics and the view of economics as the study of scarcity is no exception. **Post-Keynesian** scholars, who seek to develop the work of John Maynard Keynes (see Sections 13.4 and 14.6), assert that in certain important areas of the economy there's no scarcity whatsoever (see Figure 1.2). For example, they argue there isn't usually enough demand for labour in the economy to allow every individual who wants a job to have one, meaning that more often than not there's unemployment (see Section 11.1). In this case, economics is actually a study of abundance: a study of how to employ the abundant labour.

1.2 the dismal science?

It was largely due to English economist Thomas Malthus (see Sections 13.2 and 14.3) that the nineteenth-century historian Thomas Carlyle referred to economics as the dismal science: a science of despair and negativity. Malthus was aware of the basic economic problem and predicted that the growth of resources – particularly agricultural resources and foodstuffs – simply couldn't keep pace with population growth, thus condemning society to periodic famines and widespread destitution: a dismal state for the human population indeed. Developed economies have apparently freed themselves from this fate through technological progress, at least in the agricultural case Malthus focused on. For large parts of the human population, though, the reality of the Malthusian prediction is felt every day, and there's a possibility Malthus will be proved correct for the population as a whole, but in the case of the environment rather than agriculture. Climate change is a clear example of natural resources not being able to accommodate the growth of human activity, thereby raising the potential of widespread destruction.

It isn't surprising that with economists announcing such warnings, the subject acquired such a label. However, Malthus didn't intend to be a prophet of despair, and neither do environmental economists today. Economists pursue research in these areas in the hope of finding positive and practical outcomes. A tremendous amount of work is done by economists into the possible solutions to the severe problems experienced by less developed countries, and the same can be said about the work into the possible responses to environmental degradation. In this respect, economics is far from dismal: it's very much a hopeful subject.

However, Carlyle's label for economics had a second strand. For a subject to be considered a science it needs to be based on objective principles – tenets that are demonstrably true and not based on opinion – and it needs to involve the systematic observation and investigation of natural phenomena. Economics satisfies the second of these. Economists continually develop theories based on observations from the real world and, increasingly, from the behaviour of individuals within laboratory situations as well: this is the realm of behavioural economics (see Figure 1.2 and Box 5.5). They then empirically test the accuracy of these theories using actual data. However, it's with regard to the first condition that the standing of economics as a science is questionable. Objective principles are those that are fundamentally undeniable. They may not be as we would like them to be, but there's no question of their being correct. Taking physics as an example, the Fundamental Law of Thermodynamics categorically states that energy cannot be created or destroyed: it can only be changed from one form into another. We may want to be able to create more energy but we cannot deny that it just isn't possible to do so. It isn't clear that economics is entirely based on such objective principles.

You will hear of there being two types of economic study: **positive economics**, which is based on objective principles and so can be deemed to be scientific, and **normative economics**, which is based on economists' opinions (also known as **value judgements**). The study of the relationship between a product's price and the quantity of it demanded by consumers can be considered to be an example of the former, as predictions (hypotheses) about it can be tested against the data and so proved right or wrong. The promotion of economic growth, on the other hand, should be considered to be an example of the latter because it isn't clear whether economic growth is necessarily the best thing for a population: how can this be scientifically tested without someone making a judgement call? The issue is that value judgements are pervasive across economics – more so than is usually perceived by economists themselves – and so there's disagreement about whether the subject as a whole can claim to be based on objective principles.

An often overlooked source of these opinions is the choice as to what to include in the part of the world of economics being studied (see the Introduction). It isn't usually possible for economists to include all aspects of reality in their study – reality is just too complex for this – and so they need to simplify their work. The choice of which factors to include is usually based on opinion, and so even if the resulting hypotheses appear to be positive, they are often grounded on value judgements and so have normative elements. In fact, economics is very rarely either positive or normative – it usually comprises elements of both.

Key term: positive economics

Positive economics refers to economic assertions that are testable and so are demonstrably true or false. For example, saying the average price of housing within an economy increases at between 2 and 3 per cent each year is a positive economic statement: it's relatively easy to use data to test whether or not the statement is true.

Key term: normative economics

Normative economics refers to economic assertions based on value judgements. For example, saying a 3 per cent rise in the average price of housing each year is harmful to an economy is a normative statement. Whether something is harmful usually requires a judgement to be made, based on opinion.

Overall, economics should certainly not be labelled a dismal science. The reputation of being dismal is unfair, and although economics is certainly a science in many respects, the widespread influence of value judgements means that, by comparison with the natural sciences, it's based, usually implicitly, more on subjective than objective principles. This last point is by no means a weakness or criticism of the subject, though. Irrespective of whether or not economics is considered a true science, it involves the rigorous study of human activity and has an undeniably powerful role to play in the generation of knowledge and the development of society.

1.3 the study of money?

It isn't uncommon to hear people say economics is the study of money. This comment is understandable since money is certainly involved in a lot of economic analysis, but it cannot be used as a complete definition of the subject.

As is shown throughout this book, much of economics is focused on issues relating to money. For example, in macroeconomics a significant amount of time is devoted to assessing the size of an economy, which is measured in money, and the factors that cause it to expand (see Chapter 9); the causes and consequences of changes in the value of money (see Section 11.3); and the amount of money that flows between economies and its effects on the economies involved (see Chapter 12). Likewise, a significant amount of time in microeconomics is devoted to analysing the prices that result from different forms of market structure (see Chapter 7); the effects of government policies and other events on the prices of products in an economy (see Chapters 7 and 8); and the value of external costs, such as pollution and accidents, that individuals cause (see Section 8.3). These are just three examples among a multitude from each of the main branches of economics that in some sense involve the study of money.

However, money is far from being the sole focus of economics, and over time is becoming less so as economists increasingly widen their attention to questions and problems that don't directly involve money at all. Fields such as public choice (see Box 9.1) often have only a peripheral role for money in their analyses. A comprehensive survey of these fields isn't possible here, but it should be noted they're both fascinating and of great importance to understanding how economies and the actors within them function. Existing fields such as these are continually developing, attracting the attention and time of exceptional economists, and new directions of economic study that don't have money at their heart are continually emerging. It's becoming increasingly unsatisfactory, then, to define economics as the study of money.

1.4 a way of thinking?

An inevitable response to the discussion in Section 1.3 – and a perception of economics that's becoming increasingly common – is that it's just a way of thinking about and approaching problems.

The spread of economics can be categorised either according to its fields of study or its schools of thought. As with most subjects, there's a dominant view about what the subject should involve – a dominant way of thinking about it – that's often referred to as the existing **paradigm**. The dominant school of thought in economics at the moment is that of **neoclassical economics** (although this is a simplification as the dominant view today reflects some ideas that are not strictly neoclassical). This view emphasises the use of marginal analysis in the study of how individuals and firms behave (see Section 5.1), and analysis that looks at how changing the situation being studied (through a new tax, for instance) causes the final outcome to change rather than at how a particular outcome is actually attained. This last part is known as the method of **comparative statics**.

The neoclassical view of economics is the primary focus of both this book and the teaching in most universities around the world. Applications of it are known as **fields** within economics. Figure 1.1 illustrates just a sample of the many, varied and interesting areas into which modern economics now extends.

Key term: the method of comparative statics.

This is analysis in which final outcomes (equilibrium points) are compared rather than analysis of how those points are reached.

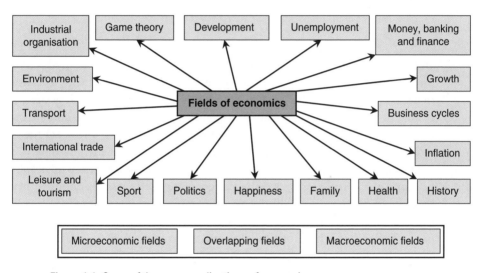

Figure 1.1 *Some of the many applications of economics*

However, not all economists agree with every element of the neoclassical view and so there exist other schools of thought promoting different views about what's important to study. The post-Keynesian and behavioural economics schools have already been mentioned. Others are outlined in Figure 1.2. It must be emphasised that the descriptions in this figure are intended to give you only a flavour of each school – they don't attempt to describe the richness and breadth of these different views – and that some schools of thought lie closer to that of neoclassical economics than others. For example, the work of behavioural economists is more readily accepted by mainstream, neoclassical economists than that of the post-Keynesians.

As in other subjects, there's also a dominant approach to how the subject should be studied – to 'doing economics'. Economists across the different schools of thought study a whole range of different social situations

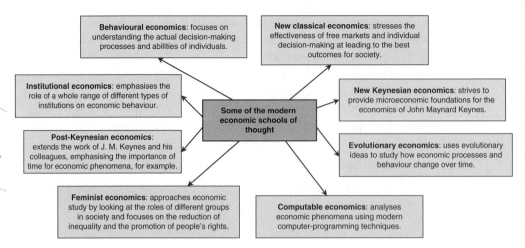

Figure 1.2 *Some of the many economic schools of thought*

and human interactions, but they largely do so according to **deductive methodology** (see Section 13.2 for the history of this). Faced with a reality that's simply too complex, and in which there's simply too much going on at any moment in time to be able to scientifically separate cause and effect, they usually replicate real situations in the form of models. These are theoretical – and often mathematical – replicas of reality that include only the most important factors for the phenomenon being studied. They're simplifications of the real world, designed to generate useful lessons about reality that would be obscured if all the actual complexities were included. This is the mainstream approach to 'doing economics', which suits nicely the dominant neoclassical school of thought; and, put together, these models form the world of economics discussed in the Introduction. Studying economics primarily involves the study of these models, and so in this book you will find lots of them.

The starting point for an economic model is a set of conditions about the situation being studied – what factors are important and should be included and what relationships exist between them. These conditions are sometimes assumed from intuition and personal experience, sometimes from actual observation of reality, and sometimes – less desirably – from a need to make the analysis possible (what economists call making the model **tractable**). Relevant information, such as the prices of products or the rate of an imposed tax, is then fed into the model. This information is manipulated according to the relationships within the model, which finally produces an output about the situation being studied – the quantity of the good demanded or the effect of the tax, for instance.

The factors determined outside the model, and used either to structure the model or as the initial input into it, are known as **exogenous variables** (*exo-* meaning outside the system). Those factors determined within the model, which are its outputs and predictions, are known as **endogenous variables** (*endo-* meaning within the system). Exogenous variables are fed into a model in order to generate endogenous output.

Such modelling is immensely powerful. It enables us to analyse situations that are highly complicated in real life, to focus on the central factors involved, enhancing our understanding of how the economy functions, and to ultimately lead to policies that may benefit us all. It's unsurprising that this modelling approach is employed by economists working in all the different fields of Figure 1.1, and that economics is often viewed as this particular way of thinking about and approaching issues rather than as the study of a specific set of issues.

1.5 a branch of maths?

If economists rely on mathematical models, is economics not simply a branch of maths? This is certainly a question that concerns many newcomers to the subject and is often given as the reason why others decide not to pursue it.

There is a considerable amount of maths involved in economics and an increasing number of universities are demanding entrants achieve good grades in the subject. A solid understanding of maths is particularly important in two aspects of economics. Pure maths is important in economic theory (see Section 4.2) and statistics is absolutely essential in econometrics (see Section 4.3). The further you take these two particular aspects of the subject the more sophisticated the maths becomes, until at the highest level the assertion that economics is a branch of maths is perhaps justified.

However, maths is simply one of a number of tools useful for economic analysis. Economics is certainly not just applied maths. Not all economics is mathematically demanding and some aspects are not mathematical at all. The mathematical content of economics courses across different universities is highly varied, and even in those universities that lean heavily on maths there's always a considerable degree of flexibility: the units demanding advanced maths can often be circumvented, and for the aspects of the core units that do involve maths, a keen intuition can get you more than a long way.

Furthermore, there are an increasing number of voices within academic economics calling for a reduction in the emphasis placed on maths. Queen Elizabeth II has – no doubt to her complete surprise – been exposed to this mounting debate. Whilst visiting the London School of Economics in November 2008 she enquired why economists failed to predict and prevent the recent global crisis. She subsequently received two responses. The first was from economists at the London School of Economics, outlining the mainstream view that economists failed to predict the crisis because they overestimated the advantages of free markets. The second was from a group of economists in other schools of thought suggesting the main reason was the way economists have overemphasised the use of maths in both their research and teaching, making the subject too far removed from the reality it seeks to understand. Even Paul Krugman, a winner of the Nobel Prize in Economics, has criticised the economics mainstream, arguing in the *New York Times* (2 September 2009) that:

[T]he economics profession [has gone] astray because economists, as a group, mistook beauty, clad in impressive-looking mathematics, for truth ... economists fell back in love with the old, idealized vision of an economy in which rational individuals interact in perfect markets, this time gussied up with fancy equations ... Unfortunately, this romanticized and sanitized vision of the economy led most economists to ignore all the things that can go wrong.

By this he means that economists have concentrated on sophisticated mathematical models, with the result that their assumptions about the real world have been unrealistic. The models may be technically impressive but have been of limited use in helping us to understand how the economy actually works.

The view is strengthening that economists' reliance on maths has advanced at a far quicker rate than the development of other essential aspects of economic understanding, and so it's likely this situation will change, with some of the emphasis being transferred from mathematical analysis to an understanding of economic history, human psychology and actual behaviour. Having said this, though, maths will always be an important part of economics, both for theory and for the crucial statistical analysis of hypotheses and economic policies. However, the mathematical element should certainly not deter you if you have a keen interest in economic behaviour.

1.6 what is economics, then?

There are common elements in all the suggested answers above. Economics is the study of choice and human interaction, usually – but certainly not always – in situations of scarcity, and is useful for informing policy that can improve the lives of all. The approach adopted in this study is predominantly based on modelling that's often mathematically based. Changes are under way regarding the methodology of economics, but the focus on choice and human interaction will certainly remain at the heart of economics.

However, it's important to recognise that economists emphasise different aspects of their subject. For example, Stephen Glaister CBE, a Professor of

Transport and Infrastructure at Imperial College, University of London, and Director of the UK Royal Automobile Club Foundation, explains that for him:

Economics is the scientific study of how to adjust public policies so as to make as many people as possible better off whilst disadvantaging as few other people as possible. It is not primarily about money, although money can sometimes be used to represent the magnitudes of costs, benefits and the distribution of who experiences them. It is about allocation of physical resources (including people's working time), the personal welfare that the consumption those resources generates and any disbenefits to others.

Economics exists because there have to be trade-offs: it's not often that you can have more of everything, whatever the politicians may seek to imply. Because one thing has to be traded against another it is essential to do everything possible to gather quantitative, statistical evidence to predict the manner and extent of people's likely responses to change, now and in the future. One of the things that distinguishes good economic policy analysis from the opinion of the person in the street is that it is properly based on the best (if imperfect) available evidence and not only on personal experience or prejudice.

Perhaps unsurprisingly, given that she was a member of the Monetary Policy Committee of the Bank of England, Kate Barker echoes many of Stephen's views, explaining that her real interest in economics also revolves around public policy and that:

For this four concepts are critical: the allocation of scarce resources, market failure, opportunity cost and unintended consequences. Economists should in principle be able to improve policy by thinking about how these concepts apply to particular proposals, and how incentives can be set, costs and benefits evaluated and risk assessed in order to reach a desired result (what is desired then involves the even more difficult issue of ethical considerations). Both micro- and macroeconomic policies also need to be evaluated by proper use of data – understanding the strengths and weaknesses of data is a vital part of an economist's toolkit.

These two highly eminent economists emphasise the study of welfare. For both, a key focus of economics is the evaluation of public policy so that such policies are to the overall benefit of society. They recognise that this often involves difficult decisions, what Stephen calls 'trade-offs'. Clearly this is only possible through the effective use of economic data, which is a second element of economics they both identify as crucial. It's clear they both view economics as the study of how society can be improved – a definition far removed from the view of economics as a dismal science.

Although the views of Stephen and Kate are in harmony, other economists stress different aspects of economics as being most important and of the greatest interest. This variety is one of the many advantages of the subject: the fact that it's such a wide-reaching discipline means individuals are able to specialise and focus on the areas in which their own interests lie. For some, the interest lies in formal mathematical modelling. For others it lies in the empirical evaluation of public policy. For others still it lies in the understanding of human decision-making. Economics successfully draws together all these strands, along with a multitude of others, into a study of choice and human interaction and into how policy can be employed to benefit society as a whole.

For me, then, and to answer the question of this chapter directly:

Economics is the study of choice and human interaction, of the implications of these for society as a whole, and of the policies that can be employed to improve the functioning and the results of both.

1.7 economics as a diverse social science

Because economics is the study of choice, human interaction and the wider effects they have, it's rightly counted among the social sciences along with subjects such as psychology, sociology, international relations, politics, education and consumer science. In fact, there are clear areas of overlap between economics and these other subjects, with scholars across them studying very similar things. For example, economists are increasingly basing their models on observations about how individuals make decisions, observations that are drawn from both reality and laboratory experiments (see Section 5.7 and Box 5.5). This fascinating work – which forms part of behavioural economics and economic psychology – clearly complements and draws upon work in psychology and consumer science, both of which also study decision-making processes and their implications in different settings. Other areas in which economics today overlaps with other social sciences include the economics of education, public choice (see Box 9.1), and health, international and feminist economics.

These various disciplines all exist to expand our understanding of the issues involved in these aspects of society, and economics is no different in this regard. However, the ways in which scholars in these various subjects approach their study tend to differ, although this is a generalisation since there are of course areas of overlap here as well. As explored in Section 1.4 above, those working within each subject tend to adopt a particular dominant approach to their study. It's these approaches that tend to set these subjects, which study very similar issues, apart from one another.

The dominant approach in economics at the moment is that of deduction, which involves the creation of simplified (and usually mathematical) models grounded on a number of assumed conditions about the issue being studied. This approach complements well the dominant neoclassical paradigm view of economics, which stresses the importance of optimal decision-making and comparative statics (see Section 1.4). These models – many of which are explored in this book – are used to generate predictions about the issues being studied, which can then be tested empirically through econometrics (see Section 4.3). This is the mainstream approach to 'doing economics' and it's this, rather than the questions it seeks to answer, that sets economics apart from the other social sciences.

However, this mainstream approach is being increasingly challenged, with economists being ever more willing to take different approaches. Those working in behavioural economics conduct experiments such as those used in psychology. Evolutionary and neuro-economists employ strategies drawn from the natural sciences, in the latter case actually using brain-scanning technology to analyse brain processes during economic decision-making. Computable economists use techniques from computer science to model economic systems. Gradually the importance of these alternative approaches is being realised and they're becoming increasingly popular within the subject, but for now the mainstream approach continues to be that of deduction.

The issue of what methodology economists should use continues to be debated. It's a thorny issue about which numerous books have been written, sometimes drawing on abstract notions from philosophy. It's lightly touched upon in various parts of this book but isn't explored in any depth since that would require entire chapters to be devoted to it and because it isn't usually addressed in degree courses (see Chapter 15 for recommendations about books that do explore these issues).

The Introduction observes that there may never have been a more exciting time to be studying economics. The neoclassical world of economics, which has been created using deductive methodology, has been found wanting as a result of the recent global financial crisis. For this reason, increasing numbers of economists are challenging both the neoclassical view of what's important for economists to focus on and the deductive approach to studying it. Ideas and methodologies from other subjects – particularly the other social sciences – are increasingly being adopted, and are helping expand our understanding of the world in which we live. Economics as a subject is changing and, although the final outcome of these changes is as yet unclear, the subject could look very different in a few years time. This is an exciting time to be engaging with this vitally important, diverse social science; and is a time in which it has never been more important to see the overlaps with the other social sciences.

1.8 summary

> Economics is the study of choice and human interaction, of the implications of these for society as a whole, and of the policies that can be employed to improve the functioning and the results of both.

> The dominant, mainstream school of thought about what economists should focus on is that of neoclassical economics, which emphasises marginal analysis and comparative statics.
> The dominant methodology used in economics is deduction – the creation of simplified models through which reality can be studied.

2 why study economics?

Being successful at economics requires you to engage with and to understand current affairs, economic modelling, politics, history and philosophy. Even if you don't find every aspect of the subject interesting, you will certainly find enough of interest to keep you motivated for at least the duration of your course. It also requires you to master skills of analysis – diagrammatical, mathematical and statistical – and to further your abilities at a whole range of transferable skills. For these reasons, economics students are highly valued in the workplace and studying the subject successfully opens up a wide array of interesting career opportunities. It's perhaps the subject that will expose you to the widest range of techniques and knowledge, help you develop the most rounded set of aptitudes and give you the broadest range of future career opportunities. As Arran Lawson, an economics undergraduate at the University of Bath, comments,

Studying economics is great. I didn't get a chance to study it at A-Level so was worried about whether or not I would understand any of it; but after getting to grips with it I would definitely tell anyone in the same position to go for it! The subject is really interesting as it applies to everything happening around you. It also gives you some really useful skills that will help your career and make you incredibly employable.

2.1 understanding the wider world

In an economics degree you learn about things wholly relevant to everyday life. You discuss issues such as the abuse of monopoly power, rush-hour congestion on public transport, the minimum wage and its effects on unemployment, the recession caused by the current financial crisis, and the effects of inflation. It enables you to turn over a page of any financial newspaper and to understand what is reported, to critique the reports and identify the biases of the journalists. It will also enable you to read the manifestos of political parties, formulate your own opinions about them and understand the causes and consequences of important events across the world, both recent and historic, such as the current financial crisis, the Thatcherite attacks on unionism in the 1980s and the Great Depression of the 1930s, to name only three. This is such a significant benefit that it stands alone.

However, it's really just the most valuable transferable skill out of many you develop as you study economics. A knowledge of economics enables you to approach most situations with some relevant understanding – a skill highly valued in the workplace. As Tom Gallagher, also an undergraduate at Bath, comments,

Since starting to study economics I have not regretted the decision one bit. There is a vast array of areas in which to specialise and it is amazing that one day you can learn something in your lessons and then when you open a newspaper or watch the news you can relate your subject exactly to what is going on in the real world.

2.2 other transferable skills

Studying economics also helps you foster a whole array of other, more practical, transferable skills, expertise useful across almost all occupations and viewed with eager anticipation by employers. If you're to be successful at economics it's imperative you become proficient at these skills (tips about how to do this are suggested in Chapter 4).

1 **writing effectively in a variety of different formats**. Studying economics helps you further enhance your skills of writing essays, short answers, projects and presentations. It involves learning how to write concise, focused and sophisticated pieces of work, a skill that comes only from practice, which studying economics certainly affords you.

2 **the ability to analyse thoroughly and to solve problems quickly and successfully**. By studying economics you also develop your aptitude for analysing models, for using maths to demonstrate whether or not assertions are correct and for examining statistics so you can test opinions and ideas against real-life data. As Chris Pinner, another undergraduate at Bath, comments,

The study of economics at university helps you to develop a thorough approach to problem solving, an aptitude to analyse and question, and an ability to reach logical conclusions when others are unable.

Studying economics requires you to extend your capacity to think through and to outline a line of argument logically, identifying the implications of each step until the overall result is ascertained. It enables you to see the 'bigger-picture' whilst maintaining a thorough grasp of the technicalities, to see things that non-economists usually overlook. It actually helps you make everyday decisions, since it helps you understand the situations you find yourself in and the implications of the different responses available to you. As Matt Nottingham, a fourth undergraduate at Bath, comments,

Studying economics helps inform your everyday decisions; turning you into the 'rational consumer' that features in much of the theory.

❸ **skills of critical evaluation and original thinking**. Faced with different models, ideas and arguments, you learn to systematically outline their strengths and weaknesses – both logically and by comparing them to reality – in order to reach your own, fully thought-through and justified opinions and judgements. The capacity to evaluate assertions critically and to think originally is a valuable skill, which economics gives you the opportunity to develop.

❹ **the ability to process information quickly but thoroughly**. Studying economics requires you to read and understand vast amounts of information, whilst learning new skills of analysis and evaluation. This is testing and hard work, but the ability to process information quickly will serve you well throughout the rest of your life. Indeed, the entry examinations of large companies, the UK's Government Economic Service and advanced teaching positions almost always include scenarios testing the efficiency of your information-processing skills. The study of economics is an effective training ground in this regard.

It's impossible to unjustifiably exaggerate just how valuable these transferable skills are in the workplace and how much they'll benefit you throughout your life. Economics isn't, of course, the only subject that helps you develop these skills, but it certainly provides you with everything you need to become proficient at them. As Maria Tubbs, a final undergraduate at Bath, summarises,

Studying economics has enabled me to develop a wide range of skills, including mathematics, critical evaluation and effective writing – all of which are highly regarded by employers. Economics is very relevant to the world today, and it is rewarding to be constantly improving my understanding of a subject that is always in the news.

2.3 employment opportunities

Considering the wide range of transferable skills that studying economics helps to cultivate, it isn't surprising that graduating economics students are welcomed, and incorporated readily, into the workplace. Figures 2.1a and 2.1b compare the general destinations of students graduating with degrees in economics, or economics with politics, from the University of Bath against those of all students graduating from that university in both 2005 and 2006 (based on those students who responded to the destination survey). In both years a greater proportion of the economics graduates immediately found employment, or employment with further study, than of the overall cohort: 71 per cent compared with 70 per cent in 2005 and 76 per cent compared with 70 per cent in 2006. Furthermore, in both years, the percentage of economics graduates still without employment in the January of the following year was lower than that of the overall cohort: 5 per cent compared with 6 per cent in 2005 and 4 per cent compared with 6 per cent in 2006. The employment opportunities for economics graduates compare, at the very least, favourably with those for graduates of other subjects.

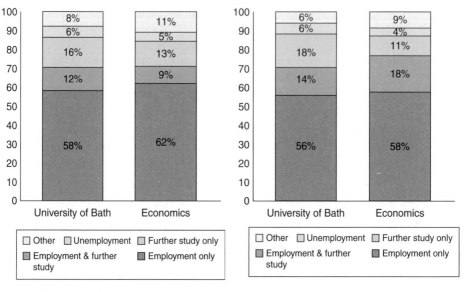

Figure 2.1a Destinations of UK and EU graduates from the University of Bath in 2005: economics, and economics and politics, against all graduates.

Source: Careers Advisory Service at the University of Bath

Figure 2.1b Destinations of UK and EU graduates from the University of Bath in 2006: economics, and economics and politics, against all graduates.

Source: Careers Advisory Service at the University of Bath

Figures 2.1a and 2.1b reflect the overall employment opportunities that studying economics successfully opens up, but they conceal the vast array of different careers available for economics graduates to choose from. For a better sense of this array consider Figure 2.2, which illustrates more finely the destinations of students graduating with degrees in economics, or economics and politics, from the University of Bath between 2006 and 2008 (again, based on those students who responded to the survey).

Consider first the financial services destination, to which 16 per cent of these graduates went in 2008, 21 per cent in 2007 and 20 per cent in 2006. Included in this category are careers in accountancy (which also includes roles in assurance and advisory, tax and corporate finance), actuary, banking, and insurance and mortgage services. The financial trading category, in which 7 per cent embarked on careers in 2008, 1 per cent in 2007 and 4 per cent in 2006, includes positions that primarily involve trading financial

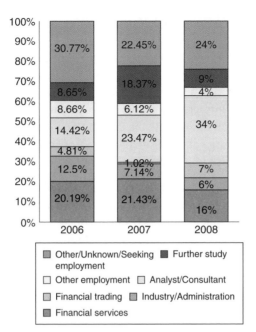

Figure 2.2 Destinations of UK and EU graduates of economics, and economics and politics

Source: Careers Advisory Service at the University of Bath (categorisation my own)

instruments. As Richard Bailey, an economics graduate from Exeter University and a chartered accountant at one of the Big Four professional services firms, explains,

As part of my job, I use my economics degree on a daily basis. Not only do I use the technical side of my degree but also the analytical thinking style that my degree helped me to develop. My economics training has given me a core understanding of the economy and markets in which my clients operate; helping me to look beyond the numbers that the client is disclosing, to think about whether they are reasonable in the context of the client's business.

The industry and administration destination, in which 6 per cent of these graduates started careers in 2008, 7 per cent in 2007 and 13 per cent in 2006, includes roles in business. For example, included in these figures are positions in strategic development, management, marketing, sales and pricing, product development, distribution and finance.

The analyst and consultant category, which in 2007 and 2008 accounted for the greatest proportion of these graduating students with 34 and 23 per cent respectively, comprises roles in private consultancy businesses, analyst and consultancy roles in large corporations, and roles in the public sector, such as analysts at the Bank of England and in the UK's Government Economic Service. Venetia Bell, an economist at the Bank of England, explains that,

My work supports the Monetary Policy Committee, which sets monetary policy in order to meet the Government's inflation target. More specifically, my work involves analysing recent developments in the economy, and assessing what they mean for monetary policy. That requires a good understanding of how the economy works, and a broad knowledge of the available data and methods that can be used to interpret economic developments. So the knowledge and skills that I learnt during both my BA and MSc in economics (from the University of Cambridge and the London School of Economics respectively) are an invaluable backdrop to my everyday work.

The analyst and consultant category also includes economic researchers for private research groups and think tanks, of which Steven Arnold at the University of Bath is an example. Having graduated with a degree in economics and international development, and a subsequent Masters of Research in economics, from the University of Bath, he's now employed by the university as a research officer in environmental economics. He explains that he uses the learning from his studies on a daily basis.

[My studies have] provided me with a wide view of economics and social science research, not just covering advanced microeconomics, macroeconomics and econometrics, but also the underpinnings of research and the opportunity to see economics alongside other research fields. Now, as a full-time researcher, I need a strong understanding of the foundations of economics, but also how to apply processes and systems of economic thought to large-scale problems such as climate change and global sustainability.

The last employment category is that of 'other'. Roughly accounting for an average of 6 per cent of the destinations of these graduates across the three years, this category includes those gaining positions in teaching, construction, event organisation, research funding, charities, the armed forces, journalism, the media and tourism. Kaazim Hussain explains how his degree has been useful in his teaching career:

I completed both my Bachelors and Masters at the University of Essex, focusing on pure micro and macro, international trade and the airline industry. For the past five years, I've been teaching mathematics and economics at secondary- and A-Level in Saffron Walden. Passionate about both subjects, I was able to analyse the job market to enter teaching as a maths teacher (where there was excess labour demand), before moving into teaching economics. I now use my knowledge to develop students' passion for the subject, getting them to think about how the models apply to the news stories of the day.

It's often thought that an economics degree inevitably leads to financial jobs. Figure 2.2 clearly demonstrates this is certainly possible, but not inevitable. Alexis Pavlou describes the variety of work he's done, which has drawn on his background in economics.

I have worked in the City of London, my undergraduate degree being key in highlighting how I can understand and evaluate economic policy, trading currencies and options and writing analysis for customers; started my own small business and bought into a second; invested in low and high yield properties; and now teach [economics] at A-Level. It is the confidence gained from my MA in economics and economic history at Edinburgh University, where I specialised in post-war UK economic policy and the Hong Kong Dollar Currency Board, and my MSc in economics from the University of Bath, where I specialised in public policy, development and behavioural economics, that has laid the foundations for a flexible and exciting lifestyle.

Successfully attaining an economics degree opens up a wealth of interesting careers, only a selection of which I've been able to mention in this section. It also opens up interesting, and potentially rewarding, avenues of further study. For instance, solely looking at those graduates represented in Figure 2.2 shows that an economics, or an economics and politics, degree can lead to further and higher degrees in economics, European business, international relations, law, international politics, carbon management, politics and markets, finance, property management and European public policy – amongst a multitude of others.

2.4 summary

> Studying economics helps you understand the wider world, and helps you develop a range of valuable transferable skills.
> Being successful at economics opens up a diverse array of interesting employment opportunities.
> Economics graduates are welcomed into the workplace.

3   what to expect from your economics course

3.1   typical structure and content

Economics undergraduate programmes tend to be very similar to one another, as the following comparison of those at three European universities demonstrates. Figures 3.1, 3.2 and 3.3 present the programmes for pure economics at the Universities of Edinburgh, Helsinki and Bath, respectively. The courses are all three years in duration, although at Edinburgh you can take a fourth year to earn a Senior Honours degree – as opposed to the Junior Honours you would leave with at the end of the third year – and at Bath you can opt for a four-year course in which the penultimate year is spent working in industry. Each module or unit is represented by a box, which may be divided into separate smaller units for each semester in the year. At Helsinki, some modules extend over two or more years. These are modules you can choose to take in any of the covered years. Each module is weighted equally at Edinburgh and Bath, but not at Helsinki: their weightings are presented in brackets.

The first observation is that in each of the three programmes you're required to take modules of introductory microeconomics and macroeconomics in

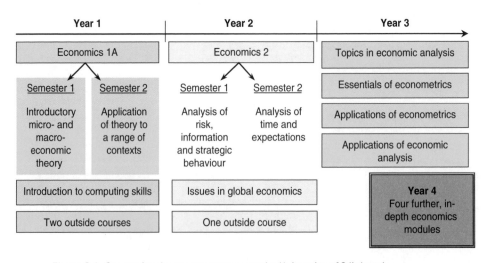

Figure 3.1   Economics degree programme at the University of Edinburgh

what it's all about and how to study it

your first year. At Edinburgh the theory elements of these modules are amalgamated into a single module taken in the first semester, leaving their applications and development in particular contexts to the second semester. At Helsinki, on the other hand, there's flexibility to take take either introductory microeconomics or introductory macroeconomics, or both, in the second year. However, despite their differing formats, they each cover essentially identical material. For introductory microeconomics they primarily include consumer behaviour, producer behaviour, market structures and welfare analysis. For introductory macroeconomics they include aggregate demand and supply, output determination, unemployment and inflation. Each of these elements is examined in detail in Parts 2 and 3 of this book.

As you progress through an economics programme, you're required to complete modules that take the analysis of these theories to increasingly more advanced levels. Consider the programme at Edinburgh, for example. The second year covers more advanced theories of risk, information, strategic behaviour, time and expectations; and in the third year you're required to choose from advanced topics such as general equilibrium and welfare, adverse selection, signalling and moral hazard: these come under the module 'Topics in economic analysis'. In the second year at Bath you're required to take courses on intermediate microeconomics and macroeconomics and in the final year their advanced counterparts.

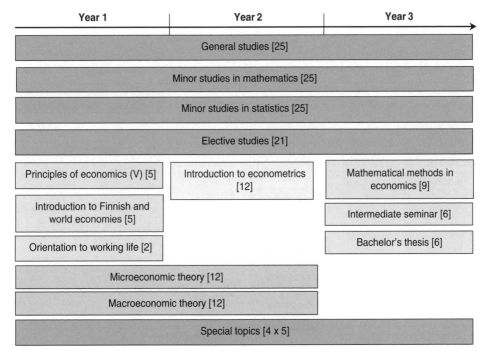

Figure 3.2 Economics degree programme at the University of Helsinki

Note: (V) stands for voluntary

Modules also usually become more specialised in later years of an economics programme. This is partly from necessity – it simply isn't possible to learn advanced theory for all parts of economics – but partly also to give you choice in what you study. Consider Helsinki, for instance. This choice manifests itself in the 'Special topics' module, which requires you to select five modules from a list including public economics (see Box 8.1), environmental economics (see Box 8.2), labour economics (see Box 11.1), development economics (see Box 9.2) and the history of economic thought (see Chapter 13). Similarly at Bath, you're increasingly able to select 'Optional units' from a list including many of the same modules as at Helsinki, as well as international monetary economics (see Box 11.4) and experimental, behavioural and neuro-economics (see Box 5.5). At Edinburgh, topics similar to these are touched upon in the module 'Applications of economic analysis' in the third year, with the further option of studying them in even more depth during the Senior Honours year.

A final requirement common across all economics programmes is to develop your skills of mathematical and statistical analysis and, in the second and/or third years, econometrics. These skills are essential if you're to be successful in economics: they are explored in Chapter 4. There are usually modules on additional transferable skills as well, such as the module on 'Research and presentation skills' in the second year at Bath and 'Intermediate seminar' in the final year at Helsinki, which is intended to prepare you for effective scientific discussion and writing.

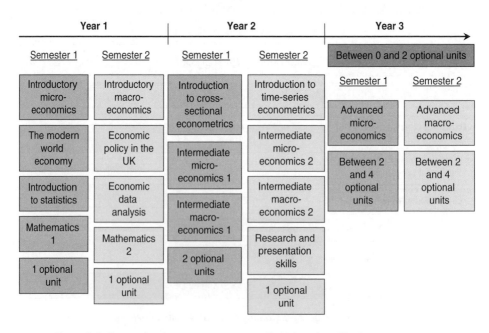

Figure 3.3 Economics degree programme at the University of Bath

3.2 selecting your course and modules

Although there are many elements common across economics courses at all universities, there are also some significant differences. These differences tend to relate to three areas of a course: the non-core but compulsory modules, the optional modules, and the possibility of wider modules. These differences should be the first consideration when choosing your course.

With regard to the non-core, compulsory modules, in the first year at Bath you're required to study 'The modern world economy', which covers issues including international trade and finance, poverty and the role of international organisations such as the World Bank and the International Monetary Fund. At Edinburgh, these topics are covered in the compulsory second-year course, 'Issues in global economics'. However, at Edinburgh you're required to study computing skills in the first year and at Helsinki you take a module about the Finnish and world economies: both of which are studied only in these universities. Such compulsory modules should influence your decisions about which course to take.

The optional modules offered at a university are largely determined by the expertise of the faculty members, meaning larger departments are usually able to offer a wider selection from which you can choose. Many are undoubtedly the same across universities, but there are likely to be some significant differences. For example, at Bath you have the option to study 'Treasury management' or 'Welfare economics and distributive justice' in the final year; during the Senior Honours year at Edinburgh you're offered the options of 'Economic transformation of East Asia' and the 'Economics of self-management'; whilst at Helsinki you're offered the options of 'Ethics and economics' and 'Women, men and economy' in your third and final year. These choices should play a significant role in your decision about which course to apply for. You should think carefully about which modules you think you will be most interested in: all universities publish information about their options and what they include on their websites.

A third major characteristic of courses you should consider is the flexibility they offer regarding the study of non-economics modules. For example, at Edinburgh you're able to study two modules at an appropriate level from any other subject in the first year and a further one in the second year. If you're doing a joint honours degree, though, one of those in the first year must be from your second subject, as must that in the second year. At Bath you're able to choose a module from another subject as your optional module, or one of your optional modules in both semesters of years one and two, as long as they're approved by the undergraduate Director of Studies. At Helsinki, though, there isn't the same flexibility to study non-economics modules. So, if you're interested in other subjects and would like to study them further, the flexibility offered should be a serious consideration.

Related to this wider flexibility is the consideration about a joint honours degree. You don't have to study economics on its own: you can combine it with other subjects. For example, at Edinburgh you're able to study for joint honours in economics with Chinese, economics with environmental studies, and Arabic with economics, naming just three; whereas at Bath you're offered a more limited range of joint courses, including economics and politics, and economics and international development. The range of joint degrees varies significantly across universities, but in all of them the economics element includes the core modules named above.

The final general characteristic to consider when deciding which course to apply for is the offer of wider opportunities. Certain universities, such as Bath, offer four-year economics courses, in which the third year is set aside for you to work for a business on a placement basis. Such a placement is usually of great benefit because of the experience it gives and the maturity it inevitably fosters. Applying as a placement student at university helps to open doors to experience in large companies that are usually otherwise closed. A placement allows you to apply and further advance your transferable skills. It also allows you to more thoroughly learn about your interests and the future career path you would like to pursue: many students come away from their placements certain of the career they would like or, equally valuably, having discovered they aren't actually interested in what they had been planning to do. As Dennis Owusu-Sem, an economics undergraduate at Bath, notes,

Working at Goldman Sachs on placement has helped me to develop a wide network of contacts, both internally and externally. It has also helped me to develop personal skills such as those of communication, creativity and leadership. The placement has given me a better understanding of what path I want to follow in the future.

A placement may also help to reinforce the learning from your course, by demonstrating how the theories and concepts are actually applied and used by businesses every day. As Dennis Hammond, a peer of Dennis Owusu-Sem who spent his placement year working in the Finance Department of IBM, comments,

I have often found some of the concepts discussed in the classroom rather abstract and theoretical. Doing a placement allowed me to actually apply these economic theories to real-life markets.

At Edinburgh, on the other hand, there's the option of spending your third year studying abroad as an exchange student. Students have spent their third years at universities in America, Canada, Europe, Asia and Australia and New Zealand. This can be a fantastic opportunity, bringing both personal and academic benefits. Not all universities offer opportunities such as these as part of their courses, and so it's an important consideration to bear in mind when choosing your course.

Soon after being enrolled on an economics course you have to make choices about which optional modules you would like to take, although the scope to do so is limited in the first year. It's important to consider two things when making these decisions. First, what areas of economics interest you? Being interested in a module is often the key to being sufficiently determined to learn its material and to develop the skills and techniques it requires. It's certainly worthwhile to devote time to ascertaining what's involved in each of the options: see the boxes in Parts 2 and 3 of this book, in which experts outline their own fields of expertise. Second, how do the different options form pathways? For example, if you're to study 'Development economics' in your final year at Bath it's a prerequisite that you have taken the corresponding module in the second year. Similarly, if you're to study 'Investment banking' in your final year at Bath, it's required that you studied 'Corporate finance and investment appraisal' as your optional module in semester two of the first year. For this reason, you need to take care not to cut yourself off from an option that you may be interested in at a later date. You should spend time looking into what future options involve and require, and to carefully plan your choices so that you don't inadvertently close interesting pathways.

3.3 summary

> Microeconomics, macroeconomics, maths and econometrics usually form the core compulsory modules of economics degree courses.
> When deciding between different economics degrees you should consider their non-core but compulsory modules, their optional modules, and the possibility of wider modules and opportunities they offer.

4 studying economics successfully

[T]he master-economist must possess a rare combination of gifts. He must reach a high standard in several different directions and must combine talents not often found together. He must be mathematician, historian, statesman, philosopher — in some degree. He must understand symbols and speak in words. He must contemplate the particular in terms of the general, and touch abstract and concrete in the same flight of thought. He must study the present in the light of the past for the purposes of the future. No part of man's nature or his institutions must lie entirely outside his regard.

As succinctly outlined above by John Maynard Keynes (see Section 14.6) in 1933, to study economics successfully you need to develop a range of general attributes. In particular, you must develop your:

1. Knowledge and understanding of the subject material, but also of the wider world and its development over time.
2. Skills of economic analysis: being able to analyse situations thoroughly, using formal logic, diagrams and maths.
3. Ability of critical evaluation.
4. Aptitude at a range of practical skills necessary for the successful completion of work and exams.

In this chapter, I present tips that should help you develop these attributes. These are tips I've learned from my own experience both as a student – unfortunately through trial and error in most cases – and as a teacher. However, it must be stressed that these are only suggestions based on my own experience – you may find alternative strategies more fruitful. They're also primarily focused on specific aspects of studying economics, and so don't include tips for studying in general. To maximise the effectiveness of your study, you should consult books on general study skills as well (see Chapter 15).

4.1 tackling all the reading

As with any subject, there's a vast amount of material you need to learn and understand if you're to study economics successfully, most of which you're required to read. Before we look at how to tackle this reading, you should be aware of the three main sources of written information in economics:

1. **Textbooks**. Lecturers usually recommend one or more core textbooks, around which they base their lectures. It's important you have access to these texts because they contain much more than your lecturers can cover in their teaching. The best textbooks I've come across for each of the subject areas covered in Parts 2 and 3 are outlined in Chapter 15.

2. **Lecture notes**. Lecturers usually distribute notes for their lectures. These are usually made available to you before the relevant lectures, and you should print them out and use them to prepare your note-taking in advance (see below, pages 31–3).

3. **Journal articles**. Original work in economics is usually published in the form of journal articles rather than books. Such articles range from 1500 to 10,000 words in length and are published in a wide variety of journals. Some journals are wide-ranging, such as the *American Economic Review* and the *Review of Economic Studies*, whereas others specialise in specific areas of the subject, such as the *Journal of Environmental Economics and Management* and *Games and Economic Behavior*. Some journals are extremely technical and mathematical, such as the *Journal of Economic Theory* and *Econometrica*, whilst others are easier to read, such as the *Journal of Economic Literature* and the *Journal of Economic Perspectives*. As you progress through your degree an increasing proportion of your reading should be focused on these articles. However, it must be stressed they're rarely easy to read and usually assume a considerable pre-existing wealth of knowledge and understanding. But by reading them you're able to avoid the 'middle-man bias' that's inevitable in the translation of original work into textbooks. You're also able to see how the ideas and techniques in the work have developed, and you're able to engage in the literature itself – a skill that's highly rewarded. It's important not to be discouraged by approaching articles and finding them too difficult to understand: you should skip over passages that are irrelevant or too technical, extracting the points that enhance your understanding and enrich your work.

what material you should cover: preparing in advance

The focus of your reading and learning should be guided by the content of your lectures and the recommended reading lists that accompany them. Your exam for a particular course is usually written by the lecturer who teaches it, and so it's most important to ensure you understand what's covered in your courses. However, university exams need to be approved by academics at other institutions to ensure comparability across universities, and they may insist on extending questions beyond the material covered in the lectures. Also, in certain universities exam questions may be written by faculty members who haven't had any direct involvement in the teaching, and they may focus on wider material as well. When deciding on what material to cover, then, you should:

❶ Attend all relevant lectures and seminar classes (a piece of obvious advice my wife finds somewhat hypocritical coming from me).

❷ Focus on the recommended reading list.

❸ Read as much additional literature as possible that isn't on the recommended reading list but is relevant to the topics covered in the lectures.

This obvious advice still leaves a significant problem, though. Recommended reading lists often go on for page after page, and sometimes simply list entire books – lists that are impossible to cover comprehensively and so require you to be selective in what you read. The key to dealing with this problem is to prepare your reading and note-taking before you pick up a single book. You should use your lectures, materials about course objectives and past paper exam questions to identify what knowledge is required. Consider, for example, the lecture (or two) on market failure (see Chapter 8) that inevitably forms part of a first-year microeconomics course. From the course outline and the relevant lectures it's clear that the types of market failure covered include externalities, merit and demerit goods, and market power. By looking at past exam papers and spending some time thinking about the sorts of questions that could be asked about market failure, you can then identify what you may need to know:

❶ The meaning of each form of failure.

❷ The way in which each is modelled/analysed by economists.

❸ Examples of each.

❹ How serious they are in reality.

❺ How economic analysis suggests they should be tackled, and the advantages and disadvantages of these policies.

Identifying areas of knowledge in this way immediately provides a structure for your notes and helps to keep them relevant. You may find it useful to structure your notes over a number of pages, so that each page is headed with a separate area of knowledge. Doing this should give you a number of benefits:

(a) **Selection**. It should help you to more easily, quickly and effectively select useful items from seemingly endless reading lists, and the useful passages within each of them. Furthermore, having identified items that are likely to be useful, you're then able to quickly flick through each of them to identify which chapters, sections and paragraphs are actually of use. You can then go back over them, only reading thoroughly those passages that are beneficial. Whole books can be covered in this way in surprising speed, as you extract only the useful information.

(b) **Avoiding waste**. It should help you to enhance your notes whilst avoiding wasteful duplication. Some items on a reading list cover virtually identical material, which can be very useful since different authors explain things differently. Reading more than one explanation of a single topic often helps to consolidate and expand your understanding of it. Preparing your notes in advance allows for such consolidation without the need to duplicate the notes themselves because additional information can be added to existing sections of notes alongside those already taken.

(c) **Future use**. Structuring your notes according to areas of knowledge rather than according to their sources will facilitate use at a later date. When writing essays, you can incorporate the information efficiently as it has already been collected into relevant groups. This also makes revision quicker.

Reading isn't the only learning that requires preparation if it's to be optimised: it's also important that you prepare your lecture notes in advance of the relevant lectures. Lecturers usually circulate their lecture slides and/or handouts in advance, which you should read before the lecture so you can identify particularly difficult areas to focus on. Being aware of the material on the slides and in the handouts, and preparing your notes to be taken in lectures, also helps you avoid the temptation of writing down everything the lecturer says.

how to maximise your time

Once you've prepared your reading or lecture notes – you've identified the required information and have structured the pages of notes you're looking to take – you then need to take your notes quickly but effectively. This is another skill that comes from practice, but there are a few tips that may prove helpful. The process of efficient reading and note-taking is illustrated in Figure 4.1. This process takes time, but the benefits of greater reading

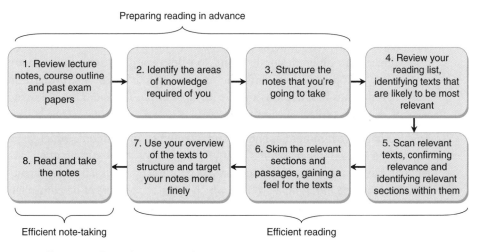

Figure 4.1 Preparing your reading

efficiency and more focused and relevant note-taking certainly makes it worthwhile.

It's necessary to read quickly because of the vast amount of material you're required to cover. Whole books have been written about speed reading, and it's certainly advisable to look into these techniques more closely (see Chapter 15). Very briefly, though, I find the **scan-skim-read** strategy helpful. **Scanning** is where you quickly search through text for specific words or phrases, enabling you to identify whether a given passage of text is relevant or not. Obviously, this can only be done after you've spent some time identifying the key words. **Skimming** is where you review an entire text without reading it fully. This gives you a feel for what the text is about as quickly as possible. I find reading the headings, sub-headings and the first and last sentences of each paragraph an effective way to get such a quick understanding of a text. Finally, **reading** is where you actually work through the text thoroughly and carefully. I find it helpful to use each of these techniques in combination: scanning a text to establish which parts of it (if any) are relevant, then skimming it to acquire a general understanding of what it says, and finally reading the relevant parts carefully to take the necessary notes.

There's a specialised vocabulary that accompanies economics, which lends itself to shorthand that's useful for taking notes quickly. Table 4.1 presents some of the shorthand that I personally find useful. This is an amalgamation of shorthand that's standard in the economics literature (such as P for price and π for profit) and notation that makes sense to me and that I've developed the habit of using. However, this is only my suggestion: you may find alternative shorthand more logical and useful. Of utmost importance when using shorthand is that it's easy to remember when taking notes, easy to decipher when reviewing the notes at a later date, and becomes second nature – and so it should be personal to you.

As well as using notation such as this to shorten words, it's important to develop a way of shortening entire sentences – removing words and phrases without losing the point being made. Unfortunately, this is something that can only be developed with practice since different words take on different levels of significance in different contexts and so rules regarding their omission are ineffective. This point, along with the use and effectiveness of shorthand in general, is perhaps best demonstrated with an example. Consider the following passage, which is typical in economics.

An injection of government spending and a reduction in taxation – which together is an example of expansionary fiscal policy – in the run-up to an election but at a time when the economy is near full employment may simply serve to increase inflation; a problem which in time may have to be controlled by a tightening of monetary policy in the form of an increase in the interest rate.

This passage can be shortened using the suggested shorthand, with no loss of detail or accuracy, as follows.

↑G + ↓T (e.g. ↑FP) in election run-up but when Ec is near FE may simply ↑inf – this may have to be controlled by ↓MP (↑r).

Please note that words such as 'an' and phrases such as 'which together is' have been removed in the note-taking in this example. In other passages it may be important to maintain these in the notes, and so it's important your shorthand is flexible, which comes from practice.

Table 4.1 *Useful economics shorthand (omitting standard mathematical symbols that are also useful in economics note-taking)*

Term	Shorthand	Term	Shorthand
Balance of payments	BoP	Income	Y
Business cycle	BC	Increase/expansion	↑
Capital	K	Inflation	Ṗ
Consumption	C	(Real) interest rate	(R)r
Decrease/contraction	↓	International trade	Intd
Depreciation	δ	Labour	L
Economy	Ec	Leads to	→
Economic growth	Gr	Market	Mkt
(Real) exchange rate	(R)er	Monetary policy	MP
Exports	X	Net national product	NNP
Fiscal policy	FP	Price	P
Full employment	FE	Production	Prd
Function	f	Profit	Π
Government spending	G	Savings	S
Gross domestic product	GDP	Subsidisation	Sub
Gross national product	GNP	Taxation	T
Imports	M	Unemployment	U

Taking notes in such a shortened way considerably speeds up the process, which is hugely beneficial for keeping up with a fast-talking lecturer or when ploughing through a pile of books. The key is to practise taking notes in this way so that it becomes second nature and instinctive.

Third, it's important to leave space in your notes so that you can incorporate additional information at a later date. Preparing your notes as suggested above lends itself to doing this, as information is immediately grouped according to topic and so further information can be added at the bottom of each section of notes. However, it's also useful to leave wide margins in your notes so that further information can be added alongside your existing notes at the relevant places.

what you should do with your notes

Gaining an understanding of the subject matter doesn't ensure your success, though. Once you understand part of the subject material – from attending lectures or from wider reading – you should do three further things:

❶ **Review it regularly**. Memory of the material can only be made long-lasting by regularly reviewing it. In practice this means not only re-reading your notes, although that's undoubtedly helpful, but also the further manipulation of them. As Simon Fowell, an undergraduate economics student at the University of Leeds, comments:

To be a successful student you have to study little but often. Don't leave learning until the last minute as you won't remember it later on. Read a little after lectures; squeeze any extra detail into your notes; and then copy them up neatly some other time so they properly stick in your mind. Never be afraid to ask lecturers or tutors any questions – they're happy to help, and know what they're talking about.

Continually condensing your notes is an effective way of reviewing the material: it also helps you develop a final set of revision notes that are succinct and quick to use.

❷ **Use it**. From my experience, subject material is not comprehensively understood until it has been used, which can take a number of forms: writing it in different formats – using it to answer practice essay and exam questions, for instance – or explaining it to, and discussing it with, other people. I often find I think I know something fully until I come to write it down or explain it to someone else, at which point I realise there are gaps in my understanding. Explaining it to non-economists is often particularly fruitful as they ask questions that lecturers and authors simply take for granted and that really test your understanding.

❸ **Apply and evaluate it**. Economics is about understanding the surrounding world, not about learning abstract theories and models. Economic theory is developed so that actual behaviour can be analysed and understood. Simply learning the theories, then, leaves your study incomplete. It's certainly necessary for you to understand economic theory, but it's also necessary for you to understand the surrounding world and to be able to assess how effectively the former explains the latter. You can only do this by reading newspapers and magazines that discuss current affairs and books that deal with the history of economic thought; but you should be aware of the bias of interpretation that inevitably accompanies such texts and you should try to see through such bias by reading different views of the same events. Successful students develop their own opinions regarding current and historic affairs and are able to draw upon these, when relevant, in their essays and other assessed work.

4.2 tackling theoretical analysis: the diagrams and maths

If you're to study economics successfully, just being able to describe the theories and empirical results learned isn't sufficient: you need to be able to thoroughly analyse them as well. In practice this means being able to understand and use diagrams and maths.

Theoretical analysis – by which I mean the study and examination of one or more economic models – is extremely important in economics because it's such a powerful tool, often leading to important and sometimes surprising results. As explained in Section 1.4, an economic model is a simplification of an aspect of the economy – usually expressed in either mathematical equations or diagrams – that economists develop because the reality is too complex to be studied directly. To develop and use a model, an economist goes through the following steps:

Step 1: Determine the question to be answered.

Step 2: Consider the aspect of the economy that this involves and decide which elements are likely to be most important to the question asked: these are the exogenous aspects of the model.

Step 3: Establish how the exogenous aspects interact with one another. These interactions are expressed as either mathematical equations or lines on a diagram, and form the final model.

Step 4: Manipulate the model to obtain an answer to the question posed.

Consider the model examined in Box 4.1, which is a simplified version of that developed by Mark Armstrong, John Vickers and Jidong Zhou in their article in the *RAND Journal of Economics* in 2009.

BOX 4.1: **Prominence and consumer search**

Imagine the following situation. You're flying off on holiday the day after tomorrow and so you go into your local town to buy a book to read on the flight. It's been a while since you last bought a book and so you aren't sure what books have recently been released or what you really want. You need to search through the shelves of your local bookstore to help you make your decision.

When you walk into the store, you find some books are being specially promoted. You're faced with an impressive display stand for one book immediately on entering, there's a big poster advertising the bookstore's 'recommended book of the month' covering one wall, and there's a list of the top ten bestsellers on another. You're being subjected to **prominence**: a marketing strategy in which one or more products are brought to the attention of consumers first.

The question is: when there's competition between books in terms of price, will the prominent book be more or less expensive than its rivals?

To answer this question theoretically, consider the simplified situation (the model) in which:

> There are a number of publishers, each of which supplies a different book.
> The publishers all set the prices for their books at the same time.
> The publishers all know the book of publisher 1 is prominent – that it will be looked at first by all consumers – and that all the other books will be searched randomly.
> Each consumer has an individual set of desires regarding books, which determines the utility they receive from buying one.

If consumers had complete information about all the books on the shelves, they would simply buy the book that maximises their **surplus utility** (see Box 7.2), the utility they receive over and above the price they have to pay. However, it's likely that consumers don't have this information and so need to search through the books. This leads to further elements of the model:

> Consumers search through the available books one at a time.
> As consumers search through the books, they discover the utility they would receive from each book and its price; but this search is costly in the sense that it takes time to look at each book.
> Consumers can freely recall the utilities and prices of all the books they've already looked at.
> Consumers have a target amount of surplus utility they want to receive from a book. Consumers look first at the prominent book. They decide whether the surplus utility they would receive from buying it is greater than their target utility, and if it is, whether the extent to which it's greater is itself equal to or greater than the cost of looking further. This sounds more complicated than it is. If the surplus utility they would receive from buying the first book is greater than their target utility, they'll be happy to buy it. However, it may be possible for them to look at another book and still come back to buy the one they looked at first if the second book isn't as good, and still obtain a surplus utility greater than their target utility. If this is the case, they continue their search. Logically, they continue to look at further books until the extent to which the surplus utility they would receive from buying the best book they've seen so far is just equal to the cost of searching further. At this point, to look at another book would incur a cost causing the final surplus utility they take home from buying the best book they've seen so far to be less than their target utility: the shopping trip would be a failure.

Let me give an example of this process. Imagine a consumer walks into a bookstore, having already decided he wants £3's worth of surplus utility from the book he buys. He immediately looks at the prominent book, which takes time that he values at 50 pence (his search cost). He finds that it's priced at £9 and would give him utility worth £11. His surplus utility if he was to buy this book would be £1.50 (utility of £11 minus the cost of £9 minus the search cost of 50 pence). This is less than his target surplus utility of £3 and so he continues his search. The second book he looks at costs £6 and would provide him with utility worth £10.50. If he was to buy this book now, his surplus utility would be £3.50 (utility of £10.50 minus the price of £6 minus the total search cost so far of £1: he has looked at two books, which costs him 50 pence each time). This is above his target utility and so he's happy to buy it. However, he can look at a third book (which would cost him 50 pence to do) and still satisfy his target utility if he decides to buy the second book afterwards. It's rational for him to do this and so he looks at a third book, finding it has a £7 price label and would give him a utility worth only £9. If he was to buy this book he would enjoy a surplus utility of only 50 pence (utility of £9 minus the price of £7 minus the total search cost of £1.50) and so he returns to the second book. Looking at the third book has reduced his surplus utility from the second book to £3 (utility of £10.50 minus the price of £6 minus the total search cost, which is now £1.50), and looking at a fourth book would reduce it to below his target level, and so he rationally ends his search now and buys the second book.

Returning to the model, then, if the prominent book gives consumers a surplus utility greater than their target utility, but not enough to make looking at other books worthwhile, they immediately stop their search and buy it. If it doesn't give them a surplus utility greater than their target, or if it does but it's still worthwhile to look further, they move on to a second, randomly chosen book. They evaluate this in the same way, and respond in one of three ways. If the second book isn't as good as the first but it's now not worthwhile looking further, they buy the prominent book. If the second book isn't as good as the first but it is still worthwhile looking further, they move on to a third book. If the second book is better than the first, but the surplus utility it gives them isn't greater than their target utility by more than the cost of looking further, they buy the second book. And so the search process continues.

The publishers of the non-prominent books know they may be at the back of the queue: they may be looked at last. They also know that if consumers look at their book, they must have thought all the other books on the shelves were either not good enough or were good enough but cost an amount that made it worthwhile to look further. This gives publishers of non-prominent books a sense of power, which they use to charge higher prices.

Overall, the publisher of the prominent book charges a lower price for its book than the other publishers charge for theirs. Also, the higher the cost of looking at additional books, the sooner consumers stop the search process and settle on a book to buy.

The four steps above are clear in the model:

Step 1: The question is straightforward: should we expect prominent goods to have higher or lower prices than their non-prominent alternatives?

Step 2: The authors have simplified the situation by including only those elements important to answering the question at hand. For example, the model includes only a single type of product and all consumers within the model are assumed to engage in the same decision-making process. These are clearly unrealistic assumptions, but they serve to make the situation simpler so an answer to the question can be found.

Step 3: It's clear how all the elements interact with one another. For example, the publishers supply the books for the shelves and the consumers search through them in a way that both producers and consumers understand.

Step 4: The elements of the model are brought together to reach an answer to the question. The answer is logical and cannot be denied given the way the model has been set up. The answer in this case is also surprising: most people would probably assume the prominent book would be sold for a higher price than the alternatives because of its prominence. This is one reason why theoretical analysis of models such as this is so important: it can lead to results that are surprising, but logical all the same.

Box 4.1 also highlights the primary reason why maths is used by economists. The article in the *RAND Journal of Economics* in which Mark Armstrong and his co-authors present their model is very mathematical. This makes the explanation of the model complicated and daunting to read, but it is also very clear and precise. Even though I've tried in Box 4.1 to describe the model as clearly as possible, the explanation of when a consumer stops his search process and buys a book is still tricky to follow, which is why I give a numerical example of it. An advantage of maths is that it's often clearer and more precise than words can be, particularly when explaining complicated models and ideas, which is why economists use it so much in their work and why mastering it is valuable to you in your study of the subject.

diagrammatical analysis

In the first year of an undergraduate degree the form of theoretical analysis you come across the most is that of diagrams. Before discussing what it means to analyse diagrams, a couple of obvious but very important points should be made:

① When drawing diagrams, you must make sure they're clear. Many students make their diagrams too small or fail to ensure they're neat, both of which can often render them unfathomable. Using a computer to draw diagrams is always preferable, but if you have to draw them by hand then you must take the time to do so carefully.

② Every single line and relevant area on a diagram, along with the axes, must be clearly and appropriately labelled. Again, too many students lose valuable marks because of sloppy, or sometimes non-existent, labelling.

Thorough diagrammatical analysis is perhaps most effectively demonstrated using a simple example, the subject material for which is outlined in Section 8.2. Consider the following question: 'Using a demand and supply diagram, analyse the effects of an indirect tax on petrol.'

The first step in diagrammatical analysis is to draw the relevant diagram, making it clear and specific to the question. This is done for the question above

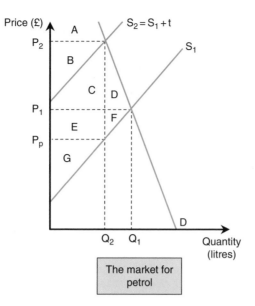

Figure 4.2 *Example of diagrammatical analysis*

in Figure 4.2. It's extremely important to make the diagram specific: it should not just be copied from a textbook. We know the demand for petrol isn't very sensitive to changes in price – the price of petrol can increase significantly and people will continue to buy a similar amount because they need it in their everyday lives – and so the demand curve in Figure 4.2 is steep, certainly more so than that for the supply of petrol. The vertical axis is labelled 'price', which is measured in money terms, and the horizontal axis is labelled 'quantity', which for petrol is measured in litres.

Once you've constructed the diagram, it's important to analyse it thoroughly. An example of this is presented in Box 4.2, which is accompanied by a commentary outlining the key elements to be included in any analysis. All the terms used are explained in Part 2.

BOX 4.2: **An example of diagrammatical analysis**

As shown in the diagram (Figure 4.2), the petrol market is initially characterised by a demand curve that is more price-inelastic than the supply curve (labelled D and S_1, respectively). Demand is price-inelastic because petrol is considered to be a necessity for the majority of the population who use cars to get to work every day; supply is less so because of the ability of producers to store surplus stocks of petrol.

The diagram is clearly referred to and its component parts – in this case the demand and supply curves – are identified and their characteristics explained.

The initial market equilibrium – the point where demand and supply are in balance and the market clears – is such that the market price for a litre of petrol is P_1, at which Q_1 litres of petrol are consumed. In this initial state, consumer welfare, represented by the amount consumers are willing and able to pay for the petrol they consume (which, in turn, is represented by the demand curve) in excess of the price they actually have to pay, is given by areas A, B, C and D – this is the initial consumer surplus. The welfare of producers, represented by the amount of revenue they receive that is in excess of the amount for which they are actually willing and able to supply the petrol they sell (which is represented by the supply curve), is given by areas E, F and G – this is producer surplus.

The initial state is clearly and thoroughly outlined, with all relevant terminology (such as consumer and producer welfare) defined and explained.

Levying an indirect tax on petrol causes its supply curve to shift inwards, from S_1 to S_2, because it has to be paid by the producer and so effectively causes the marginal cost of every quantity supplied to increase by the tax rate, which in the diagram is denoted by t. Producers are now only willing and able to supply a given quantity of petrol if the price they receive for it is increased by t. The tax, then, causes the equilibrium price to rise from P_1 to P_2 and the quantity traded to fall from Q_1 to Q_2.

The immediate effects of the tax are outlined and the intuition underlying them is explained.

The tax serves to raise revenue for the government, which is given by the tax rate multiplied by the number of litres of petrol sold after the tax has been imposed, or areas B, C and E in the diagram. Ignoring any political effects, this suggests the government is better off from the imposition of the tax. Consumers and producers, on the other hand, experience a reduction in their welfare because of the tax. Consumer welfare, represented by consumer surplus, is reduced to area A only because the market price has increased to P_2 and the number of litres of petrol they are willing and able to consume has fallen to Q_2. Producer welfare, represented by producer surplus, is reduced to area E because the price they effectively receive has fallen from P_1 to P_p (they are required to pay the tax rate, $t = P_2 - P_p$, to the government for each litre they sell) and the quantity they sell has been reduced to Q_2. The market as a whole experiences a reduction in total welfare as areas D and F are no longer enjoyed by any of the actors. This is the deadweight welfare loss of the tax and is caused because fewer litres of petrol are being traded, the price for consumers has increased and the effective producer price has been reduced.

The deeper welfare effects of the policy are clearly outlined and explained. For example, the intuition underlying the deadweight welfare loss.

Due to demand being more price-inelastic than supply, the tax burden imposed on consumers exceeds that
borne by producers. This is because producers know they
can pass the tax onto the consumers without significantly reducing the amount of petrol they sell. Consumers have to pay the portion of the tax rate given by $P_2 - P_1$
to the government for each unit they consume, whereas
producers pay only the remaining portion of the tax rate,
$P_1 - P_p$, for each unit they supply. Consumers clearly bear
the greatest part of the tax burden, which is reflected
in the fact that the reduction in their welfare is greater
than that of the producers. Also, due to the inelasticity
of demand, the reduction in the consumption of petrol is
relatively small, from Q_1 to Q_2 litres, whereas the increase
in the market price is relatively large.

If the policy is intended to reduce consumption,
perhaps due to environmental concerns, its effectiveness
may be limited; whereas if the intention is to raise
government revenue, perhaps to address the national debt
problem, it is likely to be successful.

The remaining effects, in this case regarding the distribution of the welfare effects and the likely effectiveness of the policy, are also clearly outlined and explained. For exam- ple, the intuition under- lying why consumers bear the brunt of the policy.

The above example demonstrates how you should use diagrams to analyse
questions. To summarise, the key things to ensure are:

① The diagram is clear and easy to read, and includes all relevant labelling.

② The initial situation is outlined and explained, ensuring all terminology is
defined.

③ The immediate diagrammatical effects are stated and explained, making
them absolutely clear on the diagram (shifting curves, for instance).

④ All remaining relevant effects are then identified and explained.

Throughout such analysis, the intuition underlying the effects should be
explained. For example, why does an indirect tax cause the supply curve to
shift inwards and why do consumers end up paying the biggest share of the
tax? The end result should be that there's no relevant element of the diagram
left unexplained.

mathematical analysis

As you progress through an undergraduate economics course, the emphasis
of analysis is increasingly placed on maths rather than diagrams, although
diagrams continue to be used throughout. The reasons for this are that maths
makes complicated analysis clear and precise, and so using it is an essential skill that you need to develop, and that advanced analysis is often too

complicated for diagrams (requiring diagrams to be three-dimensional, for instance).

Mathematical analysis is also perhaps most effectively examined using an example. Consider the question above, but in a slightly altered form: 'Using a mathematical exposition of the model of demand and supply, analyse the effects of an indirect tax on petrol.'

If possible, which it is here, it's advisable for you to sketch out a diagrammatical analysis of the question before attempting to analyse it mathematically: this helps you ensure that you cover all relevant points. An example of the analysis in this case is presented in Box 4.3, in which important elements are again identified. It's important to stress that you must always present each step of the calculation. Mathematical analysis in which only the final solution is presented is likely to be awarded only a minimum of marks: showing your complete working is always best. Again, this should be read in conjunction with Part 2.

BOX 4.3: **An example of mathematical analysis**

Assuming the demand and supply curves of petrol are linear, the normal and inverse forms of the curves are outlined below. The normal form of these curves express quantities demanded or supplied as functions of price, whereas the inverse forms express price as functions of quantities demanded or supplied. The parameters a and c are constants, whilst b and d are the gradients of the normal demand and supply curves respectively.

(1)

	Normal form	Inverse form
Demand	$Q^d = a - bP^d$	$P^d = \dfrac{a}{b} - \dfrac{1}{b}Q^d$
Supply	$Q^s = c + dP^s$	$P^s = \dfrac{1}{d}Q^s - \dfrac{c}{d}$

(2)

Equilibrium in the petrol market is where the quantity demanded is equal to the quantity supplied. An expression for the equilibrium price is calculated by setting the normal demand and supply curves equal to one another and then rearranging; and that for the equilibrium quantity is calculated by setting the inverse demand and supply curves equal to one another and then rearranging. Terms superscripted with an * denote equilibrium values, where demand is equal to supply.

Equilibrium price	Notes	Equilibrium quantity	Notes
$Q^d = Q^s$	(equilibrium condition)	$P^d = P^s$	(equilibrium condition)
$a - bP^* = c + dP^*$	(insert functions)	$\dfrac{a}{b} - \dfrac{1}{b}Q^* = \dfrac{1}{d}Q^* - \dfrac{c}{d}$	(insert functions)
$a - c = bP^* + dP^*$	(rearrange)	$\dfrac{a}{b} + \dfrac{c}{d} = \dfrac{1}{d}Q^* + \dfrac{1}{b}Q^*$	(rearrange)
$P^* = \dfrac{a - c}{b + d}$	(find expression for P*)	$\dfrac{a}{b} + \dfrac{c}{d} = \left(\dfrac{1}{d} + \dfrac{1}{b}\right)Q^*$	(rearrange)
		$\dfrac{a}{b} + \dfrac{c}{d} = \left(\dfrac{b + d}{bd}\right)Q^*$	(multiply out fractions)
		$Q^* = \left(\dfrac{a}{b} + \dfrac{c}{d}\right)\left(\dfrac{bd}{b + d}\right)$	(find expression for Q*)

The imposition of an indirect tax on petrol causes the price required by suppliers, for any given volume of petrol, to increase by the tax rate. Denoting the tax rate by t, the indirect tax is represented by increasing the constant in the expression of the inverse supply curve by t. In the expression for the normal supply curve, the tax causes the value of the supplier price to fall by t. These effects on the expressions for the curves are shown below.

	Normal form	Inverse form
Demand	$Q^d = a - bP^d$	$P^d = \dfrac{a}{b} - \dfrac{1}{b}Q^d$
Supply	$Q^s_t = c + d(P^s - t)$	$P^s_t = \dfrac{1}{d}Q^s - \dfrac{c}{d} + t$

It is now necessary to derive expressions for the equilibrium price and quantity in the petrol market after the imposition of the tax. To find the new equilibrium price you set the altered expression for the normal supply curve equal to the normal demand curve and rearrange. To find the new equilibrium quantity you set the altered expression for the inverse supply curve equal to the inverse demand curve and rearrange.

Equilibrium price	Notes	Equilibrium quantity	Notes
$Q^d_t = Q^s_t$	(equilibrium condition)	$P^d_t = P^s_t$	(equilibrium condition)
$a - bP^*_t = c + d\left(P^*_t - t\right)$	(insert functions)	$\dfrac{a}{b} - \dfrac{1}{b}Q^*_t = \dfrac{1}{d}Q^*_t - \dfrac{c}{d} + t$	(insert functions)
$a - c = dP^*_t - dt + bP^*_t$	(rearrange and multiply out brackets)	$\dfrac{a}{b} + \dfrac{c}{d} - t = \dfrac{1}{d}Q^*_t + \dfrac{1}{b}Q^*_t$	(rearrange)
$a - c + dt = P^*_t(d + b)$	(rearrange and simplify to isolate the price)	$\dfrac{a}{b} + \dfrac{c}{d} - t = \left(\dfrac{1}{d} + \dfrac{1}{b}\right)Q^*_t$	(rearrange)
$P^*_t = \dfrac{a - c + dt}{d + b}$	(find expression for the new equilibrium price)	$\dfrac{a}{b} + \dfrac{c}{d} - t = \left(\dfrac{b + d}{bd}\right)Q^*_t$	(multiply out fractions)
		$Q^*_t = \left(\dfrac{a}{b} + \dfrac{c}{d} - t\right)\left(\dfrac{bd}{b + d}\right)$	(find expression for the new equilibrium quantity)

Having derived expressions for the equilibrium price and quantity in the petrol market both before and after the imposition of the indirect tax, it is now possible to isolate the actual effects of the indirect tax. This is done by subtracting the expressions for the initial equilibrium price and quantity from those for equilibrium price and quantity after the tax has been imposed.

Effect on price	Notes	Effect on quantity	Notes
$P^*_t - P^*$	(expression for change in equilibrium price)	$Q^*_t - Q^*$	(expression for change in equilibrium quantity)
$\dfrac{a - c + dt}{d + b} - \dfrac{a - c}{d + b}$	(insert functions from above)	$\left(\dfrac{a}{b} + \dfrac{c}{d} - t\right)\left(\dfrac{bd}{b + d}\right) - \left(\dfrac{a}{b} + \dfrac{c}{d}\right)\left(\dfrac{bd}{b + d}\right)$	(insert functions from above)
$(+)\dfrac{dt}{d + b}$	(simplify)	$(-)t\left(\dfrac{bd}{b + d}\right)$	(simplify)

The effects of the indirect tax, then, are that the equilibrium price is increased by $dt/(d+b)$ and equilibrium quantity is reduced by $t[bd/(b+d)]$. Clearly, the size of the effects are partly determined by the value of the tax rate, t. The greater the tax rate, the greater the effects on both equilibrium price and quantity will be, which is intuitive. However, the sizes of the effects are also determined by the values of b and d, which are the gradients of the normal demand and supply curves. The greater their values, the greater the effects will be. Again, this is intuitive because steeper normal demand and supply curves imply more price-elastic inverse demand and supply curves and so consumption and production that is more sensitive to changes in price. Finally, the distribution of the tax burden between consumers and producers is determined by the relative values of b and d. When $d = b$, equilibrium price rises by half the tax rate, meaning consumers and producers each have to pay half of the tax rate for each unit traded: the burden is equally distributed. When $d > b$, equilibrium price rises by more than half the tax rate, meaning consumers pay more than half the tax rate for each unit traded: consumers bear the majority of the tax burden. Finally, when $d < b$, equilibrium price rises by less than half the tax rate, meaning consumers pay less than half the tax rate for each unit traded: producers bear the majority of the tax burden. This is also intuitive, because when $d > b$, demand is more price-inelastic than supply. Consumers are less sensitive to changes in price than producers and so more than half the tax rate is passed onto consumers to pay in the form of higher prices.

Notes:

1 The analysis begins with the initial conditions in the petrol market being clearly outlined, with explanations for each of the terms used and with all the workings needed to derive the initial equilibrium conditions.

2 The effects of the indirect tax on the equilibrium market conditions are clearly identified and the derivation of them is clearly explained.

Maths is often viewed by economics students with a sense of fear and foreboding. The seemingly bewildering array of symbols and apparently incomprehensible list of rules makes such apprehension understandable. However, such feelings are unnecessary. It's often said that some people are simply unable to master maths, but this isn't the case. Maths is very much like a language, with different symbols needing to be combined, according to specified rules, in different ways for different reasons; and I've never heard it said that some people are simply unable to learn a foreign language. Languages may come easier for some people than for others but everyone is able to learn a language if they devote the necessary time to doing so. Precisely the same is true of maths as well. Table 4.2 provides definitions of the mathematical symbols you're most likely to come across in your first year.

Table 4.2 Definitions of common mathematical symbols

Symbol	Meaning	Definition
Equality		
$=$	Equal to	$x = y$ means x has the same value as y
$\approx$	Approximately equal to	$x \approx y$ means x has approximately the same value as y
$\neq$	Not equal to	$x \neq y$ means x does not have the same value as y
$<$	Smaller than	$x < y$ means x has a smaller value than y
$>$	Greater than	$x > y$ means x has a greater value than y
$\leq$	Smaller than or equal to	$x \leq y$ means x has a value either smaller than or equal to y
$\geq$	Greater than or equal to	$x \geq y$ means x has a value either greater than or equal to y
$\equiv$	Defined as	$x \equiv y$ means x is the same as y by definition
Operation		
$+$	Plus	$x + y$ means the values of x and y added together
$-$	Minus	$x - y$ means the value of x with the value of y subtracted from it
$\pm$	Plus or minus	$x \pm y$ means the value of y either added to or subtracted from that of x
$\times$	Multiply (also denoted by $\cdot$)	$x \times y$ means the values of x and y multiplied together
$/$	Divide (also denoted by $\div$)	x / y means the value of x divided by that of y
$\prod$	Product of	$\prod_{n=0}^{n=5} y_n$ means all the values of y between (and including) y_0 and y_5 multiplied together, i.e. $(y_0 \times y_1 \times y_2 \times y_3 \times y_4 \times y_5)$
$\sum$	Sum of	$\sum_{n=0}^{n=5} y_n$ means all the values of y between (and including) y_0 and y_5 added together, i.e. $(y_0 + y_1 + y_2 + y_3 + y_4 + y_5)$
$\sqrt{}$	Square root of	$\sqrt{x}$ means the square root of x, i.e. the number that equals x when it is multiplied by itself
$\partial x / \partial y$	Partial derivative of	$\partial x / \partial y$ means the partial derivative of x with respect to y, which means the amount x changes in response to a change in y
$\int_{x_1}^{x_2} f(x)dx$	Definite integral of	$\int_{x=0}^{x=5} f(x)dx$ means the area between the horizontal axis and the graph of the function $f(x)$ between (and including) $x = 0$ and $x = 5$

Description		
$f(x)$	Function of	$y = f(x)$ means that y is a function of, or is determined by, x
|...|	Absolute value	$\|x\|$ means the absolute value of x, for example $\|(-4)\|$ would be 4
$\Rightarrow$	Implies	A = B means that if A is true then so is B
~	Probability distribution	$X \sim P$ means the variable X has the probability distribution P
$\forall$	For all	$\forall\ x: y$ means that y is true for all x
$\exists$	For at least one	$\exists\ x: y$ means that y is true for at least one x
R	The real numbers	The numbers that can be written as decimal numbers and so lie somewhere on the number line (please note, you will come across theoretical numbers for which this is not possible)
N	The natural numbers	These are the ordinary counting numbers, i.e. 0, 1, 2, 3,... (sometimes 0 is excluded)
Q	The rational numbers	These are the numbers that can be written as x/y where both x and y are integers and y is not zero
Z	The integers	These are the whole numbers, i.e. ...,-2, -1, 0, 1, 2,...

From my own experience, by far the best way to learn maths is through regular and repeated practice: by answering question after question. As you do this, you identify terminology and techniques you're unsure about, which you can look up and learn by applying it to the questions at hand. Gradually, you develop a comprehensive understanding of the techniques and the ability to apply them in a range of different contexts. By investing sufficient time, using appropriate learning materials and employing effective techniques, everyone is able to build up their mathematical ability to the required level. Maths is certainly not something you should fear.

4.3 tackling statistics

We now come to the part of economics that most students find the most daunting and difficult: **econometrics**.

Key term: econometrics

Econometrics is simply the application of statistical analysis to economic data. There are two types:

(1) **Cross-sectional econometrics** is the analysis of economic data relating to a single period in time. It usually examines the relationship between different things at a

Econometrics is absolutely vital to economics because it's only by testing our theories against actual data that we can see whether they – and the conclusions they lead to – are correct or not. It's only by doing this that we can be sure that the policies we recommend governments implement are in fact sensible. As we see in Section 5.7, many of the implications of standard consumer theory are being shown to be incorrect in reality and so to base policies upon this theory is clearly unwise.

Econometrics is often perceived by students as being complicated and boring, largely because of the mathematical proofs involved. There's certainly a lot of maths in econometrics, but this is important because only when we understand the underlying maths can we truly understand what our data and the econometric tests we apply to it actually show. However, econometrics is far from boring because it's the only way we can see how the real world actually works. As we see above, economic theory involves the logical study of a simplified version of the world – the world of economics – which we hope gives us insight into the actual world, but it's only through econometrics and the analysis of actual data that we can test whether these insights – or **hypotheses** – are correct or not. Box 4.4 presents one example of how econometrics helps us to understand our world: an example that I think is particularly interesting.

BOX 4.4: **Econometrics in action: income differences across countries**

In their article in the journal the *American Economic Review* in 2001, Daron Acemoğlu (see Section 14.13), Simon Johnson and James Robinson (AJR) used econometrics to analyse what has caused the large differences in income per person across different countries: a question we need to understand if we're to help poor countries grow. Economic theorists suggest the way in which a country is governed and structured – what economists call its **institutions** – is an important influence on its income level. AJR sought to test this against the data.

The big problem they faced was how they could measure these institutions. Data about the levels of income per person in different countries was readily available, but not about how these countries are structured. AJR took a novel approach. As they couldn't measure institutions directly, they focused on what led to different institutions in the first place: by measuring this in different countries, they could identify the different institutions within them.

Specifically, AJR looked at the period of European colonisation and noticed that European colonisers employed two different strategies. In some countries they simply extracted all valuable raw materials, leaving the countries impoverished: Belgian colonisation of the Congo is an example of this. In others they actually settled, creating modern social structures, introducing education and the like: America, Australia, Canada and New Zealand are examples of this. AJR also noticed these two types of institution – extraction and settlement – continued after colonisation and were determined by the levels of disease in the countries. In countries with high rates of disease Europeans used extraction, whereas in countries with low rates of disease they settled. This gave AJR a way of measuring institutions: by measuring levels of disease during colonisation they could indirectly measure the resulting institutions. Such indirect analysis is known as **instrumental variable analysis**: disease here being the instrumental or representative variable for institutions.

Analysing the relationship between current income per person and data on the mortality rates of European soldiers, bishops and sailors in the colonies between the seventeenth and nineteenth centuries, AJR showed that the mortality rate – and so the resulting institutions – was exceptionally important in explaining why some countries today are rich and others are poor. In fact, the relationship between them is so significant that when we control for this effect countries in Africa and those near the equator aren't actually any poorer than rich countries. As we see below, it's always important to test whether empirical results are sensitive to small changes in the data used. AJR showed how their result remains highly significant even if there are changes in the location of countries, their climate, their current levels of disease, their religion, their natural resources, their soil quality and the composition of their populations: it's an exceptionally strong result. Using very clever econometrics, AJR showed how a country's institutions are of vital importance to the wealth of its population. From this, we see how European colonisation actually determined the wealth of countries today: European countries are highly responsible for poor countries being poor.

You probably won't be expected to learn econometrics until the second and third years of your degree. However, in your first year you will be required to take courses on statistics. It's exceptionally important for you to gain a good understanding of statistical analysis during your first year so you can tackle econometrics later on: the latter builds very much on the former.

4.4 thinking critically

The most highly prized skill you should strive to develop during your course is that of critical evaluation. The longer, most heavily weighted questions in economics exams are usually those requiring you to evaluate a statement or model and to justify your own opinion about it; and the highest marks for coursework are awarded to those students who not only demonstrate the abilities to describe and analyse but also the higher-order abilities to evaluate and justify personal judgements.

Evaluation means weighing up both sides of an argument. For example, evaluating a statement such as 'free trade is of vital importance to less developed countries' requires the arguments both for and against the statement to be explained and for them to be weighed against one another, leading to a fully justified overall judgement. Similarly, evaluating a model, such as the IS-LM model (see Section 9.5), requires the positive aspects of the model to be explained and weighed against its weaknesses, again leading to a justified overall judgement. Demonstrating your ability to do this thoroughly and to formulate and justify your own opinions is a key to success.

When evaluating a theoretical model you should consider and comment on three things:

1. **Its realism.** All models are based on assumptions to simplify the situation being studied. Does the model include all the elements from reality important to the question asked? Are the assumptions made about how those elements behave and interact with one another realistic? The assumptions made should be supported by evidence.

2. **Its usefulness and generality.** A good model leads to interesting and useful conclusions. Does the model you're evaluating lead to interesting, perhaps even surprising, results, or does it simply tell us something that was obvious from the outset? Does it generate conclusions that could assist policymakers in devising policies to make the economy function better? A good model is also one that can be modified to suit different situations. Does the model you're examining allow you to change the situation and to look at the effects of those changes, or is the model suited to only a narrow situation?

3. **Its complexity.** In the fourteenth century, English philosopher William of Occam suggested that it's wasteful to make things more complicated than they need to be. This principle is now known as **Occam's razor** or the **principle of parsimony**, and is an important criterion against which models should be evaluated. In effect it's the opposite of the first criterion above: simple (parsimonious) models are likely to be unrealistic, but realistic models are likely to be complicated. There needs to be a balance struck between these two: a good model should be just simple enough that it's workable whilst still reflecting the important aspects of reality.

When evaluating a piece of empirical/econometric analysis, you should consider and comment on four different things:

(a) **The data.** The source of the data used should be made clear. It should be reliable, unbiased and voluminous enough to give a true reflection of what's being studied. For example, if the study is about the changing level of governmental corruption in a developing country, data acquired from the government itself is likely to be biased and unreliable; and if the views of only fifty citizens of that country are included, the dataset isn't large enough to generate results representative of the country as a whole. The data should also successfully measure what's being studied. Taking the example of corruption again, using data reporting the number of government officials resigning from the government each month may not be an effective measure.

(b) **The methodology used**. Empirical work usually involves processing – sometimes called 'cleaning' – the data to make it usable. For example, this could involve the removal of strange data-points or its rescaling. Is it likely that the processing used in the work you're evaluating has changed the results at all? Has it introduced further biases into the work? Then there's the actual analysis of the data. Is it appropriate for the question being asked? Are all the steps in the analysis justified and are the reasons given sensible? Are all the elements that are important to the question included within the study? For example, if a study is looking at the difference between wages paid to men and women but fails to include the occupations of the men and women represented in the data, its results are going to be misleading: occupation is perhaps the most important determinant of wage rates.

(c) **The results**. It's always important that results are subjected to sensitivity analysis and diagnostic checks. Are the results based on a particular assumption or methodology, and if that's altered do the results change significantly? For example, a study of corruption in a particular country may show that it has increased over the past decade if it uses survey results from businessmen, but that it has fallen if it uses data from an independent observer. In this case the results are sensitive to the choice of data used and it's important this is reflected in the conclusions. This is the idea of sensitive analysis: how much do the results change if different data or tests are used? Strong results are robust to such changes. A good empirical paper also tests its results for statistical weaknesses, such as bias, and reports the outcome of these whilst adjusting the results accordingly. This is known as diagnostic testing. Does the work you're evaluating do these things? Have its results been tested and demonstrated to be strong?

(d) **Usefulness**. Similarly to a good theoretical model, a piece of empirical work should generate results that are interesting and potentially useful for policy-makers, rather than simply showing us something that was obvious from the start. Does the work that you're evaluating do this?

However, having said all this, a word of warning is needed. It's extremely important to be sure of how much critical thinking your lecturers want you to demonstrate in exams. Some lecturers encourage it, rewarding it highly when marking; but you should be aware that others want you to focus on explaining the models as they are, rather than critiquing them. You need to get the balance right – and that balance differs from lecturer to lecturer.

4.5 summary

> When reading and taking notes you should prepare your notes in advance, develop your ability to take notes quickly, and review, use and apply the notes you've taken.
> When using diagrams you should make sure they're clear, specific and fully labelled, and that your analysis is thorough.
> When using maths you should show all your workings, carefully going through each step in turn, and ensure that your analysis is thorough.
> It's important that you're able to think critically about all the economic ideas and theories you learn, but that you're careful to get the balance between explaining economic models and critiquing them right in exams and coursework.

introducing smaller-scale analysis: the microeconomic world

the next four chapters

Microeconomics is primarily concerned with three types of individual agent: consumers, producers and the government. They're collectively referred to as **economic actors** throughout this book, but in other books they're called economic agents. They interact with one another in markets, where they engage in some sort of trade. This is usually, but not necessarily, the trading of products for money: there's also the market of the household, for instance, in which family members interact with one another to make family decisions.

The ultimate goal of studying microeconomics, then, is for us to understand how these markets function: how the prices of products – by which I mean goods and services – are determined, what products are produced and sold, and in what quantities, and how beneficial this is to society as a whole. This is only possible by studying how economic actors make their decisions about what to produce and buy – and so what those decisions actually are – and what results when they make them. This is what micro-economics is all about.

Key term: microeconomics

Microeconomics is the study of the decision-making behaviour of economic actors and of how their interaction with one another in markets determines what products are produced and sold, and in what quantities, what prices they're traded at, how beneficial this is to society and what problems are caused, and how it can be improved.

The purpose of the following four chapters is to introduce and examine each of these actors and the markets in which they interact. They will cover:

1. How consumers decide what to buy (Chapter 5).
2. How producers decide how much to produce and sell (Chapter 6).
3. How consumers and producers interact with one another to determine the prices of products and the quantities of them produced and sold (Chapter 7).
4. Why governments intervene within markets, how they do this and the effects it has (Chapter 8).

The intention is not for these four chapters to take the place of your textbook for microeconomics. As indicated by the discussion in Section 4.1, it's impor-tant for you to use the books recommended to you by your microeconomics lecturers: it will be on these that your exams are likely to be based. The purpose of these four chapters is simply to introduce you to these topics in an accessible way, to introduce all the key terms and techniques that you will come across as you study them, and to explain why they're so important, placing them in con-text. I hope these chapters will act as the first point of reference for you as you study microeconomics.

its importance

To my mind, the purpose of studying economics is to enable us to under-stand how peoples' lives and society as a whole can be improved: to under-stand what the government can do to make society a better place in which to live (see Section 1.6). Microeconomics is crucial for this as it helps us see what motivates actors to make the decisions they make and the various prob-lems this causes for society: problems that include us having to pay extremely high prices for poor quality services and essential utilities, the growing levels of harmful addiction within society and the global threats caused by climate change. Only by fully understanding the microeconomics underlying these problems can we hope to devise policies to resolve them. This is what the next four chapters help us to do, and this is why they're so important and exciting.

5 what consumers buy

In this chapter we examine the behaviour of **consumers**, looking at what products they buy and how much they're willing to pay for them. This is the first step towards developing a complete understanding of how markets function, which, as mentioned above, is the ultimate goal of microeconomics.

Key term: consumer

A consumer is an actor within the economy who uses his income to buy products.

We assume consumers are individual decision-making units. This means it doesn't matter whether they're individuals or groups such as households: they behave as if they're single people. Later on in degree courses the actual decision-making processes within households and other groups is analysed in detail, but for now this assumption helps us maintain the clarity of the analysis.

There are two elements to how economists model consumer decision-making. The first is an examination of what consumers would like to buy and the second is an examination of what they can afford to buy. Once we understand each of these elements we can then determine what consumers actually buy, completing our model of consumer behaviour, which can then be extended in various ways.

It should be stressed the model we explore here is the standard model of consumer behaviour. Alternative models exist – the reasons why they've been developed are discussed in Section 5.7 – but the primary focus of this chapter is on the model you will be taught during your first year. This is the neoclassical model of consumer behaviour.

5.1 the products consumers would like to buy

Consumers can choose from a whole range of different products. The starting point of our model, then, is to examine which of these they would like to buy, and in what quantities. For ease of explanation, let's look at a typical consumer rather than looking at all consumers at the same time. We take this consumer to be representative of all others in the economy. Let's also simplify the situation so it involves only two products, which we call products X and Y. This allows us to represent them on a two-dimensional diagram.

We've immediately distorted the model away from the real world by making these simplifying assumptions, but this is necessary so we can keep the model solvable (or tractable, as economists say). The intention when creating any model is to keep it as simple as possible (the principle of parsimony: see Section 4.4) whilst including all the elements important for answering the question at hand. Modelling the world as consisting of only two products and identical consumers should make the analysis easy to follow, whilst leading to all the important conclusions about consumer behaviour. At the end of the chapter you should decide whether it achieves the correct balance between realism and parsimony.

Perhaps surprisingly, we don't actually look at the separate products available to the consumer. Instead, we look at the available *combinations* of the products, known as **consumption bundles**. We assume the consumer is able to compare different bundles and to identify which provides him with most utility. In fact, we assume he's able to rank all available bundles in order according to the utility they give him. He's able to create a **preference ordering** of all available bundles, with the bundle that gives him most utility (and so the one he prefers) at the top and that which gives him least utility (and so the one he desires least) at the bottom. In a preference ordering, it's fine for some bundles to be given equal rank if they give the consumer the same amount of utility. We say that he's **indifferent** between bundles that have the same rank.

Key term: consumption bundle

A consumption bundle is a combination of available products. Consider, for example, the situation in which the consumer is only able to buy lager and nuts. One consumption bundle is composed of three bottles of lager and two packets of nuts, and another of one bottle of lager and five packets of nuts. There actually exist an infinite number of such bundles, each with a different combination of the two products. What we're interested in is which bundle the consumer chooses to buy.

Key term: preference ordering

A preference ordering is a list of available consumption bundles according to the amount of utility they give the consumer. The consumer places the bundle that gives him greatest utility at the top and that which gives him least utility at the bottom. In a preference ordering it's fine for some bundles to be given the same rank if the consumer is indifferent between them. Taking the example above, the consumer may place the bundle with three bottles of lager and two packets of nuts above that with one bottle of lager and five packets of nuts in his preference ordering.

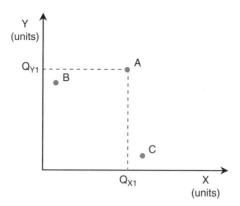

Figure 5.1 Consumption bundles

We represent these bundles on a diagram such as that in Figure 5.1, which measures the number of units of X along the horizontal axis and the number of units of Y along the vertical axis. Three possible bundles are identified in the figure. Bundle A, for instance, is composed of Q_{X1} units of X and Q_{Y1} units of Y. Every point in the space of the diagram represents a possible bundle, with bundles lying on an axis comprising zero units of one of the products and the bundle lying at the origin being the **null bundle**: meaning it's composed of zero units of both products.

To help the analysis that follows, we now need to make three further assumptions relating to the consumer's preferences:

❶ Preferences are complete: the consumer is able to compare every possible bundle and to create a preference ordering that contains every single bundle available to him. No bundle exists that he cannot place in his ranking, and so he can say which bundle he prefers when given a choice between any two of them.

❷ Preferences are reflexive: if the consumer is faced with two identical bundles, he's indifferent between them. In other words, the consumer gives two or more identical bundles exactly the same rank in his preference ordering. This is a common sense assumption, but it is needed to prevent strange effects when the model is put together.

❸ Preferences are transitive: if the consumer prefers bundle A to bundle B, and prefers bundle B to bundle C, then he must prefer bundle A to bundle C. It means the consumer's preference ordering is always in the form of a list and doesn't have any points which go round in circles.

Preference orderings are represented in diagrams such as that of Figure 5.1 by **indifference curves**.

Economists usually make two final assumptions about preferences, ensuring the indifference curves representing them take on the standard, well-behaved shape:

❶ **They're monotonic**: the consumer prefers to have more rather than less of the products. For example, if there are two products available and bundles A and B have equal amounts of one but bundle A has an additional unit of the second product to bundle B, the consumer prefers bundle A to bundle B.

❷ **They're strictly convex**: the consumer prefers average amounts of the available products to large amounts of some and very little of others. This reflects **diminishing marginal utility** (see page 62).

Given the assumptions of completeness, reflexivity, transitivity, monotonicity and strict convexity, indifference curves look like those in Figures 5.2a and 5.2b. In Figure 5.2a there's a single indifference curve, labelled IC$_1$. Every bundle along that curve – bundles A, B and C, for instance – gives the consumer an identical amount of utility. He's completely indifferent between them. Figure 5.2b shows a family of such curves, which we call an **indifference map**.

Please note the following about the diagrams:

❶ **All bundles on a given indifference curve give the consumer an identical amount of utility.** For example, bundles A, B and C – which all lie on IC$_2$

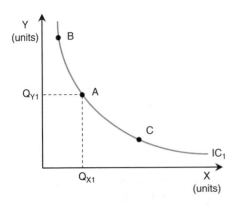

Figure 5.2a *A well-behaved indifference curve*

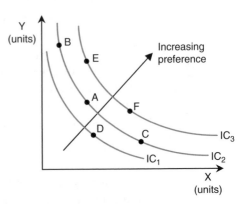

Figure 5.2b *A well-behaved indifference map*

in Figure 5.2b – give the consumer the same amount of utility; and bundles E and F – which lie on IC_3 – also give him the same amount of utility, but an amount that's different from that of A, B and C.

❷ **Preference increases as bundles contain more of both products.** The bundles on IC_3 are preferred to those on IC_2, which are preferred to those on IC_1. This is because of the assumption of monotonicity.

❸ **The indifference curves bend towards the origin** because of the assumption of strict convexity. The consumer prefers to have average amounts of both products, and so is indifferent between bundles that are closer to the null bundle but contain a more equal combination of products and those that are further away from the null bundle but are characterised by an unbalanced combination of products.

When you're drawing indifference curves, you should always make it clear in which direction preference is increasing by including a labelled arrow as in Figure 5.2b. You should also make sure your indifference curves never cross. Consider Figure 5.3. The consumer is indifferent between bundles A and B because they lie on the same indifference curve, but he's also indifferent between bundles B and C for precisely the same reason. This logically means he's indifferent between bundles A and C, but this cannot be the case because A contains more of both products than C. You may not be failed for crossing indifference curves, but you will certainly have marks deducted.

At this point we need to introduce a vital piece of terminology: a **marginal** figure. Whenever economists talk about a marginal something, which they do a lot, they're referring to a very small change in whatever that something is. The **marginal utility of X**, then, is the additional utility the consumer gets from buying one more unit of X. Consider, for example, a consumer who gets a utility of 135 utils from buying eight units of X and nine units of Y. If his utility increases to 145 utils when he buys nine units of both products, his marginal utility from the ninth unit of X is 10 utils. See Box 5.2 (pp. 63) for more on the derivation of marginal utility.

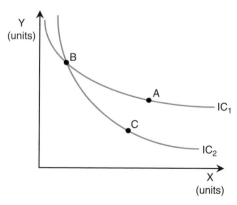

Figure 5.3 *Why indifference curves should not cross*

Marginal utility is an important concept because the slope of an indifference curve, known as the **marginal rate of substitution** (MRS) between the two products, is given by the negative ratio of the marginal utilities of the products. This is shown in Equation 5.1, where MU_X is the marginal utility of X and MU_Y is the marginal utility of Y.

$$MRS = -\frac{MU_X}{MU_Y}$$

(Equation 5.1)

Key term: marginal rate of substitution (MRS)

The MRS is the amount of one product the consumer needs to give up if his utility is to remain the same after receiving more of another product. More formally, the MRS is the negative ratio of the marginal utilities of the products. Consider, for example, a consumer who buys ten DVDs and two novels. He gets 10 utils from the tenth DVD and 30 utils from the second novel. The MRS of his chosen bundle, then, is $-30/10 = -3$, meaning for that specific bundle he needs to give up three DVDs for an additional novel in order to maintain his current level of utility. MRS is negative for well-behaved preferences because as the amount of one product increases, the amount of the other must fall if the utility is to remain the same. The MRS is a measure of the slope of an indifference curve.

With well-behaved indifference curves, such as those in Figure 5.2a, the MRS is different at every point on the curve. For bundles with large amounts of Y compared to X, such as bundle B, it's large: it takes a relatively large increase in Y to offset the utility effects of reducing the amount of X by one unit. Conversely, for bundles with large amounts of X compared to Y, such as bundle C, it's small: it takes a relatively small increase in Y to offset the utility effects of reducing the amount of X by one unit. In both cases, it takes a relatively large increase in the already abundant product to offset the utility effects of a relatively small reduction in the scarce product. This is strict convexity and diminishing marginal utility at work.

Key term: diminishing marginal utility

Diminishing marginal utility is the idea that the additional utility a consumer enjoys from consuming one more unit of a product declines as his total consumption of that product increases. Consider, for example, the utility you enjoy from eating an ice cream. Then consider the additional utility you enjoy from eating a second, and then a third, and then a fourth. No doubt your marginal utility falls as your consumption increases: at some point it may even become negative!

Given his preferences, the consumer would like to buy the bundle that maximises his utility: to buy the bundle positioned at the top of his preference ordering and on his preferred indifference curve. In other words, the consumer's utility is determined by the amounts of the products within the bundle he buys, which we can represent mathematically by a **utility function** (see Box 5.1), and he would like to buy the bundle that maximises this.

BOX 5.1: **Functions**

The mathematics used in economic analysis is primarily based on the notion of a function: a mathematical construct stating what determines a particular variable.

Example 1: $U_A = f(Q_X, Q_Y)$. This simply says the utility of consumer A (U_A) is determined by the amounts of X and Y she consumes $(Q_X$ and Q_Y respectively). Notice this function doesn't specify precisely how the consumption of the two products determines her utility: X could be an **economic bad**, which reduces her utility.

Example 2: $B = b(T,S,C)$. This function says the number of sunbathers on a privately owned beach (B) is determined by – or more formally is a function of – the temperature (T), the amount of sunshine (S) and the cost of accessing the beach (C). It's likely that as each of the first two of these increases, the number of sunbathers also increases; but as the third increases, the number of sunbathers declines. Notice the functional relationship doesn't necessarily have to be denoted by 'f'.

BOX 5.2: **Marginal utility**

Marginal utility refers to the utility the consumer receives from buying one more unit of a particular product. Following on from Box 5.1, a very simple utility function can be expressed as $U = f(Q_X)$, meaning utility is solely a function of the amount of X bought. In this case the marginal utility of X, denoted by MU_X, is derived through the **total differentiation** of the utility function:

$$\frac{dU}{dQ_X} = MU_X$$

However, throughout this chapter we assume the consumer's utility is actually determined by the amounts he buys of two products. Mathematically this means his utility is a function of both these products (or even more formally, his utility function is composed of two arguments): $U = f(Q_X, Q_Y)$. In this case, the marginal utility of X is given by the **partial derivative** of the utility function with respect to the amount of X, and the marginal utility of Y is the partial derivative of the utility function with respect to the amount of Y:

$$\frac{dU}{dQ_X} = MU_X$$

$$\frac{dU}{dQ_Y} = MU_Y$$

Marginal values are used throughout economics and they're always derived through either total or partial differentiation. It's extremely important you're comfortable with and proficient at differentiation: you will need it during your first-year exams!

5.2 the products consumers can afford to buy

Now we've examined what the consumer would like to buy, we need to look at what he can actually afford to buy. We all have a list of products we would like, but mostly we don't act upon it because we simply cannot afford to buy them. The same is true of our consumer here. So what can he afford?

Let's start by assuming he has a finite amount of money to spend on the two available products, which we denote by B_1. This is his **budget**. He cannot spend more than this amount on the two products. This is his **budget constraint**. Denoting the number of units of X he buys by Q_X and the price of X by P_X, and the number of units of Y he buys by Q_Y and the price of Y by P_Y, his budget constraint can be expressed formally as Equation 5.2. The term $P_X Q_X$ is the total expenditure on X and the term $P_Y Q_Y$ is the total expenditure on Y. Adding these two together gives the total expenditure on the products, which must be either equal to or less than his budget.

$$P_X Q_X + P_Y Q_Y \leq B_1 \qquad \text{(Equation 5.2)}$$

Key term: budget constraint

A budget constraint is the total amount of money that can be spent: expenditure must be equal to or less than this amount. For example, a consumer may have a budget of £55. He cannot spend more than £55 on a consumption bundle: this is his budget constraint.

The consumer can spend his entire budget on X, in which case he can afford B_1/P_X units of it. Alternatively, he can spend it all on Y, in which case he can afford B_1/P_Y units of it. For example, if he has a budget of £45 and the price of X is £15 and that of Y is £5, he can afford at most three units of X (and zero units of Y) or nine units of Y (and zero units of X). These simple calculations provide the points for plotting his **budget line**. An example is presented in Figure 5.4 and labelled BL_1. This line traces the boundary of the bundles he can afford: the bundles on the line or between it and the null bundle are

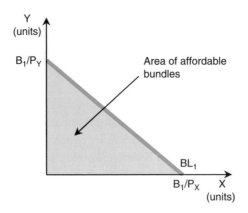

Figure 5.4 The budget line

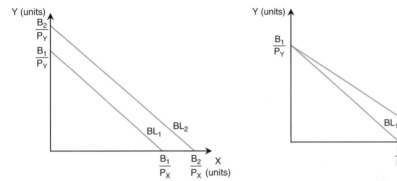

Figure 5.5a The budget line and increased income

Figure 5.5b A change in the price of X

affordable. Continuing the example from above, the budget line intersects the horizontal axis at three units and the vertical axis at nine units.

The slope of the budget line is the negative ratio of the prices of the two products: $-P_X/P_Y$. In the example above it's $-15/5 = -3$. This means the consumer needs to give up three units of Y if his total expenditure is to remain unchanged at £45 after he buys one additional unit of X.

Figure 5.5a illustrates the effect of an increase in the consumer's income, which causes his budget to rise from B_1 to B_2. Assuming the prices of X and Y remain unchanged, the budget line shifts outwards to BL_2. He's now able to afford a greater number of bundles: the area between his budget line and the null bundle has expanded. With the prices of the two products unchanged, the price ratio is unaffected and so the new budget line must be parallel to the initial line: its slope doesn't change.

Figure 5.5b illustrates the effect of a change in the price of one of the products, in this case a reduction in the price of X from P_{X1} to P_{X2}. The maximum amount of Y the consumer can afford isn't affected because his budget and the price of Y haven't changed, and so the budget line continues to intersect the vertical axis at the same point. However, X is now cheaper and so the amount of it he can afford is increased. This is shown by the budget line pivoting from BL_1 to BL_2: the budget line now intersects the horizontal axis at a higher number of units of X.

Following precisely the same logic, an increase in the price of X causes the budget line to pivot around the same point, but inwards towards the null bundle. Changes in the price of Y have similar effects, but pivot the budget line so that the maximum amount of X the consumer can afford remains unchanged. A proportional change in the prices of both products, perhaps due to inflation (see Section 11.3), causes the budget line to undergo a parallel shift. In effect, a proportional change in prices that leaves the price ratio unchanged is a change in the budget constraint.

5.3 the products consumers actually buy

We're now in a position to analyse what the consumer actually buys. We know he wants to buy the bundle that gives him most utility, that lies on his highest indifference curve and that maximises his utility function. We also know he can only afford bundles that cost him an amount equal to or less than his budget. Putting the two together means he buys the affordable bundle that gives him most utility, that is on his highest attainable indifference curve and that maximises his utility function subject to his budget constraint.

This result is illustrated in Figure 5.6. The consumer buys bundle A, which is on indifference curve IC_3. No other bundle exists in the figure that gives him a greater level of utility and is affordable. Bundle A is the optimal choice.

Figure 5.6 illustrates an important result: we find the optimal bundle at the point at which an indifference curve just touches the budget line. More formally, we find it at the point at which the two lines are tangential, and so the MRS is equal to the negative ratio of the two prices (Equation 5.3). If this

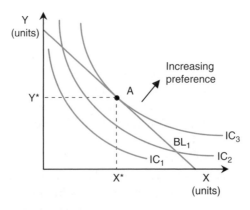

Figure 5.6 The consumption decision

condition isn't met, the consumer can increase his utility by choosing a different bundle.

$$-\frac{MU_X}{MU_Y} = -\frac{P_X}{P_Y}$$

(Equation 5.3)

This condition is central to the neoclassical model of consumer behaviour and holds for the majority of cases with well-behaved preferences. For preferences that aren't well behaved the condition doesn't necessarily hold; here, the optimal choice will simply be the bundle on the most preferred indifference curve that's attainable given the budget constraint.

5.4 consumer demand

The result in Equation 5.3 is one of the most important results in microeconomics. Using it we can identify the precise bundle the consumer buys given logical assumptions about his preferences and budget. It also allows us to extend the analysis to make it more useful: to examine the effects of price and income changes.

changes in the price of a product

Figure 5.7a illustrates how the chosen bundle changes as the price of one of the products, in this case X, changes. Initially the price of X is P_{X1}, the budget line is given by BL_1 and the chosen bundle is A, which contains X_1^* units of X. Let's now reduce the price of X to P_{X2}. This causes the budget line to pivot to BL_2, meaning the consumer is now able to afford bundles on higher indifference curves: bundles he prefers to A. He changes his chosen bundle to B, which contains X_2^* units of X. Let's do this again, reducing the price of X to P_{X3}. This causes the budget line to further pivot outwards to BL_3 and the chosen bundle to change again, this time to C, which contains X_3^* units of X. Plotting these bundles traces the **price offer curve**.

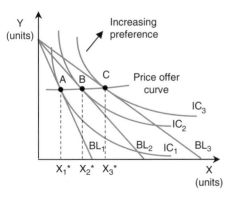

Figure 5.7a Price offer curve

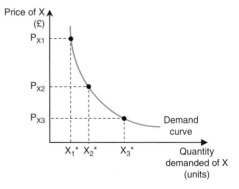

Figure 5.7b Demand curve

In Figure 5.7b the three different prices of X are plotted against the quantities bought, generating the **demand curve** for X. Unfortunately, there's an element of confusion in the analysis here. You will have learnt that mathematical relationships are illustrated by graphs that have the dependent variable on the vertical axis and the independent variable on the horizontal axis. We've derived Figure 5.7b by examining how demand for X alters as a result of changes in its price. In other words, we've been assuming the quantity demanded is a function of price, $Q_{dX} = f(P_X)$, meaning the quantity demanded is the dependent variable and the price is the independent variable. If we're to follow mathematical convention, we should put the quantity demanded on the vertical axis and the price on the horizontal. Figure 5.7b, though, has the reverse, meaning it's actually showing the functional relationship $P_X = f(Q_{dX})$. This confusion is understood and accepted by economists because Figure 5.7b can be interpreted as showing what price the consumer is willing and able to pay for every given quantity demanded. Formally, though, the functional relationship of $Q_{dX} = f(P_X)$ refers to the **normal demand** curve, and when economists draw demand curves such as that in Figure 5.7b they're actually constructing **inverse demand** curves, which are often more convenient for economic analysis. This confusion dates back to Alfred Marshall (see Sections 13.3 and 14.5). It isn't something to be concerned about, but you should always be careful to use the most appropriate version: see Box 4.3 for an example of when it's important to understand the distinction.

Key term: demand curve

There are two types of demand curve. The **normal demand curve** for a particular product shows the quantity of it bought – or demanded – at each and every price. It has the quantity demanded on the vertical axis and the price on the horizontal axis. In mathematical terms it's expressed as $Q_{dX} = f(P_X)$. However, it's the **inverse demand curve** that's most often used by economists. This shows the maximum price consumers are willing and able to pay for each quantity of the product; this is expressed as $P_X = f(Q_{dX})$, and has quantity demanded on the horizontal axis and price on the vertical axis.

changes in the level of income

We can analyse the effect on consumption of changes in income in a similar fashion. Consider Figure 5.8a. Initially the budget line of the consumer is represented by BL_1. The prices of the two products are P_X and P_Y respectively, and he buys a bundle with X_1^* units of X. This is the affordable bundle that gives him most utility and so is his optimal choice. Let's now increase his budget, causing his budget line to shift outwards to BL_2, parallel to BL_1 because the prices of the two products haven't changed. He can now afford bundles on higher indifference curves, which he prefers to the bundle he initially bought, and he buys a bundle with X_2^* units of X, moving onto the higher indifference

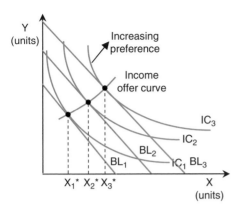

Figure 5.8a *Income offer curve for a normal product*

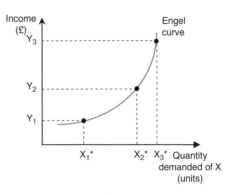

Figure 5.8b *Engel curve for a normal product*

curve IC_2. Let's repeat this once more, increasing his budget further so his budget line shifts to BL_3. He now buys a bundle that has X_3^* units of X and lies on IC_3. Plotting these points on the diagram gives the **income offer curve**.

In Figure 5.8b the quantity demanded of X at each of the three income levels is plotted, generating the **Engel curve.**

Key term: Engel curve

An Engel curve traces the income levels at which different quantities of a product are demanded. It's expressed mathematically as $Y = f(Qd_x)$, where Y represents income level, which is a function of the quantity demanded of product X. It does for income levels what the inverse demand curve does for the price levels of the product.

BOX 5.3: **Constrained optimisation**

Neoclassical economics assumes a consumer buys the bundle that maximises his utility given his budget constraint. This can be calculated mathematically through **constrained optimisation** – the optimisation of utility is being constrained by the budget – using the **method of Lagrange multipliers**.

Example: Suppose a consumer's utility is determined by his consumption of two products, X and Y: $U=f(Q_x,Q_y)$. To be more precise, utility is actually given by: $U=2Q_xQ_y$. Also suppose the price of X (P_x) is £2, that of Y (P_y) is £3 and the consumer has a budget (B) of £45.

To calculate how much of each product the consumer optimally buys we need to work through a number of steps:

Step 1: Write out the budget constraint. The generic form of a budget constraint is given in Equation B5.3.1: the total amount spent on X (its price multiplied by the number of units bought) plus the total amount spent on

Y (calculated in the same way) must equal the budget (to be precise it isn't necessary for it to equal the budget, but for ease it's usually written as an equality). The budget constraint specific to this example is that of Equation B5.3.2, which is then simply rearranged to be Equation B5.3.3.

$$Q_X P_X + Q_Y P_Y = B \qquad \text{(Equation B5.3.1)}$$

$$2Q_X + 3Q_Y = 45 \qquad \text{(Equation B5.3.2)}$$

$$45 - 2Q_X - 3Q_Y = 0 \qquad \text{(Equation B5.3.3)}$$

Step 2: Construct the **Lagrange equation** (L). The generic form of this is given as Equation B5.3.4, and that specific to this example as Equation B5.3.5. The lambda (λ) represents the **Lagrange multiplier**. This is a mathematical device required for the calculation which drops out later.

$$L = \text{(function to optimise)} + \lambda \text{(rearranged budget constraint)} \qquad \text{(Equation B5.3.4)}$$

$$L = 2Q_X Q_Y + \lambda(45 - 2Q_X - 3Q_Y) \qquad \text{(Equation B5.3.5)}$$

Step 3: Partially differentiate the Lagrange equation with respect to each quantity and the Lagrange multiplier. This generates the first-order partial derivatives. Differentiating with respect to Q_X gives the partial derivative of Equation B5.3.6. Doing the same with respect to Q_Y gives that of Equation B5.3.7. Doing the same with respect to λ gives that of Equation B5.3.8.

$$\frac{dL}{dQ_X} = 2Q_Y - 2\lambda = 0 \qquad \text{(Equation B5.3.6)}$$

$$\frac{dL}{dQ_Y} = 2Q_X - 3\lambda = 0 \qquad \text{(Equation B5.3.7)}$$

$$\frac{dL}{d\lambda} = 45 - 2Q_X - 3Q_Y = 0 \qquad \text{(Equation B5.3.8)}$$

Step 4: Equate the partial derivatives to zero, thereby creating the **first-order conditions** for constrained optimisation – this has been done in the expressions above – and solve for the variable values using a method of solving simultaneous equations. One way of doing this is to:

1. Rearrange Equation B5.3.6 to show the amount of Y consumed is equal to the value of lambda. This gives Equation B5.3.9.
2. Rearrange Equation B5.3.7 and then substitute lambda for Q_Y, which have just been shown to be equal to one another. This gives Equation B5.3.10, which expresses the amount of X in terms of the amount of Y.
3. Substitute this expression for the amount of X into Equation B5.3.8 so this equation is now solely in terms of the amount of Y and can be solved. Solving this demonstrates that 7.5 units of Y are consumed (Equation B5.3.11).

Finally, substitute the solution into Equation B5.3.10. This shows that 11.25 units of X are consumed (Equation B5.3.12).

$$2Q_Y - 2\lambda = 0 \rightarrow 2Q_Y = 2\lambda \rightarrow Q_Y = \lambda \qquad \text{(Equation B5.3.9)}$$

$$2Q_X - 3\lambda = 0 \rightarrow 2Q_X = 3\lambda \rightarrow 2Q_X = 3Q_Y \qquad \text{(Equation B5.3.10)}$$

$$45 - 2Q_X - 3Q_Y = 0 \rightarrow 45 - 3Q_Y - 3Q_Y$$

$$= 0 \rightarrow 45 - 6Q_Y = 0 \rightarrow Q_Y = \frac{45}{6} = 7.5 \qquad \text{(Equation B5.3.11)}$$

$$2Q_X = 3Q_Y \rightarrow 2Q_X = 3(7.5) \rightarrow 2Q_X = 22.5 \rightarrow Q_X = 11.25 \qquad \text{(Equation B5.3.12)}$$

For the consumer to optimise his utility subject to his budget constraint, he must consume 11.25 units of X and 7.5 units of Y. You should always check your solutions by seeing whether the budget constraint holds, which it does.

5.5 determinants of demand

As the analysis so far in this chapter suggests, the primary determinant of the quantity demanded of a product is usually its price. This is why economists draw demand curves with axes representing quantity demanded and price. It's also usual for demand curves to be downward-sloping as in Figure 5.7b. This represents the **law of demand**. Changes in the quantity demanded of a product caused solely by a change in its price, such as those shown in Figure 5.7b, are known as **movements** along the demand curve.

Key term: the law of demand

The law of demand states that as the price of a product increases the quantity demanded falls. This holds for the vast majority of products, although there are some exceptions, such as **Giffen** and **Veblen goods** (see below, p. 74).

income and substitution effects

We now turn to the part of the model that students usually find most difficult to grasp: the analysis of income and substitution effects. This part of the model has been developed because economists aren't wholly satisfied with the law of demand. The reason for this is that a change in the price of a product has two simultaneous effects. Consider an increase in the price of X whilst the price of Y and the consumer's budget remain unchanged. The first effect of the change is to reduce the total amount the consumer can buy. His budget hasn't changed but the average price of the two products has increased. This must mean that, on average, he can now afford fewer products with his budget. This is the **income effect**. The second effect is that Y is now relatively cheaper compared with X than it was previously, which is likely to cause the consumer to buy more units of Y and fewer units of X. This is the

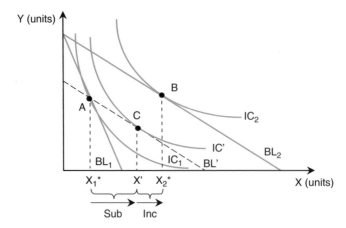

Figure 5.9 Substitution and income effects

substitution effect. Each of these effects separately causes the consumer to alter his consumption choice, but the law of demand simply shows the overall effect of both. Economists want to be able to separate out the two effects.

There are two ways of doing this. One is to use the **Slutsky decomposition**, named after Russian economist Eugene Slutsky who developed the method in the early part of the twentieth century, and the other is to use the **Hicksian decomposition**, developed by Sir John Hicks (see Section 14.8). The two methods of analysis are closely related, the difference being that with the Slutsky method the consumer's purchasing power remains constant, whereas with the Hicksian method the consumer's utility is constant. Here we only examine the first method; you should look up the other one in a textbook (see Chapter 15).

Key term: income effect

The law of demand states that as the price of a product increases the quantity demanded falls. The income effect is the part of this change in quantity demanded caused solely by the effect of the price change on the consumer's purchasing power. For example, consider a consumer who spends his entire budget of £100 on cinema tickets and sandwiches, which cost £10 and £5 each respectively. He buys five cinema tickets and ten sandwiches. Now think what happens if the price of cinema tickets rises to £13. The consumer simply cannot afford the same amount of the two products as he did before – doing so would cost him £115 and his budget is still £100 – and so it's necessary for him to change what he buys. This is the income effect of the increase in price on his consumption choice.

Key term: substitution effect

Following on from the definition of the income effect, the substitution effect is the part of a change in quantity demanded caused solely by the effect of the price change on ⌄

the relative prices of the products. Consider again the example from above in which a consumer spends his £100 budget on cinema tickets, costing £10, and sandwiches, costing £5. If the price of a cinema ticket rises to £13, sandwiches become even cheaper in comparison with them than they were before, which makes sandwiches appear more attractive. The consumer switches some of his expenditure away from cinema tickets and towards sandwiches as a result. This is the substitution effect of the increase in price on his consumption choice.

Consider Figure 5.9. Initially the prices of X and Y combine with the consumer's budget to establish a budget line of BL_1. Given this budget constraint and the consumer's preferences, he chooses bundle A, which comprises X_1^* units of X. Let's now reduce the price of X, but keep that of Y and the consumer's budget constant. This causes the budget line to pivot to BL_2 and the consumer to change his choice to bundle B, comprising X_2^* units of X. The overall effect of the price change is for him to purchase $X_2^* - X_1^*$ additional units of X.

Let's now separate this overall effect into its two components. We do this by determining how much income would need to be taken from the consumer after the price change so that his overall purchasing power is the same as it was before. To do this we need to shift the new budget line (BL_2) towards the null bundle such that it passes through the old consumption bundle (A). This creates the hypothetical budget line, BL', which represents the situation in which the consumer has the same purchasing power as before the price change – he's again just able to purchase his original consumption bundle, A – but faces the new relative prices (this budget line is parallel to that after the price change, BL_2). Given this hypothetical budget line, he optimally buys bundle C on the indifference curve IC'. This bundle, in which there are X' units of X, represents his choice if he had the same purchasing power as before but faced the new relative prices of the products. This now allows us to see the following:

1 The change in the consumption of X caused solely by the original budget line pivoting around the original consumption bundle – which represents only the effect of the change in relative prices – is the substitution effect. It's denoted by *Sub* in the diagram.

2 The change in the consumption of X caused solely by the budget line shifting outwards from BL' to BL_2 – which reflects only the increase in the consumer's purchasing power – is the income effect. It's denoted by *Inc* in the diagram.

The substitution effect increases the quantity demanded of X from X_1^* to X'; and the income effect increases it from X' to X_2^*. We've successfully separated the overall effect into its two component parts.

In this case both effects are in the opposite direction to the price change. The price of X falls and both the income and substitution effects cause an increase in demand. However, this isn't the case for all products. In fact, there are three different types of products according to their substitution and income effects:

❶ If the substitution and income effects operate in the same direction, as they do here, the product is said to be a **normal good**. An increase in the price of the product leads to a reduction in consumption, and a fall in the price of the product leads to more of it being consumed. Most products are normal goods.

❷ If the effects operate in opposite directions but the substitution effect is greater than the income effect, the product is said to be an **inferior good**. The substitution effect always operates in the opposite direction to the price change. If the price of a product increases, the substitution effect reduces the amount of it consumed, and if its price falls the substitution effect means more is consumed. This never changes. An inferior good, then, is a product for which the income effect operates in the opposite direction to the change in purchasing power: an increase in purchasing power leading to less of it being consumed, and a reduction in purchasing power leading to more being consumed. Overall, though, the substitution effect outweighs the income effect, and so if the price increases (and purchasing power falls), less is actually consumed, and if its price falls (and purchasing power increases), more is actually consumed. Examples of inferior goods include VHS video recorders and personal cassette players.

❸ If the effects operate in opposite directions and the substitution effect is less than the income effect, the product is a **Giffen** or **Veblen good**. With these products, an increase in its price actually leads to an increase in its consumption, whilst a reduction in its price leads to less consumption – thereby breaking the law of demand.

(a) There's only been one observed case of a Giffen good (attributed to Scottish economist Sir Robert Giffen, who worked primarily in the second half of the nineteenth century): that of potatoes during the Irish potato famine. As the price of potatoes rose, families were unable to purchase as much meat and potatoes as they could before. They found they could survive on a diet solely of potatoes, but not on a diet of more meat and fewer potatoes than before: the meat was still too expensive for them to be able to purchase enough to sustain them. Faced with this dilemma, they cut back on meat so that they could buy enough of the now more expensive potatoes to survive. The increase in the price of potatoes actually led to increased demand for them.

(b) Veblen goods (identified by American economist Thorstein Veblen, who worked in the late nineteenth to early twentieth century) are products consumers buy because they're expensive and exclusive. Top fashion brands and models of car are often bought for this reason. An increase in the price of such a good may attract more wealthy consumers to buy it. If the additional demand from the wealthy is sufficient to offset the reduction in demand from the existing less wealthy buyers, the total quantity demanded increases as a result of the price rise.

determinants of demand other than price

As well as the price of a product, various other factors can influence the quantity the consumer demands at each price. Many of these determinants are common across all products but some are product specific. Those common across all products include:

1. **The price, availability and quality of substitute products,** that is, products purchased instead of the original product. For example, if ferry fares from England to France fall, the demand for Eurostar train tickets is likely to fall as well, as the consumer switches to the now cheaper mode of transport.

2. **The price, availability and quality of complementary products,** that is, products necessary to accompany the original product. For example, if the price of plants dramatically increases, the demand for plant feed is likely to fall as the consumer buys fewer plants and so needs less feed.

3. **Income changes.** If the disposable income of the consumer increases – perhaps due to economic growth or a reduction in income tax – the quantity he demands of most products will also increase. Until very recently, incomes have tended to rise by 2 or 3 per cent per annum above inflation (see Section 11.3), implying that they double every thirty-five or twenty-three years. This causes large increases in the demand for most products.

4. **Popularity effects.** If a product becomes less popular, perhaps due to it becoming less fashionable or because of a health or safety scare, the consumer's demand for it is likely to fall. This was observed in the market for airline tickets immediately after the terrorist attacks of 2001.

Any non-price changes that increase the quantity demanded of a product cause its demand curve to **shift** outwards, and any non-price changes that reduce the quantity demanded of a product cause its demand curve to shift inwards. An example is displayed in Figure 5.10, which shows the likely effect of a product becoming more fashionable: the price of the product remains at P_1 but the quantity demanded increases from Q_1 to Q_2.

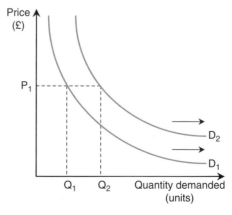

Figure 5.10 Outward shift in demand

BOX 5.4: Linear demand curves, and normal and inverse demands

Until now, demand curves have been drawn as actual curves. This is arguably the most correct form as it suggests the price cannot go so high that consumers purchase a negative amount and the price cannot be negative. However, demand curves are usually drawn as straight lines because it makes further analysis easier. In particular, it means they can be represented by equations such as Equation B5.4.1, which is of a normal demand curve:

$$Q_d = a - bP \qquad\qquad \text{(Equation B5.4.1)}$$

This means quantity demanded is a negative function of the price, and so as the price increases, the quantity demanded falls, but there's also a maximum amount, a, that's purchased if its price is zero. To draw the inverse demand curve from this, which is the convention, we need to rearrange Equation B5.4.1 so price is a function of quantity demanded. Doing this leads to Equation B5.4.2.

$$P = \frac{a}{b} - \frac{1}{b}Q_d \qquad\qquad \text{(Equation B5.4.2)}$$

The inverse demand curve has a slope of $-1/b$ and a vertical intercept of a/b. This is why it's so important to be careful about which type of demand curve is being used, the normal one or the inverse.

Such an inverse demand curve – linear demand curves are still known as curves – is illustrated in Figure B5.4. At a price of P_1, the quantity demanded of the product is $a - b(P_1)$. A shift in the curve is simply represented by a change in the value of a/b: an outward shift is shown by an increase in a/b, and an inward shift by a reduction.

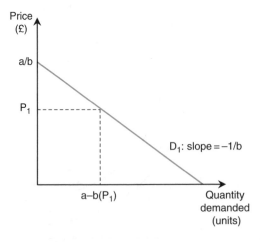

Figure B5.4 *Linear inverse demand curve*

5.6 elasticity of demand

There's one final step in our model that we need to examine. In analysis it's necessary for economists to be precise about how large the change in the quantity demanded will be in response to a change in one of its determinants. The concept of **elasticity** denotes this, the general formula for which is that of Equation 5.4: ΔA represents the change in variable A, ΔB represents the change in variable B, and A_1 and B_1 represent the initial values of the two variables. The output from this formula shows how responsive variable A is to a change in variable B, in percentage terms.

$$\text{elasticity} = \frac{\%\Delta A}{\%\Delta B} = \frac{\Delta A}{\Delta B} \frac{B_1}{A_1} \qquad \text{(Equation 5.4)}$$

There are three particularly important demand elasticities that you need to be aware of: own-price elasticity of demand, income elasticity of demand, and cross elasticity of demand.

own-price elasticity of demand

Own-price elasticity of demand (P_{ed}) measures the responsiveness of the quantity demanded of a product, in percentage terms, to a percentage change in its own price. It's calculated using Equation 5.5, in which ΔQ_d represents the change in quantity demanded, ΔP the change in its price, Q_{d_1} the initial quantity demanded and P_1 its initial price.

$$P_{ed} = \frac{\%\Delta Q_d}{\%\Delta P} = \frac{\Delta Q_d}{\Delta P} \frac{P_1}{Q_{d1}} \qquad \text{(Equation 5.5)}$$

Own-price elasticity of demand is negative in all situations in which the law of demand holds and so economists often take this for granted, omitting the negative sign from their results. For the purpose of clarity, though, you should insert the negative sign in brackets in front of the result, particularly during exams.

If own-price elasticity of demand is between 0 and –1, the quantity demanded is relatively unresponsive to a change in price. Such products are said to be **price-inelastic**. If it's less than –1 (for example –1.5 or –2), the product is said to be **price-elastic** and the quantity demanded is relatively responsive to a change in price. Finally, if the coefficient is equal to –1, the product is said to be **unitary price-elastic:** a change in price causes an equal but obverse percentage change in the quantity demanded.

It's important to note that own-price elasticity isn't the same as the gradient of a demand curve. The own-price elasticity of demand is different at every point along a linear demand curve, whereas its gradient is obviously constant. In fact, the own-price elasticity of demand along a linear demand curve changes in a particular way: the central point of a linear demand curve is unitary elastic, its upper section is price-inelastic and its lower section is price-elastic.

Own-price elasticity of demand is useful for both producers and the government as it identifies the effect that changing price – directly by producers or indirectly through taxes and subsidies (see Section 8.2) – has on quantity demanded. For example, suppose the government wants to reduce alcohol consumption by 5 per cent over the next few years. Knowing the own-price elasticity of demand for alcohol enables it to implement the necessary tax rises to achieve its target. At the same time, knowing the own-price elasticity of demand for their products means alcohol producers can forecast how their revenues will change as a consequence of any increase in taxation, enabling them to plan for the future regarding production costs and profits. On this note, there's a simple rule of thumb for producers: if their product is price-inelastic they should increase its price because this causes a smaller percentage reduction in quantity demanded than the percentage increase in price, thereby increasing revenue; but if their product is price-elastic, to increase revenue they need to reduce its price as the resultant increase in quantity demanded will outweigh the reduction in price per unit. However, it's always important to remember that the own-price elasticity of demand of a product is likely to vary along its demand curve, and so while this rule of thumb is reasonable for minor alterations in price it is not necessarily so for larger changes.

There are five main determinants of how own-price-elastic a product is:

1. **Proportion of consumer expenditure**. The smaller the proportion of total expenditure that a product accounts for, the more own-price-inelastic it's likely to be. This is because any change in price is less noticeable and so is more easily absorbed. For example, matches usually account for a very small proportion of the cost of a family's shopping basket and so their price can double without the family noticing it. Fillet steak, on the other hand, usually accounts for a much larger proportion of the family budget and so if its price doubles, the family would perhaps be less inclined to purchase it, choosing a cheaper cut instead. The matches are relatively price-inelastic whereas the fillet steak is relatively price-elastic.

2. **Addictiveness**. The more addictive a product is, the more price-inelastic it is because the consumer is more willing to pay any price increase in order to obtain it. Alcohol and cigarettes are typical examples of this: their prices can increase dramatically without causing the demand from addicts to fall significantly.

3. **Level of necessity**. Following the same logic, the greater the necessity of a product, the more price-inelastic it is. For example, commuters who travel to work in London by rail are likely to be much more willing to pay higher train fares than those who use the railway for only the occasional day trip. The former are compelled to accept the higher fares because of their need to get to the office, whereas the latter have more flexibility to find alternatives.

④ **Time scale**. The longer the time period under consideration, the more price-elastic the product is likely to be. The best example of this is that of the OPEC (Organization of Petroleum Exporting Countries) price hikes in the 1970s and 1980s. OPEC produces the majority of the world's oil, and has done for many decades. In the 1970s it substantially increased the price of a barrel of oil. Western economies – by that time heavily reliant on oil – had no available alternatives and were forced into recession as they paid the increased prices. Seeing how profitable it had been, OPEC repeated the price hike in the following decade. However, by this time Western economies had realised how vulnerable they were to oil price changes and so had invested in alternative fuels: the UK started to extract North Sea gas and France developed a network of nuclear power stations. When OPEC increased its prices the second time, Western economies simply reduced the amount of oil they purchased. In the immediate term, oil was highly price-inelastic but over the longer time period it became more elastic as viable alternatives were developed.

⑤ **Closeness of substitutes**. A close substitute is one that's very similar to the product in question, in both price and functionality. The greater the number and closeness of available substitutes a product has, the more price-elastic it is. This is simply because the consumer is less willing to continue buying it if its price increases as there are satisfactory alternatives available. For example, a rural train service without any competing bus services and in a region with an exceptionally poor road infrastructure is likely to be much more price-inelastic than a similar route with two competing bus providers and good roads for car users.

other elasticities of demand

There are two other important elasticities of demand you should be aware of: **income elasticity of demand** and **cross-price elasticity of demand**.

Key term: income elasticity of demand

Income elasticity of demand measures the responsiveness of the quantity demanded of a product to a change in the income of consumers. It's calculated using Equation 5.5, but with the price of the product replaced with the income of consumers. If it's positive, an increase in the income of consumers is associated with an increase in the quantity demanded of the product, suggesting that an increase in income causes an increase in demand: the product is a normal good (see Section 5.5). If it's negative, an increase in the income of consumers is associated with a reduction in the quantity demanded of the product, suggesting that an increase in income causes a reduction in demand: the product is an inferior good (see Section 5.5). Whether income elasticity of demand is positive or not tells us whether the Engel curve (see Section 5.4) for the product is upward-sloping (a normal good) or downward-sloping (an inferior good): income elasticity of demand is to the Engel curve what own-price elasticity of demand is to the demand curve.

Key term: cross-price elasticity of demand

Cross-price elasticity of demand measures the responsiveness of the quantity demanded of one product to a change in the price of another. It's calculated using Equation 5.6, in which Q_{dA} represents the change in the quantity demanded for product A, ΔP_B represents the change in the price of product B, P_{B1} is the initial price of product B, and Q_{dA1} is the initial quantity demanded of product A.

$$X_{\varepsilon d} = \frac{\%\Delta Q_{dA}}{\%\Delta P_B} = \frac{\Delta Q_{dA}}{\Delta P_B} \frac{P_{B1}}{Q_{dA1}}$$

(Equation 5.6)

If cross-price elasticity of demand is positive, an increase in the price of product B is associated with an increase in the quantity demanded of product A, suggesting that an increase in the price of product B causes an increase in the demand for product A: the products are substitutes. If it's negative, an increase in the price of product B is associated with a reduction in the quantity demanded of product A, suggesting that an increase in the price of product B causes a reduction in the demand for product A: the products are complements. If it's zero, the two products are apparently unrelated.

5.7 criticisms of the standard model

We've now come to the end of our examination of the standard, neoclassical model of consumer behaviour. It's undeniably an exceptional theoretical model. Starting with a handful of very logical assumptions about consumers' preferences and budget constraints, and then progressing through a series of logical steps, it allows us to:

1. Predict the precise bundles consumers buy.
2. Analyse how consumers change what they buy in response to changes in the price of products, their incomes and other influences.
3. Analyse why consumers change what they buy in response to these influences, enabling us to group products into different categories.
4. Analyse how much consumers change what they buy in response to these influences.
5. Develop strategies to shape consumer behaviour in the interests of society.

It's no wonder this theory lies at the heart of microeconomics, and has done so for more than half a century.

However, it also has weaknesses and is seriously criticised by some economists for both empirical and theoretical reasons. These criticisms, which are growing in strength and number, have led some economists to propose alternative ways of modelling consumer behaviour.

empirical criticisms

The standard model of consumer behaviour makes three very important assumptions about the preferences of consumers, that they are complete, reflexive and transitive. Implicitly, it also assumes consumers maximise their utility: that they choose bundles that give them the greatest satisfaction. Of course, no economist suggests consumers actually go through the process we went through as we constructed the model – clearly consumers don't think about finding the bundle that equates their MRS with the negative ratio of prices – but what they do argue is consumers behave **as if** they're doing this. The problem is, however, that there is an increasing body of evidence that suggests preferences aren't complete, reflexive and transitive, and that consumers don't behave as if they're maximising utility.

Evidence suggests consumers find it difficult to compare and rank bundles, particularly if they're very different to one another. This contravenes the assumption of completeness. For example, leading behavioural economist Daniel Ariely describes the following experiment in his excellent book *Predictably Irrational*. A group of MBA students and financial professionals were presented with two options for subscribing to *The Economist* magazine:

❶ Online only subscription for $59.
❷ Online *and* hard copy subscription for $125.

Roughly half the subjects chose each option (which would you choose?). The same group was then presented with a second list of subscription options, in which the first two options were the same as before:

❶ Online only subscription for $59.
❷ Online *and* hard copy subscription for $125.
❸ Hard copy only subscription for $125.

From this second list, the vast majority of subjects chose the online and hard copy subscription. The third option is known as a **decoy** because it causes consumers to focus on a particular aspect of the products on sale. What's happening here is consumers find it difficult to compare the first two options because they're so different, and so the publisher offers a decoy option that gives them an additional piece of information, in this case the price of the hard copy only subscription. With this extra information consumers can compare the first two options more easily, and as they do so they see the second option effectively gives them everything in the first option for free, and so they choose option two. The problem for the standard economic model is that this evidence suggests consumers – even MBA students and financial professionals – aren't always able to create complete preference orderings, and this contravenes the first essential assumption of the model.

There's also evidence that preferences aren't reflexive and transitive. In an article in the journal *Science* in 1981, Amos Tversky and Daniel Kahneman, two other leading behavioural economists, presented the Asian disease experiment. People were informed about a disease that threatens 600 citizens and were asked to choose an option from two different lists. In the first list they had to choose between:

❶ Being certain of saving 200 lives.
❷ Having a one-third chance of saving all 600 citizens but a two-third chance of saving no one at all.

Most subjects in the experiment chose the first option (which would you go for?). The subjects were then presented with the second list of options:

1 Being certain that 400 citizens will die.

2 Having a two-thirds chance of 600 citizens being killed and a one-third chance of no one dying.

Most subjects chose the second option. The problem for the standard model is that the two sets of options are identical: they are just worded differently. The standard model, assuming reflexivity and transitivity, suggests people make the same choice from both lists. As they clearly don't do this, these two essential assumptions of the model are contravened.

Daniel Kahneman and his colleagues have also presented evidence that's troubling for the assumption that individuals behave as if they're maximising their utility. In one work they focused on a sample of patients undergoing colonoscopies. For half the patients the medical examination was conducted as usual. For the other half the physician left the colonoscope in place for a minute after the examination had ended, extending the duration of discomfort but not in itself causing much pain. The assumption of utility maximisation would suggest that those patients who had undergone the extended treatment with greater discomfort and pain would evaluate the procedure less favourably than those who had received the standard examination. In fact, in violation of this assumption, those patients who had received the extended examination evaluated the procedure more favourably. Evidence such as this suggests individuals don't make decisions as if they're maximising their utility at all. Instead, they employ rules of thumb – known as **heuristics** – to help them make their decisions more easily, but this sometimes causes the decisions made to be suboptimal. In this particular case, it seems patients employed what the authors called the **peak-end rule**, which involves them judging the procedure primarily according to the level of pain immediately before the colonoscope was removed.

These are just three pieces of evidence from an ever expanding number suggesting that preferences don't conform to the standard model of consumer behaviour and that individuals don't always make decisions as if they're maximising their utility.

theoretical criticisms

It isn't just because of the contradictory evidence that the standard model of consumer behaviour is criticised, though. There are also three critical theoretical arguments.

1 **It's unrealistic.** The evidence that the model, and the assumptions upon which it's based, is simply unrealistic is mounting. The theoretical argument here is that models should be based on realistic assumptions. Only realistic models can lead to conclusions we can be confident are true and useful for policy-makers trying to improve the functioning of markets. Basing policy on the results of unrealistic models is always potentially dangerous. Also, if the aim of microeconomics is truly to understand how markets function, then having models based on the actual behaviour of economic actors is vital.

2 **It isn't computable**. This is a more recent criticism of the standard model. The argument here is that the utility maximisation assumption – that consumers find the bundle at which their MRS is equal to the negative ratio of prices – cannot be put into a computer program. In other words, it isn't possible to programme a machine to find the optimal bundle in this way, and to assume such behaviour is to completely ignore the process through which the decision may actually be made. For an increasing number of economists, such as Kumaraswamy Velupillai and Suren Basov, this is a serious limitation of the model; they argue that we should seek to understand the actual processes by which consumers make decisions.

3 **It limits our ability to alter behaviour**. To assume consumers simply behave as in the standard model means economists can only alter the amount of a particular product consumed by changing its price (through taxation and subsidisation), its availability (by making it illegal), its popularity (through advertising and the provision of information), the incomes of consumers (through taxation and benefits) or the characteristics of substitute and complementary products (their prices, popularity and availability). By dispensing with the assumption that consumers behave as if they're maximising their utility and examining how they actually make decisions, we can potentially also alter consumption behaviour by influencing the actual processes used in decision-making. The standard model restrains our policy options unnecessarily.

a call for alternatives

Given the mounting empirical evidence against the standard model and the growing theoretical criticisms of it, economists are calling for and developing alternative models of consumer behaviour. Here we take a quick look at the most important of these alternatives.

The first is the model of **bounded rationality**, developed by Nobel Laureate Herbert Simon (see Section 14.10). The behaviour outlined in the standard model of consumer choice is known as objectively (or globally) rational behaviour. Herbert Simon argued that this simply isn't realistic. Rather than being characterised by objective rationality, consumers are boundedly rational, meaning their ability to make decisions isn't sufficient to deal with the complexity of the decisions they have to make. Instead of making optimal decisions, then, they resort to **satisficing** – the making of decisions that are just good enough – and to using heuristics to help them make their decisions quickly.

The second model is that of **prospect theory**, developed by Daniel Kahneman and Amos Tversky. Prospect theory models choice as a two-phase process. In the first phase, consumers edit the information about the options they have using a range of heuristics that are supported by evidence from the real world. For example, they use the heuristic of **simplification**: the rounding of information to handle figures more easily. In the second phase they use the altered information to make their choice, taking into account attitudes that have actually been observed of consumers.

The third is the theory of **mental accounting** proposed by Richard Thaler, another leading behavioural economist. Mental accounting addresses the issue of how individuals make decisions about how to spend their money, asserting there are three relevant elements of such decisions. Based on prospect theory, the first element involves editing the financial information according to a number of actually observed heuristics. The second involves assigning budgets to specific categories of spending: these are the mental accounts. For example, a consumer may have separate mental accounts for groceries, transport and entertainment. These accounts are often **non-fungible**, meaning a consumer won't use the money assigned to one account to pay for a different type of expenditure. Once the money for entertainment, for instance, has been spent, they won't buy any more in that category that week. Some consumers have been observed to have a set of envelopes, one for each account, into which they actually put money each week. It's a heuristic that can be helpful to the consumer in ensuring that they don't spend more money than they think they should. The third involves determining the time periods to which different accounts relate. For example, the transport account may need to stretch across only a week, whereas the entertainment account might be for the entire month.

Each of these alternative models – and many others that we haven't looked at here – explains some of the behaviour the standard model fails to do. However, despite the progress made with them, there isn't yet a single one that can rival the strengths of the standard model in terms of its simplicity and generality, and so the standard model remains at the heart of microeconomics.

BOX 5.5: **Behavioural economics**

Paul Dolan (Imperial College, University of London) and Robert Metcalfe (University of Oxford)

The standard economic model assumes individuals make choices that are concerned only with end-states, that are time-consistent, affected only by their own pay-offs and independent of the context of the choice. Behavioural economics shows that our behaviour is often affected by changes rather than final states, that it is time-inconsistent, affected by the pay-offs of other people and influenced by the context within which the choices are made. Essentially, behavioural economics attempts to increase the explanatory power of the standard model by providing it with more realistic psychological foundations.

Preferences have been shown to be time-inconsistent. The standard economic model, however, assumes the decision-maker has the same preferences about future plans at different points in time. There's now overwhelming evidence that discounting is steeper in the immediate future than in the distant future. For example, it's been found that people are generally indifferent between $15 now and $20 in one month (an annual discount rate of 345 per cent) and between $15 now and $100 in ten years (an annual discount rate of 19 per cent).

Issues of fairness have also become important for behavioural economics. The standard model assumes consumers are purely self-interested, and utility depends only on their own pay-offs. There's evidence that this is not entirely true. More recent research in behavioural economics examines the impact of context on choice. This relates to how salient choice attributes are; how people are persuaded to behave in a certain way (through a social norm); and how emotions and subtle primes (such as the decoys mentioned above) impact on choices. Much of the work to date has been in laboratory settings, but more and more of the evidence comes from natural and field experiments (real-life situations).

The lessons from behavioural economics have been used for public policy. A prominent example is the Save More Tomorrow (SMT) plan proposed by Richard Thaler and Shlomo Benartzi. The SMT plan gives workers the option of committing themselves today to increase their savings rate later (through their bonus or a percentage of their salary). Once they join the plan, their contributions to the plan increase, beginning with the first pay cheque and increasing with each scheduled raise until the contribution rate reaches a preset maximum. The employee can opt out of the plan at any time but SMT plays on people's time inconsistency and inertia. The first implementation of the SMT plan yielded dramatic results. The average saving rates for SMT plan participants more than tripled, from 3.5 per cent to 11.6 per cent, over the course of twenty-eight months.

To date, behavioural economics has challenged the standard economic model, but as more researchers are coming into this area, we will gain a better understanding of how more realistic assumptions about human behaviour can be used in economic models, and how much explanatory power they actually have.

Key reading:

> C.F. Camerer, G. Loewenstein and M. Rabin, *Advances in Behavioral Economics* (Princeton University Press, 2003).
> S. DellaVigna, 'Psychology and Economics: Evidence from the Field' *Journal of Economic Literature*, 47 (2009): 315–72.
> J. Henrich, R. Boyd, S. Bowles, C. Camerer, F. Fehr and H. Gintis, *Foundations of Human Sociality: Economic Experiments and Ethnographic Evidence from Fifteen Small-Scale Societies* (Oxford University Press, 2004).

5.8   summary

> The neoclassical model of consumer behaviour is composed of two elements: what the consumer would like to buy (represented by indifference curves) and what he can afford to buy (represented by the budget line). The bundle that a consumer chooses is that for which the marginal rate of substitution is equal to the negative ratio of prices.
> The demand curve shows how the amount of one product within the chosen consumption bundle changes as a result of changes in its price. There are two types of demand curve: normal and inverse curves.

> The Engel curve shows how the amount of one product within the chosen consumption bundle changes as a result of changes in the consumer's income.

> A change in the quantity demanded of a product caused by a change in its price is composed of two parts: an income effect and a substitution effect. These are separated using the Slutsky or Hicksian decompositions.

> Changes in a product's price cause movements along its demand curve, whereas any other changes that cause the quantity demanded to change are shown as shifts of the demand curve.

> The responsiveness of quantity demanded to changes in the product's price, the consumer's income and changes in the price of another product are given by own-price, income and cross-price elasticity of demand respectively.

> The neoclassical model of consumer behaviour has been criticised for both empirical and theoretical reasons. More realistic, but more specific, alternatives have been proposed.

2

6 how much producers make and sell

After working through the previous chapter we have an understanding of how consumers behave. However, consumers aren't alone in markets: they interact with **producers**. It's in that interaction that we're ultimately interested because that's what determines the products that are produced and traded, and in what quantities, the prices at which they're sold, and how beneficial this is for society as a whole: the questions we primarily seek to answer by studying microeconomics. The next step towards the goal of understanding these issues, then, is for us to examine how much producers make and sell. This is the subject of this chapter.

Key term: producers

A producer is an economic actor that buys and organises the factors of production – with labour it buys labour-hours rather than the workers themselves (see Section 1.1) – in order to produce goods to sell to consumers.

We saw in Chapter 5 that the model of consumer behaviour is composed of two parts: the preferences of consumers and their budget constraints. It's only by examining each of these parts separately, and then putting them together into a complete model, that we can understand consumer decision-making. This can similarly be said of the model of producer behaviour, as the decisions producers make are also influenced by two general factors: their production costs and the revenue they receive from selling their output. Each of these is investigated separately, allowing us then to construct and analyse the complete neoclassical model of producer behaviour. Criticisms of this standard model are addressed in Section 6.5.

The primary aim of this chapter is for us to analyse and understand how much producers decide to make and sell. To keep the explanation of what follows clear, it's useful to assume all producers are identical. This allows us to talk about 'the producer': a producer representative of all those in the market. We also need to assume the producer is able to make decisions as though it is a single entity; that is, if the producer decides to maximise its profit, it's able to do so, and all the workers it employs alter their behaviour to enable this goal to be achieved.

6.1 production costs

Before proceeding to our analysis of production costs, it's important to be precise about the time period for which the producer's decisions are being analysed. In economics there are two distinct theoretical time periods: the **short run** and the **long run**. Being precise in their definition – which requires an understanding of the factors of production (see Section 1.1) – is important because the time period has significant implications for production. In economics these time periods aren't defined as certain numbers of months or years: they're theoretical in nature.

Key term: the short run

The short run is defined as a period of time in which the amount of at least one of the factors of production that the producer possesses is fixed. This is most likely to be the case with land because the actual amount of actual physical land possessed by the producer is often much more difficult to expand than the amounts of the other factors.

Key term: the long run

The long run is defined as a time period in which the amounts of all the factors of production that the producer possesses are variable. If the producer wants to increase its floor space then it can do so freely in the long run, in the same way as it can alter the amounts of the other factors as well.

Irrespective of the time period involved, in order to produce anything, the producer has to buy and organise the four factors of production and so necessarily has to pay production costs. These costs comprise half of the foundations on which the model of producer behaviour is based.

Costs can be categorised according to their relationship with the level of output produced:

① **Fixed costs** are costs that are constant for all levels of output. For example, the monthly rent a shopkeeper has to pay for the premises from which to sell her wares. It doesn't matter how many items she sells each month, the cost of her rent remains the same.

② **Variable costs** are costs that change as the level of output changes. For example, the total cost of purchasing raw materials from suppliers. As a factory's output expands, greater volumes of raw materials are required and so supply costs increase.

③ **Semi-variable** (or **semi-fixed**) **costs** are costs that are fixed up until a certain output level, at which point they change to a level at which they're then constant until the next output threshold is reached, and so on. Staffing costs are a good example. One worker can cope with production up until a certain output level, beyond which a second worker needs to be employed, causing the wage bill that had been constant up to that point to jump to a higher level. These two workers can then cope with production up until another output level, beyond which a third worker is required, causing the wage bill that had been fixed at the rate of pay for two workers to jump again. This process repeats itself, forming a wage bill that has the shape of steps. In reality all costs are actually semi-variable. Consider again the shop-keeper and the factory above. For the shopkeeper there inevitably comes a point as the amount she sells increases when she needs to hire larger premises, causing her rent bill to jump to a higher level; and the factory can probably increase its output a little by using its existing resources more efficiently: a range of output, albeit small, over which the cost is fixed.

Alternatively, costs can be categorised according to their scale:

1 **Total cost**, denoted by TC, is the figure generated by adding up all production costs. In other words, total cost is the sum of all fixed costs, variable costs and semi-variable costs. Total cost is a function of the output (Q) produced, which we can express as TC = f(Q).

2 **Average cost**, denoted by AC, is calculated by dividing total cost by the number of units of output produced, as in Equation 6.1. It represents the total cost per unit of output. To be more precise, this is the average total cost of production. We can also calculate the average fixed cost and the average variable cost of production by dividing the total fixed cost and the total variable cost by output. These combine to give the average total cost.

$$AC = \frac{TC}{Q} \qquad \text{(Equation 6.1)}$$

3 **Marginal cost**, denoted by MC, is the additional total cost incurred by producing one extra unit of output. For example, if the total cost of producing 367 units of output is £6,729 and that of producing 368 units is £6,764, the marginal cost of the 368th unit is £35. We calculate marginal cost by totally differentiating total cost with respect to output as in Equation 6.2. Total differentiation (denoted by d) is used here because total cost is a function of output alone, and we want to ascertain how total cost changes as a result of a change in output.

$$MC = \frac{dTC}{dQ} \qquad \text{(Equation 6.2)}$$

For us to be able to analyse producer behaviour comprehensively, we first need to examine in considerably more detail the nature of average and marginal costs in both the short and long run.

As mentioned above, average total cost – from here on simply referred to as average cost – is composed of average fixed cost and average variable cost. For us to understand how average cost changes in the short run as output expands, it's necessary for us to see how each of these elements changes individually.

As output increases, average fixed cost falls as it is dispersed over greater output. This effect is strong as output initially expands, but as output increases further there are ever smaller reductions in average fixed cost as these costs cannot be significantly more dispersed. Consider, for example, an extremely small producer that produces 100 units of output and has to pay fixed costs of £600 to do so. Its average fixed cost is £6 per unit of output. Now consider the effect on its average fixed cost as it doubles its output to 200 units: it's halved to £3. Finally, now consider the effect on its average fixed cost of it expanding its output by another 100 units to 300 units: it's reduced to £2. Further increases in output cause smaller and smaller reductions in average fixed cost.

The response of average variable cost to changes in output is more complex. To produce a further unit of output, the producer needs to incur an increase in variable cost because it needs to buy additional inputs. It's inevitable that the average variable cost rises increasingly quickly as output expands in the short run because one of the factors of production is fixed. The other factors are increased in order to expand output, but the fixed factor increasingly reduces their productive effect. Consider, for example, a producer that's able to increase its labour and capital freely but whose landholding is fixed. Initially it can increase its output by increasing the two variable factors: the land doesn't hinder it at all. However, once its factory floor is full, additional capital and workers actually begin to get in the way of existing workers and their machines, causing productive efficiency (see Section 1.1) to fall. Additional units of labour and capital generate smaller and smaller increases in output, and at some point may actually cause a reduction in output. This is known as **diminishing marginal returns**, in this case of labour and capital, and it causes average variable cost to rise increasingly quickly as output expands.

Let's now combine these two effects. As output increases in the short run:

1. The average fixed cost initially falls strongly, but its reduction gets smaller as output continues to expand.
2. The average variable cost rises, initially slowly but getting increasingly faster as output continues to expand.

These two effects logically mean the **short run average cost** (SRAC) curve is U-shaped, as shown in Figure 6.1. Short run average cost initially falls as output expands because at first the average fixed cost effect outweighs the average variable cost effect; but, as output expands further, at some point the average variable cost effect begins to outweigh the average fixed cost effect, causing short run average cost to rise again. The bottom of the curve is the point at which the producer is productively efficient: where it's producing the level of output at which it's minimising its average cost (see Section 1.1). In cases where there's actually a range of output at which the producer is productively efficient – meaning the average cost curve has a flat base to it – the lowest output of the flat section of the curve is known as the **minimum efficient scale** (MES). It's the minimum output at which the producer is productively efficient.

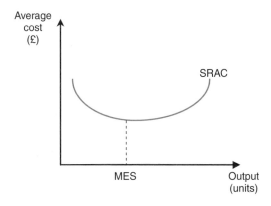

Figure 6.1 The short run average cost curve

average costs in the long run

In the short run, the producer is anchored to its short run average cost curve by the amount of its fixed factor of production. The producer is only able to determine where on this curve it operates. However, in the long run the producer is able to change the amount of all its factors of production, allowing it to switch to a new short run average cost curve.

The various possible short run average cost curves, then, form the **long run average cost curve**: the long run average cost curve envelops the short run curves as shown in Figure 6.2. To understand this diagram, consider a small-scale producer that's fixed to the short run average cost curve furthest to the left in the diagram. It expands its output and so moves down the curve until it hits its short run productively efficient output. It isn't sensible for the producer to expand its output further in the short run because that would only move it up the right-hand side of its short run average cost curve, increasing its average cost. In the long run, though, when its fixed factor of production becomes variable, it increases all its factors and so moves onto the short run average cost curve

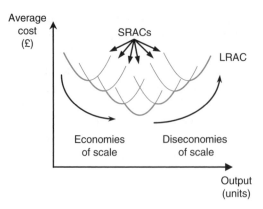

Figure 6.2 *Short and long run average cost curves*

to the right of the original curve. It now effectively enters a second short run period, in which it increases output again until it reaches its new short run productively efficient output. This process continues, tracing out the long run average cost curve. In effect, the long run is simply a sequence of short run periods.

The long run average cost curve is also likely to be U-shaped, with the short run curves lying inside it. The long run average cost curve is this shape not because of the effect of decreasing average fixed costs and then increasing average variable costs as in the short run, but because of **economies** and **diseconomies of scale**.

Key term: economies of scale

This refers to the phenomenon of falling long run average cost caused by output being expanded. It's purely a long run phenomenon because it requires all factors of production to be variable. There are four sources of economies of scale: technical, managerial, marketing and financial.

1 **Technical economies of scale**. As the producer expands its output, it can employ larger, more efficient capital, which reduces its long run average cost.

2 **Managerial economies of scale**. As the producer expands its output and improves its reputation, its ability to employ the very best management and employees may be enhanced. Individually these workers demand higher salaries, but if they increase efficiency to the extent that fewer workers need to be employed, they can potentially lead to a reduction in long run average cost.

3 **Marketing economies of scale**. Expanding output enables the producer to purchase its raw materials in bulk, giving it more bargaining power with suppliers. Suppliers are usually keen to maintain their business with

a growing producer and so are often willing to accept lower prices for their supplies, reducing the producer's long run average cost.

④ **Financial economies of scale.** Banks and other financial institutions are generally more willing to lend money to larger producers as they are seen to be less risky. This means larger producers have sources of finance available to them that smaller producers don't: sources that involve lower rates of interest.

All these effects cause long run average cost to fall as output expands, but gradually their strength diminishes and diseconomies of scale begin to dominate. These pull long run average cost back up again.

Key term: diseconomies of scale

This is the opposite of economies of scale: it refers to the phenomenon of increasing long run average cost caused by output being expanded. As with economies of scale, it can only occur in the long run because it requires all factors of production to be variable. There are two common sources of diseconomies of scale: bureaucracy and communication troubles.

① **Bureaucracy.** As the producer expands, the volume of paperwork and administration involved in its day-to-day operations inevitably increases as it becomes more difficult to coordinate its production. Increased bureaucracy hinders efficiency as time is wasted completing forms and conducting checks, causing long run average cost to rise.

② **Communication troubles.** The larger the producer becomes, the more difficult it is for management to pass directions down the chain of command and to receive feedback from the workers below. The number of instructions being ignored, lost in the chain of command or distorted rises as a result, and management becomes less responsive to the labour force, leading to increased dissatisfaction and demotivation of workers. Less efficient workers cause the long run average cost to rise.

marginal cost in the short and long run

There is a relationship between marginal cost and average cost, both in the short and long run. If average cost is falling, marginal cost must be lower than it, and if average cost is rising, marginal cost must be greater than it. This is because the only way to reduce an average is to add numbers to it that are less than it, and the only way to increase an average is to add numbers to it that are more than it. This means marginal cost must be equal to average cost at the lowest point on the average cost curve, both in the short and long run. This makes intuitive sense as the way to keep an average constant is to add numbers that are equal to it.

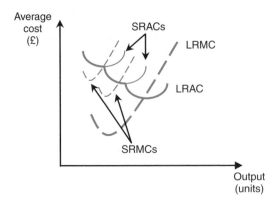

Figure 6.3 *Average and marginal cost curves in the short and long run*

This leads us to the shapes of the short run and long run marginal cost curves (SRMC and LRMC, respectively), and their relationship to their respective average cost curves, shown in Figure 6.3.

6.2 revenue

Now that we've examined the different types of production costs the producer has to pay and how they're related to one another, we need to turn to **revenue**: the money the producer receives from selling its output. This is the second part of the standard theory of producer behaviour we're constructing.

As with costs, revenue can be categorised according to scale:

1 **Total Revenue**, denoted simply by R, is the total amount of money the producer receives from selling its output to consumers. Assuming it sells its products to all consumers at the same price (P), total revenue is simply price multiplied by the number of units sold (Q): $R = PQ$.

2 **Average Revenue**, denoted by AR, is the amount of money the producer receives for each unit of output it sells. It's calculated by dividing total revenue by the quantity sold, as in Equation 6.3. If the producer sells its products at a constant price, average revenue is equal to price.

$$AR = \frac{R}{Q} \qquad\qquad\qquad \text{(Equation 6.3)}$$

3 **Marginal Revenue**, denoted by MR, is the additional total revenue the producer earns from selling one extra unit of output. It's calculated by partially differentiating the total revenue function with respect to output, as in Equation 6.4. Partial differentiation (denoted by ∂) is used here because total revenue is a function of both price and output, and we want to ascertain how total revenue changes solely as a result of a change in output. For example, if the total revenue of selling 2,091 units of output is £4,182 and that from selling 2,092 units is £4,184, the marginal revenue from selling the 2,092nd unit is £2. Once again, if the producer sells its products at a constant price its marginal revenue is simply price.

$$MR = \frac{\partial R}{\partial Q}$$
(Equation 6.4)

We represent each of these types of revenue as a curve which is important for the analysis to follow. The average revenue curve shows the revenue per unit sold for each level of output. It shows the relationship between price and output: exactly the same relationship shown by the inverse demand curve (see Section 5.4, pp. 68), because as the producer determines the price of the product, consumers determine the amount of it they buy. A producer's average revenue curve, then, is the demand curve it faces. We know from the analysis in Chapter 5 that this curve is usually downward-sloping on a graph, with price measured on the vertical axis and quantity demanded (or sold) on the horizontal axis, and that it's fine to represent it as a straight line.

Marginal revenue has a relationship with average revenue. Both curves are downward-sloping on a price-output graph, but the marginal revenue curve is steeper than its associated average revenue curve. To be more precise, where the average revenue curve is a straight line, the associated marginal revenue curve is also a straight line but one with exactly twice the degree of slope (see Box 6.1). The reason for this is that when the producer reduces its price, it has to do so for all the output it sells. Consider, for example, a producer that currently produces ten units of output, selling them for £6 each. Its total revenue is £60 and its average revenue is £6. It increases its output by one unit, but in order to get consumers to buy this extra unit it needs to reduce the price it charges to £5.80. It's not able to charge £5.80 for this eleventh unit alone, though: it needs to reduce the price for all eleven units. Its total revenue increases to £63.80 and its average revenue falls to £5.80. The marginal revenue of the eleventh unit, then, is £3.80. It now increases its output by a further unit, reducing the price it charges for each of the twelve units to £5.60. Its total revenue rises to £67.20, its average revenue falls to £5.60 and the marginal revenue of the twelfth unit is £3.40. Looking at these figures, we can see that increasing output from eleven units to twelve units has caused the average cost to fall by 20 pence, from £5.80 to £5.60. The change in marginal revenue, though, is 40 pence, from £3.80 to £3.40. The fall in marginal revenue is twice that of the fall in average revenue.

For low output levels marginal revenue is positive, as in the example above. The producer has to reduce its price if it's to sell additional units of output, but because it isn't selling many units in the first place the additional revenue it receives from selling an extra unit of output outweighs that it loses from having to reduce the price it charges for the units it's already selling. However, as the level of output it sells continues to expand and the price it charges for each of its units continues to fall, there's a point at which selling an additional unit actually causes its total revenue to fall. At this point, the extra revenue it receives from selling an additional unit of output is outweighed by the revenue it loses from having to reduce the price it charges for the units it's already able to sell: the marginal revenue becomes negative. This point is precisely in the centre of the average revenue – and so the demand – curve. The average and marginal revenue curves are illustrated in Figure 6.4.

6.3 how much output producers make and sell

We now combine these two elements to form the neoclassical model of producer behaviour. This involves us making an important assumption: the producer always aims to maximise its **profit**.

Key term: profit

Profit is defined as the amount of revenue a producer receives in excess of the total cost it has to pay. We can express this as $\Pi=R-TC$, where Π stands for profit. However, this definition is too simple in economics as there are two different types of profit: **normal profit** and **abnormal profit**. These are examined below.

In order for the producer to maximise its profit it must make its marginal cost equal to its marginal revenue. This is the extremely important **profit-maximising condition**. Look at Figure 6.4, which combines our analyses of costs and revenue, and it's possible to see why this is. As the producer initially expands its output, marginal cost increases and marginal revenue falls. This means **marginal profit** – the additional profit from producing and selling one extra unit of output, calculated as marginal revenue minus marginal cost – falls but remains positive. In fact, marginal profit remains positive up to and including the level of output at which marginal cost and marginal revenue are equal (point A). At this point, marginal profit is zero. The producer should produce and sell all units up to and including this unit because they each generate additional profit (apart from the unit at which marginal cost is equal to marginal revenue: for that particular unit marginal profit is zero). It certainly shouldn't produce more than this level of output, though, because for all greater output levels marginal cost exceeds marginal revenue. This means each additional unit beyond the profit-maximising level actually reduces total profit: marginal profit is negative. The profit-maximising level of output is denoted by Q_1 on Figure 6.4.

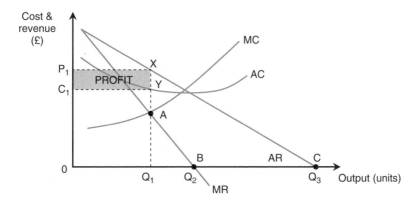

Figure 6.4 Profit maximisation

At the profit-maximising level of output the producer is able to sell each unit of its output for price P_1. This is the amount consumers are willing and able to pay for this level of output, represented by the demand curve (which as we saw above is identical to the average revenue curve). The producer's total revenue at the profit-maximising level of output, then, is given by the area $0P_1XQ_1$, meaning the area with 0, P_1, X and Q_1 at its four corners.

The average cost of producing this level of output, which can be read from the average cost curve, is given by C_1. This means the producer's total cost of production from making and selling the profit-maximising level of output is given by the area $0C_1YQ_1$. The producer's profit, the amount of revenue received over and above that necessary to cover costs, is given by $0P_1XQ_1 - 0C_1YQ_1 = C_1P_1XY$. This is the shaded area in Figure 6.4.

To be precise, the shaded area in Figure 6.4 actually represents **abnormal** (or **supernormal**) **profit**. The producer has to pay for its four factors of production. Labour receives wages, land and capital receive rent or their purchase price, and entrepreneurship receives **normal profit**. This last payment is the minimum amount of revenue, over and above all the other costs, an entrepreneur requires to maintain production. If an entrepreneur doesn't receive his normal profit, he closes down production and moves onto something new. All these costs, including normal profit, are incorporated into the cost curves, and so any area of revenue over and above costs, which can be shaded as in Figure 6.4, represents abnormal (or supernormal) profit – profit in excess of normal profit.

Figure 6.5a illustrates a producer that's just covering its costs and so is making an amount of profit precisely equal to the entrepreneur's required level of normal profit. In this situation the entrepreneur continues production: he's satisfied with his return. No abnormal profit is being made but that doesn't mean the producer isn't profitable in the eyes of accountants: it's making a profit, just the minimum necessary to keep the entrepreneur employed. Figure 6.5b, on the other hand, illustrates a producer failing to cover its costs. It's making **subnormal profit** or an **economic loss**. In this case, the entrepreneur walks away and production stops.

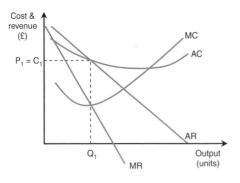

Figure 6.5a Producer making normal profit

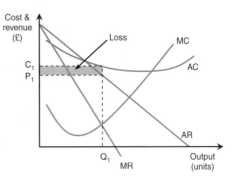

Figure 6.5b Producer making sub-normal profit

6.4 supply

By drawing together all this analysis of producer behaviour, we can derive the producer's supply curve. In Section 6.3 we assumed the producer maximises its profit by producing and selling the level of output at which its marginal cost is equal to its marginal revenue. If we assume the producer has to charge the same price for each and every unit it sells, its marginal revenue is equal to its average revenue, which is equal to the price it charges (see Section 6.2). If we combine these two observations, we see the producer makes and sells the level of output at which its marginal cost is equal to the price it charges. This means the marginal cost curve of the producer is in fact its **supply curve**. More precisely, the marginal cost curve is the **inverse supply curve**, but for clarity the convention is to refer to it simply as the supply curve (which we do from here on). However, you should be aware of the difference between inverse and **normal supply curves** and when they should each be used.

Key term: supply curve

The supply curve shows the minimum price the producer requires for each unit at a particular level of output sold. As with demand, the supply curve can be drawn as either the **inverse supply curve**, which measures price on the vertical axis and quantity supplied on the horizontal axis, thereby representing price as a function of quantity supplied, $P=f(Qs)$; or the **normal supply curve**, which measures quantity supplied on the vertical axis and price on the horizontal axis, and so represents quantity supplied as a function of price, $Qs=f(P)$. Economists usually use the inverse form for diagrams and the normal form for mathematical calculation (see Section 5.4 and Box 6.2 for discussion of this point).

However, there are two caveats to this rule, which are illustrated in Figure 6.6 in which the average cost (AC), average variable cost (AVC) and marginal cost (MC) curves of the producer are presented. The difference between the average cost and average variable cost curves is accounted for by average fixed cost, which, following our analysis above, diminish as output expands: shown in the figure by the average cost and average variable cost curves converging as output expands.

First, we see that there may be prices, such as P_1, that are associated with the two points on the marginal cost curve: a downward-sloping point and an upward-sloping point. The producer won't choose points on the downward-sloping section of the marginal cost curve because expanding output further reduces the average cost – the average cost curve is downward-sloping at these points – and so by expanding its output beyond these points and selling the additional units at the given price, it's able to increase its total profit.

Second, the producer has to pay its fixed costs irrespective of the volume of output it produces – even if it produces zero units of output it still needs to pay them – but it doesn't need to pay any variable costs because it always has the option of not producing any units at all. From this we can see it's rational for the producer only to produce and sell units of output if doing so at least covers the variable costs involved in production. If the revenue raised is insufficient to cover its variable costs, the producer has to pay both its fixed costs and whatever amount of the variable costs isn't covered. It's better off producing zero units of output and paying only its fixed costs. The producer's **shut-down point**, then, is that at which its revenue just covers its average variable costs.

The first caveat implies the supply curve of the producer is only the upward-sloping section of its marginal cost curve. The second, restricting this further, implies its supply curve is only the upward-sloping section of its marginal cost curve that's above its average variable cost curve.

determinants of supply

In Chapter 5 we examined how the quantity demanded of a product is primarily determined by its price, which is why we draw demand curves on graphs with price measured on the vertical axis and quantity demanded measured on the horizontal axis. Precisely the same is true of the quantity supplied, and so of the supply curve. As the price of the product changes, the producer alters the amount it makes and sells (supplies), maintaining the equality of marginal revenue and marginal cost. As with demand, changes in price cause **movements** up and down the supply curve.

However, there are many other factors that influence the output quantity the producer is willing and able to supply at each price. In fact, as the producer's supply curve is the upward-sloping portion of its marginal cost curve above its average variable cost, anything that changes it's marginal cost for each

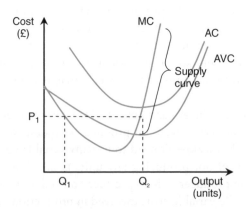

Figure 6.6 Marginal cost and supply curve

level of output supplied ultimately changes the amount of output it is willing to supply at each price. For example:

1 **Changes in the cost of the factors of production**. If the cost of land, capital or labour changes, the marginal cost curve shifts and so the quantity supplied also changes. For example, if the cost of coffee beans suddenly increases because of a natural disaster striking Sumatra, the marginal cost of producing freeze-dried coffee increases for all levels of output – the marginal cost curve shifts upwards – and so less is supplied at each price level.

2 **Changes in entrepreneurial motivation**. The cost of entrepreneurship – the level of normal profit required by the entrepreneur to continue production – wasn't mentioned in the point above because it can incorporate many other determinants: those that influence the motivation of the entrepreneur. For example, if supplying frozen meals to homebound pensioners became socially rewarding, perhaps because of an increase in the status associated with it, the entrepreneur might forgo some normal profit in order to expand supply and maximise his social status. This causes the marginal cost of production to fall for all levels of output, the marginal cost curve shifts downwards and the amount supplied increases. Changes in supply such as this, although caused by changes in the cost of entrepreneurship and so in marginal cost, are motivated by a very different line of reasoning.

3 **Changes in the profitability of products in joint supply**. Products in joint supply are those necessarily produced together, for example, leather and steak. If the profitability of steak increases, because of an increase in demand due to newly recognised health benefits or because of a reduction in its production costs, the supply of leather is also likely to expand. More cattle are reared and slaughtered for steak, causing the cost of their hides to fall. This reduces the marginal cost for all levels of leather production, causing the marginal cost curve to shift downwards and the quantity supplied to expand.

These determinants are all likely to change the quantity supplied of a product– even if the price the producer can charge for it remains unchanged – by causing the marginal cost (supply) curve to shift. Any non-price changes that increase the quantity supplied of a product cause its supply curve to shift outwards (downwards), and any non-price changes that reduce the quantity supplied of a product cause its supply curve to shift inwards (upwards). An example is displayed in Figure 6.7, which shows the likely effect of the producer enjoying lower production costs: even if the price remains at P1 the supply curve shifts outwards from S1 to S2 and the quantity supplied increases from Q1 to Q2.

own-price elasticity of supply

In a way that mirrors own-price elasticity of demand (see Section 5.6) the proportional responsiveness of the quantity supplied of a product to a change

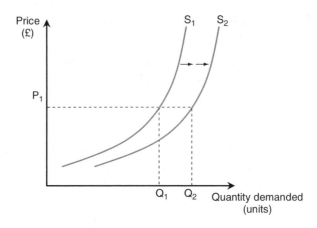

Figure 6.7 Outward shift in supply

in its price is measured by **own-price elasticity of supply** (P_{es}). This is calculated as Equation 6.5, in which ΔQ_s denotes the change in quantity supplied, ΔP is the change in price, P_1 is the initial price and Q_{s1} is the output initially supplied.

$$P_{es} = \frac{\%\Delta Q_s}{\%\,\Delta P} = \frac{\Delta Q_s}{\Delta P}\frac{P_1}{Q_{s1}} \qquad \text{(Equation 6.5)}$$

Unlike demand, own-price elasticity of supply is usually positive because quantity supplied usually changes in the same direction as price: as the price of a product increases, it's likely the producer supplies more because its marginal profit is increased. If own-price elasticity of supply is between 0 and 1 the product is said to be **price-inelastic in supply**, meaning supply is relatively unresponsive to a change in price. If it's greater than 1, the product is said to be **price-elastic in supply**, meaning it's relatively responsive to a change in price. If it's equal to 1 the product is said to have **unitary price elasticity of supply**.

The determinants of own-price elasticity of supply include the following:

1 **The producer's ability to keep stocks.** Consider a producer that's able to build up stocks of the unsold final product: the product is not perishable, for instance. It's likely this producer is able to alter supply quickly in response to changes in the price of the product. If the price rises, it's able to sell some of its surplus stock whilst organising an increase in production; and if the price falls, it's able to add to its stocks instead of supplying the market, again whilst reorganising production. This producer's supply is likely to be price-elastic. Now compare this to a producer that isn't able to store surplus stocks of the final product and so isn't able to respond quickly to changes in its price. If the price increases, it has to actually produce more

in response, which inevitably takes time. This second producer's supply is likely to be price-inelastic.

2. **Production time.** Producers that take longer to produce their goods are likely to have more price-inelastic supply because it takes them longer to expand or contract production. The own-price elasticity of supply of agricultural produce, therefore, is likely to be less elastic than that of stationary because once the seed has been planted producers cannot easily change the amount being grown, whereas the stationary producer is probably able to change its level of production fairly quickly.

3. **Flexibility of suppliers.** A producer using supplies that are price-elastic in supply is likely to produce a product that's also price-elastic in supply. This is because its suppliers are able to alter their volumes of resources quickly, enabling the producer to adapt its final supply rapidly in response to changes in the price of its product.

4. **Time horizon.** As with demand, the time period of supply is an important determinant of elasticity. Products are likely to become increasingly price-elastic in supply as the time horizon expands because producers are able to make alterations to their suppliers and their production methods, so the three determinants above become more responsive to change.

It should be noted that if a product is characterised by one of these determinants in a way that suggests it's price-elastic in supply, it doesn't necessarily follow that it will be so because one or more of the other determinants may actually cause it to be price-inelastic. However, they do usually coincide.

BOX 6.2: Linear supply curves, and normal and inverse supplies

As with demand curves (see Box 5.4), it simplifies our analysis if we draw supply curves as straight lines. In particular, it means normal supply curves can be represented by equations such as Equation B6.2.1.

$$Q_s = dP - c \qquad \text{(Equation B6.2.1)}$$

It's again important to be clear about the form a supply curve should take. Usually supply curves are expressed mathematically in their normal form – i.e. as in Equation B6.2.1 – but drawn as inverse supply curves. An expression for the inverse form is easily derived by rearranging Equation B6.2.1 to Equation B6.2.2.

$$P = \frac{1}{d}Q_s + \frac{c}{d} \qquad \text{(Equation B6.2.2)}$$

Equation B6.2.2 shows the price at which producers supply their output increases as their output expands. In other words, in order to induce producers to supply more it's necessary to increase the price they receive for each unit they sell. It also demonstrates the minimum price, $1/d + c/d$, that producers require if they're to supply a single unit of output. This is equivalent to the variable cost of the first unit.

The inverse supply curve has a slope of $1/d$. Such a curve – linear supply curves are still known as curves – is illustrated in Figure B6.3. At a price of P_1, the quantity supplied is $d(P_1)-c$. A shift in the curve is simply represented by a change in the value of c/d: an outward (downward) shift is shown by a reduction in its value and an inward (upward) shift by an increase (due to the associated change in production costs).

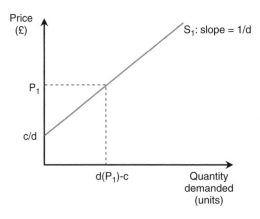

Figure B6.2 Linear inverse supply curve

6.5   criticisms of the standard model of producer behaviour

There are two general criticisms of the standard, neoclassical model of producer behaviour we've just constructed. The first regards the assumption of profit maximisation and the second the assumption that the producer is able to make decisions as though it's a single entity.

profit maximisation and alternative objectives

Many producer objectives other than that of profit maximisation have been proposed by economists because they're perhaps more realistic reflections of business practices in the real world. It isn't possible for us to cover all the proposed alternative objectives here, but a few are identified and related to Figure 6.4 (page 97).

1 **Revenue maximisation**, presented by William Baumol at the end of the 1950s. William Baumol argued that producers aim to maximise their revenue rather than their profit so that consumers, financial institutions and

suppliers see their buoyant sales and deal with them positively. Revenue is maximised at the level of output at which marginal revenue is equal to zero. This is shown as point B and output Q_2 in Figure 6.4.

2 **Output maximisation**. It's argued that some not-for-profit organisations, such as charities, may seek to maximise the level of output they produce even though this means they make a loss. The maximum output such a producer can supply is that at which average revenue, and so price, is equal to zero. This is shown as point C and output Q_3 in Figure 6.4.

3 **Managerial utility maximisation**, proposed by Oliver Williamson in the early 1960s. The argument here is that managers – those who actually make the decisions – each seek to maximise their own personal utility at work, which is determined by factors such as their salary, status and power. Managers choose to spend money on enhancing these factors – something known as **managerial expenditure** – rather than to try to maximise the profit of the producer.

4 **Growth maximisation**, suggested by Robin Marris in the early 1960s. Robin Marris suggested producers focus on long-term considerations, namely rate of growth, rather than on current size and profit. This complements Williamson's managerial utility objective because it's likely a manager in charge of a growing producer or department enjoys increasing power and status as a direct result of its growth. It's in the personal interest of the manager, then, to make decisions with the goal of growth maximisation in mind.

5 **Behavioural theories**. Herbert Simon (see Sections 5.7 and 14.10) argued from the 1950s onwards that the objectives of a producer are determined by its specific organisational structure. The logic here is that what we've been calling producers are in fact complex collections of different groups of stakeholders – people with an interest in a company, such as shareholders, consumers, managers and employees – each of which want different things. Because of this, the overall objectives of a producer are likely to be the result of interaction between these stakeholders and are likely to be determined through negotiation and compromise rather than by the simple maximisation of a particular variable such as profit. Richard Cyert and James March, in their 1963 article in the *American Economic Review*, extended the initial work in this area by suggesting producers are composed of constantly changing coalitions: groups of stakeholders in agreement about its objectives. The dominant coalition changes over time, causing producer objectives to continually change as well.

the theory of X-inefficiency

In a series of articles from the 1960s onwards, including some in the *American Economic Review* and the *Journal of Economic Literature*, Harvey Leibenstein developed the theory of **X-inefficiency**. Put simply, this theory suggests we cannot assume producers make and implement decisions as though they're single entities. A producer is actually composed of a whole structure of employees – from the management at the top of the hierarchy, through the middle managers to those working on the shop floor (for want of a better phrase) – and each of these individual employees makes decisions of his own.

Following on from the work on satisficing by Herbert Simon (see Sections 5.7 and 14.10), Harvey Leibenstein developed a model of producer behaviour that focuses on the employee rather than on the producer as a whole. An employee has to decide how much effort to put into his job. Pressure from superiors and his own career ambitions induce him to work harder, but his own desire for an easy life and pressure from fellow workers not to show them up induce him to work less hard. It's by balancing these conflicting pressures that he decides how much effort to put into his work, a level of effort that's likely to be less than his superiors would ideally like.

Looking at the whole producer, then, the workers on the shop floor don't work as hard as the middle managers would like them to, and the middle managers don't work as hard as the top managers would like them to either. This less than optimal effort, which exists at every level of a producer's structure, is known as X-inefficiency. Logically, the larger a producer becomes, the greater the X-inefficiency it's characterised by.

The top management of a producer can set the objective of profit maximisation, which if it's to be achieved requires the producer as a whole to have the level of output at which marginal revenue is equal to marginal cost. It also needs it to be productively efficient (see Section 1.1). This is simply assumed as being so in the standard model of producer behaviour, but according to the theory of X-inefficiency it cannot be taken for granted and is actually unlikely to be realised. The top management can set an objective for the producer, but because of X-inefficiency it will never actually be achieved.

Harvey Leibenstein demonstrated that in order for us truly to understand the way a producer behaves we need to understand and examine its internal workings. He also supported his model and argument with considerable evidence that X-inefficiency is a serious cause for concern.

evaluation

It's too simplistic to assume all producers have the same objective. In reality, different producers strive for different things, and the objectives of a single producer change over time. It's also too simplistic to assume producers are able to make and implement decisions as though they're single entities. To fully understand how producers behave we need to understand how they're structured and how the individuals within them behave. However, economic models need to strike the correct balance between usefulness and realism. You should think about whether the standard model, which assumes profit maximisation and single entity producers, gets this balance correct or not (see Section 4.4).

6.6 summary

> The neoclassical model of producer behaviour is composed of two elements: the cost of production and revenue. A producer supplies the amount of its product at which its marginal cost and marginal revenue are equal: this is the profit maximisation condition.

> The supply curve shows the relationship between the quantity supplied of a product and its price. As with the demand curve, there are two types: normal and inverse curves.

> The inverse supply curve of a producer is the upward-sloping portion of its marginal cost curve above its average variable cost curve.

> A producer's average revenue curve is identical to the demand curve it faces.

> Changes in the quantity supplied of a product caused by changes in its price are shown by movements along the supply curve, whereas changes in quantity supplied caused by changes other than in its price are shown as shifts of the curve.

> Own-price elasticity of supply shows the responsiveness of the quantity supplied of a product to a change in its price.

> The neoclassical model of producer behaviour has been criticised because of its assumptions of profit maximisation and that producers make decisions as single entities. Alternative models have been proposed.

7 when consumers and producers interact

Now we've examined the standard models of consumer and producer behaviour, we can place their weaknesses (see Sections 5.7 and 6.5) to one side and examine the complete neoclassical model of **market** interaction. We do this so we can understand how prices are determined in the economy, what quantities of different products are produced and sold, and how beneficial this is to society as a whole. These are the questions we're ultimately interested in when we study microeconomics, and it's to these we now turn.

Key term: market

A market is a venue, be it physical or technological, in which consumers and producers interact, exchanging money for products. It's through this interaction that market prices and the quantities of the different products traded are determined.

We start by examining the simplest model of markets, that of demand and supply. From this we can then make our analysis more sophisticated, examining each of the four primary types of **market structure** in the economy.

Key term: market structure

The term 'market structure' refers to the nature of a market: the number of producers and consumers within it – and so the degree of competition it exhibits – as well as the characteristics of the products traded. There are four primary types of market structure, which form **the spectrum of competition** shown in Figure 7.1. The structure of perfect competition is the most competitive, that of pure monopoly is the least so, and those of monopolistic competition and oligopoly lie in between.

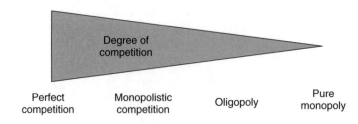

Figure 7.1 The spectrum of competition

7.1 market demand and supply analysis

In Chapters 5 and 6 we examined the behaviour of the representative consumer and the representative producer. In a market, though, there are likely to be both many different consumers and many different producers, all interacting with one another. Because of this, we need to examine demand and supply at the market level rather than at the level of these representative actors if we are to understand how markets function. Market demand and supply curves are simply derived by adding up all the demand and supply curves of the individual actors within the market. The normal market demand curve shows the total quantity of the product that all consumers in the market demand at each price, and the normal market supply curve shows the total quantity of the product that all producers in the market make and sell at each price. The inverse market demand and supply curves can then be interpreted as in Sections 5.3 and 6.4, but at the level of the market as a whole.

Combining the inverse market demand curve with the inverse market supply curve allows us to analyse markets in the most simplistic, but still informative, manner (from here on these will be referred to simply as the market demand and supply curves, unless specified as their normal types). Following on from Chapter 5, the market demand curve represents the maximum price for the product consumers are willing and able to pay if they're to buy a particular quantity; and from Chapter 6, the supply curve represents the minimum price for the goods producers require if they're to sell a particular quantity. The point at which these curves intersect is known as **market equilibrium**. This is the price that induces producers to make and sell precisely the amount of output consumers buy. It's at market equilibrium, then, that we find the market price of the product and the quantity of it that's produced and sold: market price and quantity are determined by the interaction of consumers and producers. This is illustrated in Figure 7.2, in which the market price is established at P_1 where Q_1 units of the product are produced and sold.

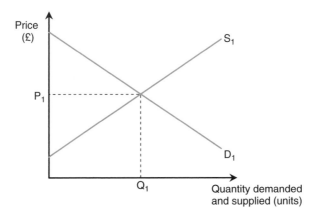

Figure 7.2 Market equilibrium

Market price and quantity are established at market equilibrium because it's only at that point that price and quantity are under no pressure to change. Consider prices greater than P_1 in Figure 7.2. At each of these prices producers want to supply more to the market than consumers are willing and able to purchase, meaning there's **excess supply**. In such situations producers have to reduce the price they charge if they're to sell all their stocks, and so the market price falls. Now consider prices less than P_1 in the diagram. At each of these consumers want to purchase more of the product than is being supplied by producers, and so there's **excess demand**. In situations of excess demand consumers compete with one another for the units of the product available, thus driving the price upwards. It's only at the equilibrium price P_1 that the amount supplied is equal to the amount demanded and there's no pressure for the price to change. Market equilibrium is often known as the **market-clearing point** because it's at this point that all excesses in demand or supply are cleared.

Whenever one of the non-price determinants of demand or supply – which we examined in Sections 5.5 and 6.4 – changes, the market moves out of equilibrium and so the market price and quantity change to re-establish equilibrium. This can be seen in Figure 7.3a, which shows the UK market for firelighters. The initial market equilibrium established a price P_1 at which Q_1 bags were bought and sold. Suppose that suddenly and unexpectedly the weather becomes extremely hot and the population immediately wants BBQs. The quantity of firelighters demanded expands dramatically at every possible price, shifting the market demand curve from D_1 to D_2. Consumers compete with one another for the bags available, driving the price up to P_2. Firelighter producers respond by expanding their output so that they can take advantage of the opportunity of greater profits. The market resettles at a new equilibrium, with a market price P_2, at which Q_2 bags are traded.

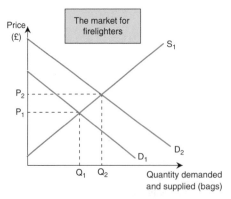

Figure 7.3a Equilibrium and a shift in demand

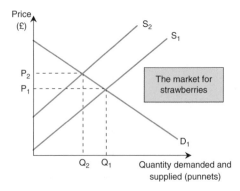

Figure 7.3b Equilibrium and a shift in supply

Figure 7.3b illustrates a separate example, this time of the market for strawberries at Wimbledon. Suppose the unexpected heatwave of the previous paragraph occurs shortly before the Wimbledon Tennis Championship is held, taking strawberry growers completely by surprise and decimating their harvest. There's insufficient time for the caterers at Wimbledon to source new suppliers, and so the effect of the heatwave is to increase the marginal cost of supplying strawberries at the Championship at every output level. This causes the market supply curve to shift inwards (upwards) from S_1 to S_2. The supporters in Centre Court, and on 'Henman Hill' (or alternatively 'Murray Mount' depending on your allegiance), compete with one another for the available strawberries, with the result that suppliers increase the price they charge. The price of a punnet of strawberries at the Championship therefore increases from P_1 to P_2 and the quantity traded falls from Q_1 punnets to Q_2 punnets.

The comparison of equilibrium points like this is known as comparative statics (see Section 1.4). This lies at the heart of neoclassical economic analysis that is the basis of all the analysis in this book. Other schools of thought disagree with such analysis because it fails to explain how equilibrium is actually reached in the first place.

BOX 7.1: **Market equilibrium**

Market demand and supply equations are two simultaneous equations in which there are two unknowns. This means that a standard method for solving simultaneous equations can be used to find the price and quantity at which they intersect.

Example 1: Suppose the normal market demand curve for a type of fine port is given by $Q_d = 3050 - 25P$ and the associated normal market supply curve is given by $Q_s = -250 + 5P$. We want to calculate the market price for this type of port and the number of bottles traded. We know in market equilibrium the quantity supplied is equal to the quantity demanded, meaning:

$$Q_d = Q_s \qquad \text{(Equation B7.1.1)}$$

We now need to substitute the demand and supply equations into Equation B7.1.1, rearrange and solve for the market price:

$$3050 - 25P = -250 + 5P \rightarrow 30P = 3300 \qquad \text{(Equation B7.1.2)}$$

$$P = \frac{3300}{30} = 110 \qquad \text{(Equation B7.1.3)}$$

The market price is £110 per bottle of port. To calculate the number of bottles traded at this price, all we now need to do is substitute this value into either the demand or supply equation:

$$Q_s = -250 + 5(110) = 300 \qquad \text{(Equation B7.1.4)}$$

At this price 300 bottles are bought and sold. Checking this with the quantity demanded equation shows that this is the correct solution.

Example 2: Consider the generic case. $Q_d = a - bP$ and $Q_s = c + dP$. In market equilibrium, the quantity demanded is equal to the quantity supplied, and so:

$$Q_d = Q_s \quad \text{(Equation B7.1.5)}$$

$$a - bP = c + dP \rightarrow dP + bP = a - c \rightarrow (d+b)P = a - c \quad \text{(Equation B7.1.6)}$$

$$P = \frac{a - c}{d + b} \quad \text{(Equation B7.1.7)}$$

Equation B7.1.7 is the generic solution for the market price when the market demand and supply curves are linear. In the first example a = 3050, c = −250, b = 25 and d = 5. If we substitute these values into Equation 7.1.7 we generate a price of £110, which is the correct solution for example 1. From the market price, the market-clearing quantity can then be ascertained.

Using linear market demand and supply curves dramatically simplifies our calculations of market equilibrium.

7.2 market welfare

Having examined how the interaction of consumers and producers within a market determines the price of a product and the quantity produced and sold, it's a logical next step to examine how beneficial this is for the actors involved. To do this we need to examine the resulting level of **market welfare**. One of the most important advantages of the standard model of markets is that it offers us an objective way of measuring this seemingly subjective, but nevertheless important, concept.

Key term: market welfare

Market welfare refers to the utility or satisfaction of consumers and producers from trading in a particular market. It's measured by **consumer** and **producer surplus**.

The concept of market welfare is grounded on the notions of consumer and producer sovereignty. In market equilibrium the price represents the amount of money consumers are willing to pay for the last unit of output they buy. It represents their own judgement about the value of that unit relative to all the other products they can spend their money on. For producers, on the other hand, the market price is equal to the marginal cost of producing the last unit they produce and sell. In market equilibrium the views of these two groups of actors are consistent with one another: there's a balance, and so no reason for change. Looking at it in this way, market equilibrium offers us an objective, coherent view of how actors value products.

We've already examined how the market demand curve shows the amount consumers are willing and able to pay for each quantity of the product. This means that for each of the units of the product that consumers buy, apart from the final unit they buy, consumers aren't actually paying the full amount that they're willing and able to: the market price is lower than the value indicated by the market demand curve for those units. For example, in Figure 7.4 consumers are willing to pay P_2 for the single unit denoted by Q_2, but they actually pay only the market price P_1. The difference between the maximum price consumers are willing to pay for a unit and the market price they actually pay is called the **consumer surplus** from that particular unit. Adding up the consumer surpluses from all the units bought in the market – in other words, calculating the size of the whole area between the market demand curve and the market price up to the final unit bought in the market – represents the consumer surplus in the market as a whole. As consumers are only willing to pay an amount for a product that's at most equal to the satisfaction they get from it, consumer surplus is a representation of their welfare: it shows the extra satisfaction they get from a product, which they don't actually pay for.

We've also examined how the market supply curve shows the minimum price at which producers are willing and able to supply each quantity of the product to the market. Up to the final unit made and sold in the market, producers receive a price for the units they sell that exceeds the minimum they're willing to sell those units for. Consider again Figure 7.4. Producers are willing to supply the unit denoted by Q_2 for a price P_3, but they actually receive the market price P_1 for it. The difference between the minimum price they would supply a unit for and the price they actually receive for doing so is known as the **producer surplus** from that particular unit. The sum of the producer surpluses from each individual unit up to the final unit sold – the area between the market supply curve and the market price up to market equilibrium – is known as the producer surplus in the market as a whole. As with consumer surplus, it's a representation of producer welfare since it shows the extra revenue producers receive over and above their minimum requirements. In fact, with a little reflection you can see that producer surplus is the same thing as the excess of revenue above variable cost, which is known as **operating profit**.

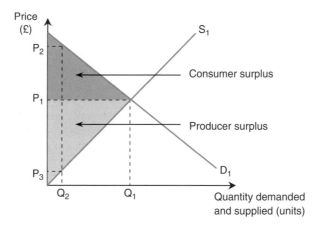

Figure 7.4 Market welfare

Total market welfare is consumer surplus plus producer surplus. It's a useful measure because it indicates the different degrees of welfare at different points of market equilibrium, and so can be used to indicate the welfare effects of any changes in market conditions, for the market as a whole as well as for the consumers and producers separately.

BOX 7.2: **Consumer surplus**

Consumer surplus is simply the area beneath the market demand curve and above the market price up to the final unit bought in the market. It's calculated using **integration** – calculating the total area under the market demand curve up to and including the last unit bought and sold, and then subtracting the amount consumers actually pay for these units. The general rule for calculating consumer surplus (CS), then, is given as Equation B7.2.1, in which Q^*_d is the quantity bought and sold in the market, 'equation' is the expression for the market demand curve, and P^* is the market price. Please note: it's important to use the inverse market demand curve equation if integrating with respect to the quantity bought and sold. Alternatively, you can use the equation for the normal market demand curve but you will need to integrate with respect to the market price.

$$CS = \int_{Q_d=0}^{Q_d=Q^*_d} (\text{equation}) dQ_d - (P^* Q^*_d) \qquad \text{(Equation B7.2.1)}$$

Again, having a linear curve dramatically simplifies this calculation as it means consumer surplus is a triangle.

Example: Consider again the market for fine port in Box 7.1. The normal market demand curve is given by $Q_d = 3050 - 25P$ and the market-clearing price and quantity are £110 and 300 bottles, respectively. We can derive the equation for the inverse market demand curve by rearranging that for the normal curve, making price a function of quantity demanded:

$$Q_d = 3050 - 25P \rightarrow 25P = 3050 - Q_d \rightarrow P = 122 - 0.04Q_d \qquad \text{(Equation B7.2.2)}$$

This market demand curve is illustrated in Figure B7.2, along with the area representing consumer surplus.

Integrating this equation with respect to quantity demanded between quantities of zero and 300 bottles gives us the total area under the curve up to and including the 300th bottle of port. The initial integral is given as Equation B7.2.3 and its solution is given in Equation B7.2.5. This represents the total utility (TU) enjoyed by consumers from consuming these bottles of port.

$$TU = \int_{Q_d=0}^{Q_d=300} (122 - 0.04Q_d)\, dQ_d = 122\, Q_d - 0.04\frac{Q_d^2}{2}\Big|_{Q_d=0}^{Q_d=300} \qquad \text{(Equation B7.2.3)}$$

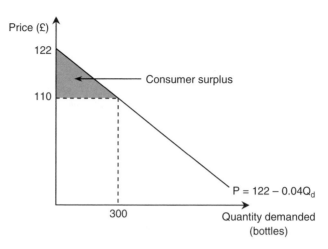

Figure B7.2 *Consumer surplus*

$$= \left[122\,(300) - 0.04\frac{300^2}{2} \right] - \left[122\,(0) - 0.04\frac{0^2}{2} \right] \qquad \text{(Equation B7.2.4)}$$

$$= 36600 - 1800 = 34800 \qquad \text{(Equation B7.2.5)}$$

Overall, consumers enjoy utility from these 300 bottles of port to the value of £34,800: it is very good port after all. However, they're required to pay £110 for each bottle, meaning they together pay a total amount of £33,000. Consumer surplus, being the amount that consumers are willing and able to pay for the units they buy over and above what they actually pay, is given by the difference between these two values: CS = 34,800 – 33,000 = 1800. Consumers are willing and able to pay an additional £1800 to consume their 300 bottles of port: this is their consumer surplus and so their welfare.

It's always important to check answers such as these. This is easy to do in this case since the market demand curve is linear and so the consumer surplus is a simple triangle with height 12, base 300 and so area of $0.5 \times 12 \times 300 = 1800$.

As with differentiation, you should be comfortable with and fluent in integration. Unfortunately, space precludes a full treatment of the technique here, but you can find sections outlining the relevant rules in all good mathematics for economics textbooks (see Chapter 15 for suggestions). Once the rules are mastered, integration is straightforward.

BOX 7.3: **producer surplus**

We can use the same procedure to calculate producer surplus – calculating the size of the area above the market supply curve and beneath the market price up to the final unit traded. With a linear market supply curve producer surplus can be easily calculated by computing the area of the triangle using the $\frac{1}{2} \times$ base $\times$ height method. For market supply curves that are actually curves, it's more complicated because we need to calculate the area under the curve using integration and to then subtract this from the rectangle representing producerrevenue. The general rule for calculating producer surplus, then, is given as Equation B7.3.1, in which Q^*_s is the quantity bought and sold in the market, 'equation' is the equation of the market supply curve, and P^* is the market price. Please note: as with consumer surplus, it's important to use the inverse market supply curve equation if integrating with respect to the quantity bought and sold. You can use the equation for the normal market supply curve, but you then need to integrate it with respect to the market price rather than quantity.

$$PS = \left(P^* Q^*_s\right) - \int_{Q_s = 0}^{Q_s = Q^*_s} (\text{equation}) \, dQ_s \qquad \text{(Equation B7.3.1)}$$

Example: Consider again the market for fine port in Box 7.1. The normal market supply curve is given by $Q_s = -250 + 5P$ and the market-clearing price and quantity are £110 and 300 bottles respectively. We can derive the equation of the inverse market supply curve by rearranging that of the normal curve, making price a function of quantity supplied:

$$Q_s = -250 + 5P \rightarrow 5P = Q_s + 250 \rightarrow P = 0.2Q_s + 50 \qquad \text{(Equation B7.3.2)}$$

This market supply curve is illustrated in Figure B7.3, along with the area representing producer surplus.

Rearranging the market supply curve equation in this way leads to an additional insight about producers: they're unwilling to produce even a single bottle for a price less than £50. This must truly be good port!

By integrating the equation of the inverse market supply curve with respect to quantity supplied between quantities of zero and 300 bottles we can derive the total area under the curve up to and including the 300th bottle of port. The initial integral is given as Equation B7.3.3 and its solution as Equation B7.3.5. This

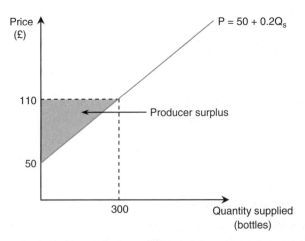

Figure B7.3 *Producer surplus*

introducing smaller-scale analysis: the microeconomic world

represents the minimum total amount producers require if they're to supply this output to the market. We call this their **reserve earnings** (RE).

$$RE = \int_{Q_s=0}^{Q_s=300}(0.2Q_s + 50)dQ_s = 0.2\frac{Q_s^2}{2} + 500_s \Big|_{Q_s=0}^{Q_s=300}$$ (Equation B7.3.3)

$$0.2\left[\frac{(300)^2}{2} + 50(300)\right] - \left[0.2\frac{(0)^2}{2} + 50(0)\right]$$ (Equation B7.3.4)

$$= 9000 + 15000 = 24000$$ (Equation B7.3.5)

This means producers have reserve earnings of £24,000 if they're to supply 300 bottles of port to the market. However, by producing and selling this amount they actually receive £110 for each bottle, meaning they earn total revenue of £33,000. Producer surplus – the amount producers earn over and above the minimum amount for which they would supply the output to the market – is given by the difference between these two values: PS = 33,000 – 24,000 = 9000. Producers, then, earn £9000 from supplying the output that's over and above their reserve earnings. This is the producer surplus in the market, which is a measure of producer welfare.

As always, we need to check this calculation. This is easy to do in this case because the market supply curve is linear and so the producer surplus is a simple triangle with height 60, base 30 and so an area of 0.5×60×300=9000.

7.3 perfect competition

Let's now turn to the first specific market structure, that of **perfect competition,** which is the market structure represented by the simple market demand and supply analysis above. The purpose of analysing perfect competition is to understand what the outcomes would be if markets were characterised by extreme competition between producers and were left to function without any intervention from government. It's not intended that such a market structure should be realistic. There's no example of a perfectly competitive market in the real world: the assumptions upon which it's based are simply too demanding. Instead, this market structure is used as a benchmark against which actual markets can be compared, which helps us to understand what happens in reality.

For a market to be perfectly competitive it needs to satisfy a number of strict assumptions:

1. There needs to be **an uncountable number of small producers and consumers,** each of which accounts for such a small proportion of the market supply and demand that they have absolutely no influence over the market price. We say they're **price takers** since they simply have to accept the price determined by the market.

2. All units of the product supplied to the market – irrespective of the producer that supplies them – need to be absolutely identical in all respects. We say **the products need to be homogeneous.**

③ Producers need to be able to enter and exit the market completely freely. There can't be anything that hinders them from doing this: there can't be any **barriers to entry or exit** (see Section 7.4).

④ There needs to be perfect knowledge within the market. This means that all consumers and producers must be fully aware of what every other actor is doing within the market at all times.

⑤ There needs to be completely free movement of products so that supply is responsive to market forces.

Only if all these conditions are satisfied is a market perfectly competitive – which is why we never see a perfect example in the real world.

A perfectly competitive market and a single perfectly competitive producer are illustrated in Figures 7.5a and 7.5b respectively. As producers and consumers are price takers, the price of the product being bought and sold is purely determined by the market, by the interaction of market demand and supply as in the previous section. Following the logic from the analysis above, this establishes a market price P_1, at which Q_m units are produced and sold (Figure 7.5a).

We saw in Chapter 6 that when a producer sells each and every unit produced at the same price, its average revenue and its marginal revenue both equal that price. The implication of this for a perfectly competitive producer that has to sell every unit it produces at the market price is that its average revenue and marginal revenue curves are identical and perfectly horizontal at the market price P_1. As a producer's average revenue curve is the same as its demand curve, this means a perfectly competitive producer's demand curve is perfectly elastic at the market price (see Section 5.6).

As all products in a perfectly competitive market are homogeneous, consumers are completely indifferent about which producer they buy from. This – in addition to the perfect information and the completely free movement of products that characterise such a market – means consumers in a perfectly competitive market always make their purchases from the cheapest producer. Producers have to compete with one another to sell their products, but they can only do this by reducing the price they charge: there's no point in advertising because consumers know that all their products are the same. Through price competition, producers drive the market price down to the price that just covers their costs. They all have the same minimum costs because the perfect information in the market enables them to all use the same production technologies and the same suppliers. A market price greater than this minimum price creates an incentive for one of the producers to reduce its price slightly and capture the whole market: consumers come running to the producer that offers the lowest price. All producers do just this and so the market price returns to the price that just covers producers' costs, the price at which average revenue is equal to average cost and only normal profits are made. This is exactly price P_1 in Figures 7.5a and 7.5b.

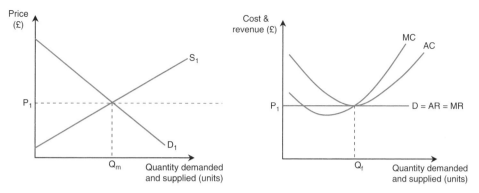

Figure 7.5a *A perfectly competitive market*

Figure 7.5b *A perfectly competitive producer*

In choosing the level of output to supply at the market price, and being driven by the desire to maximise profits, each producer equates its marginal cost with its marginal revenue: the profit maximisation condition (see Section 6.3). This means a perfectly competitive producer, like that illustrated in Figure 7.5b, supplies an output Q_f to the market at the market price P_1. As Figure 7.5b shows, a perfectly competitive producer supplies the amount of output at which its average cost, marginal cost, average revenue and marginal revenue curves all intersect.

Now suppose the market price is higher than the average cost of the individual producers currently in the market, enabling them all to earn abnormal profits (see Section 6.3). This is illustrated in Figures 7.6a and 7.6b, in which the initial market price is P_1, the initial market supply is Q_{m1} units, and each producer is supplying Q_{f1} units to the market, earning them each the abnormal profit shown as the shaded area. Unfortunately for the producers, this situation is only short-lived because entrepreneurs outside the market, who observe existing producers making abnormal profits, take advantage of the completely free entry into the market in order to enjoy this profitability as well. The market supply curve shifts outwards to the right as a result – more is produced in the market at the current market price – suppressing the market price as it shifts. New producers continue to enter the market until the supply curve reaches S_2, establishing a market price P_2 that's equal to average cost and at which all abnormal profit is eliminated. At this point the mechanism stops, since any further producers have no incentive to enter the market because if they did so the price would be reduced to a loss-making level. The final situation is identical to that in Figures 7.5a and 7.5b. This mechanism works in reverse as well. If the initial market price is such that producers are making a loss, entrepreneurs close their productions down. This shifts the market supply curve inwards to the left, driving the market price upwards until there's precisely the number of producers remaining in the market for the perfectly competitive market equilibrium to be attained.

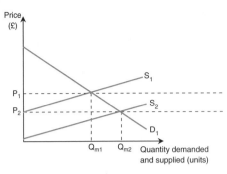

Figure 7.6a A perfectly competitive
market adjusting to
equilibrium

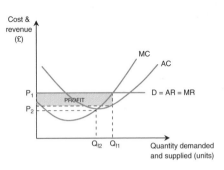

Figure 7.6b A perfectly competitive
producer adjusting to
equilibrium

perfect competition and welfare

We've effectively described the equilibrium towards which perfectly competitive markets tend and the mechanism by which they get there; but we haven't
said anything about how desirable such markets are. To do this, economists
talk about **efficiency**, a term used to show how closely a market structure satisfies a given criterion. There are three main types of efficiency against which
to compare a market structure: productive efficiency, allocative efficiency and
Pareto efficiency. These were introduced in Section 1.1. Let us analyse the
structure of perfect competition against each of these.

❶ **Perfect competition and productive efficiency**. For a producer to be
productively efficient means it operating at the lowest point on its average
cost curve and so maximising its output from a given volume of inputs.
Figure 7.5b demonstrates that a perfectly competitive producer is productively efficient. It has to be because the market price is equal to its minimum average cost, and so if its average cost isn't minimised, it makes a loss.

❷ **Perfect competition and allocative efficiency**. Allocative efficiency refers
to the way that factors of production and final products are distributed. An
allocatively efficient market is one that uses its factors of production to produce the optimal amount of output. A more formal definition is that allocative efficiency is achieved when the **price is equal to marginal cost**: P=MC.
This is true because the price consumers are willing to pay for a product
shows how they value the last unit produced and sold, and marginal cost is
the cost of the extra factors of production necessary to produce that last unit
of output. If price is higher than marginal cost, consumers are willing to pay
more for additional units than it costs producers to supply them and so the
product is under-supplied; and if price is lower than marginal cost, producers aren't receiving enough revenue to cover the cost of the extra production and so there's too much being produced and consumed. Only when
price is equal to marginal cost is the market allocatively efficient, which is
the case under perfect competition (see Figure 7.5b).

❸ Perfect competition and Pareto efficiency. Pareto efficiency is the state in which no actor can be made better off without making another actor worse off, with the result that total welfare is maximised. It's necessarily the state in which there's both productive and allocative efficiency: if the market isn't productively efficient, total utility can be increased simply by using the available resources in a way that increases production; and if it isn't allocatively efficient, total utility can be improved simply by redistributing factors of production so that the optimal amount of output is being produced. As Pareto efficiency is the maximisation of market welfare, it requires the entire area between the market demand and supply curves and to the left of the market-clearing point to contribute to either consumer or producer surplus (see Section 7.2). Figure 7.5a shows that this is the case for perfect competition: we see below that it isn't the case for the other market structures.

It was mentioned at the start of this section that perfect competition isn't realistic and so there's no actual example of it. However, this doesn't negate the importance or the usefulness of the model. Perfect competition is arguably the ideal situation – achieving as it does Pareto optimality – and as such it's useful as a benchmark against which all the other, more realistic, market structures can be compared. In fact, we compare each of the other market structures in this chapter to that of perfect competition in order to assess the implications they have for welfare.

7.4 pure monopoly

A second form of market structure, at the other extreme of the spectrum of competition compared to perfect competition, is **pure monopoly**. This is a market in which there's only a single producer. To maintain a monopoly position there has to be at least one **barrier to entry** that prevents additional producers entering the market. These can include:

❶ High set-up costs coupled with restricted access to financial capital, meaning that additional producers simply can't afford to enter the market.

❷ High sunk costs, which are costs a producer has to pay if it's to enter a market and which are unrecoverable on exit from the market.

❸ Brand loyalty, which makes it difficult for new entrants to attract consumers away from existing producers.

❹ Economies of scale. An existing producer that's able to expand to such a size that it's operating on a significantly lower short run average cost curve than is possible for new entrants is able to sustain a price against which new entrants cannot compete.

❺ Patents and licences. These are forms of fixed-term legal protection against competition that allow a producer to enjoy abnormal profits for a specified duration. Patents are usually awarded to producers developing new technology, whilst licences are granted to reduce harmful or unnecessary competition and to encourage investment into the affected product.

❻ Anti-competitive behaviour: deliberate action by existing producers specifically intended to drive competition from the market. Such behaviour can take on many forms, all of which are illegal according to the competition policy of the European Commission. For example:

a. **Predatory pricing through cross-subsidisation**. Consider a producer that operates in two markets, A and B. Cross-subsidisation is where it uses the abnormal profit it earns in market B to subsidise its operations in market A. It might adopt this strategy in order to finance the losses it makes in market A from reducing the price it charges in that market to such a low level that competitors are forced out: predatory pricing.

b. **Vertical restraints**, which is where an existing producer gains control – perhaps through exclusive dealing contracts – of either its suppliers or its outlets, making it impossible for new entrants to function in the market.

c. **Negative branding**: existing producers using the media to establish a negative view of competitors amongst consumers.

Protected by its barriers to entry, and enjoying a complete absence of competition, a pure monopoly is able to determine the price it charges. We say it's a **price maker**. Alternatively, it's able to determine the quantity of the product it sells in the market: it cannot do both, though, because it's constrained by consumer demand. Seeking to maximise profit, the monopoly determines either the price it charges or the output it sells such that its marginal cost and marginal revenue are equalised (see Section 6.3). This is illustrated in Figure 7.7a – the pure monopoly diagram – by the output Q_M and the price P_M. This combination of price and quantity produced affords the monopoly abnormal profit represented by the shaded area, which is the greatest possible profit it can earn. We only need to have one diagram for pure monopoly because the producer is the market.

pure monopoly and perfect competition compared

Let's assume the cost curves are the same irrespective of whether the market is characterised by pure monopoly or perfect competition. This allows us to make direct comparisons between the two structures. Consider Figure 7.7b. Making this assumption means the monopoly's marginal cost curve is the same as the market supply curve (see Section 6.4) and the monopoly's average revenue curve is the same as the market demand curve (see Section 6.2). As such, the market equilibrium under perfect competition is where these intersect, a quantity Q_{PC} and a price P_{PC}. A pure monopoly in the same situation produces output Q_M and charges a price P_M. From the figure it's apparent that:

❶ The price charged by a pure monopoly is higher, and the quantity of output produced and sold lower, than if the market was perfectly competitive.

❷ A pure monopoly, unlike perfectly competitive producers, fails to operate at productive efficiency: it doesn't operate at the lowest point on its average cost curve.

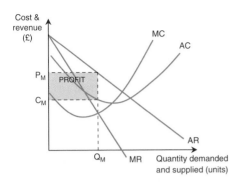

Figure 7.7a Pure monopoly

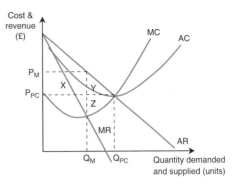

Figure 7.7b Pure monopoly and perfect competition

❸ The price charged by a pure monopoly exceeds its marginal cost at the level of output it produces, meaning it fails to achieve allocative efficiency and over-charges for the output it produces. This is rational behaviour on the part of a pure monopoly because it maximises its producer surplus. Compared with the market under perfect competition, the producer surplus of a pure monopoly is increased by area X but reduced by area Z. As the former is by far the larger of the two, a pure monopoly enjoys a significantly larger welfare by charging this higher price.

❹ A pure monopoly is Pareto inefficient. We saw in Section 7.3 that a perfectly competitive market is Pareto efficient, meaning it's impossible to make one actor better off without making another worse off. The increased producer surplus enjoyed by a pure monopoly, then, inevitably comes at a cost to consumers who see a reduction in their surplus of areas X and Y. A pure monopoly extracts welfare from consumers. In fact, a pure monopoly actually reduces total market welfare. Looking at Figure 7.7b, we see that area X is transferred from consumers to the producer, but areas Y and Z are completely lost. These lost areas make up what's known as the **deadweight welfare loss of monopoly**, and show that a pure monopoly must be Pareto inefficient because it's possible to make consumers better off without it being at the expense of the producer simply by eliminating the welfare loss.

These analytical conclusions suggest that it's preferable for a market to be characterised by perfect competition rather than by pure monopoly. This result is at the heart of **competition policy** that seeks to promote the level of competition in markets (see Section 8.1). However, a pure monopoly has some positive elements:

❶ The abnormal profit a pure monopoly earns enables it to invest in research and development, improving the quality of the product and reducing the production costs. This simply isn't possible for perfectly competitive producers to do because they don't earn any abnormal profit. A pure monopoly may be able to reduce its costs through research and development to such a degree that the price it charges can be reduced to a level below that possible under perfect competition. However, this possibility relies entirely upon the altruism of the entrepreneur and there would still be inefficiency under pure monopoly, just at a lower price.

❷ There have been many cases of harmful competition. A recent, light-hearted example is that of the 'river wars' in Cambridge during the summer of 2009. Small businesses offering tourists punting trips up and down the River Cam resorted to a variety of underhand tactics to gain an advantage over their rivals – which included taking chainsaws to one another's punts – spurring the local police force to employ three special officers specifically to deal with the problem: this represented a non-trivial cost to the town. In fact, Cambridge has experienced a number of cases of costly competition: only a few years early a similar situation arose between families selling ice-creams, which ended in violence as the families each defended their patch. With a pure monopoly such harmful competition is avoided.

non-pure monopolies

A pure monopoly is the situation in which there's only a single producer in a market. This means that one or more barriers to entry must be completely prohibitive: it must be impossible for new producers to enter. In reality such situations don't exist. All monopolies in the real world have a certain amount of competition but they dominate the market sufficiently to enjoy some degree of market power. The UK government considers a single producer in control of 25 per cent or more of a market as being a potentially concerning monopoly. We call these **non-pure monopolies**. Our analysis above still applies to these producers, but in a weakened form: realistic monopolies exhibit characteristics that are closer to those of perfect competition than our analysis above suggests.

price discrimination

As a monopoly is a price maker, whether it's a pure monopoly or not, it isn't only likely to set a price higher than that under perfect competition, it's also potentially able to engage in **price discrimination**. The purpose of price discrimination is to increase profit beyond the maximum that a single price can achieve, thereby maximising producer welfare by changing as much consumer surplus to producer surplus as possible.

Key term: price discrimination

Price discrimination is a pricing strategy by which the producer sells the same products to different consumers for different prices. Only monopolies can engage in price discrimination since they need to possess some control over the price they set. There are three general types of price discrimination: perfect, second-degree and third-degree. We see price discrimination around us every day.

1 **Perfect** (or **first-degree**) **price discrimination**. This is the strategy by which a monopoly sells each individual unit of output to the consumer who is willing to pay the most for it. This is illustrated in Figure 7.8a, in which the first unit is sold to a consumer for P_1 whereas the second unit is sold for the lower price P_2. The producer is theoretically able to convert all consumer surplus to producer surplus as each consumer can be made to pay precisely the maximum price s/he's willing to pay for it. The markets for second-hand cars and housing are effective, albeit imperfect, examples of producers employing such a strategy.

2 **Second-degree price discrimination** (also known as **excess capacity pricing**). This is the strategy by which a monopoly charges a lower price to consumers in order to sell any remaining spare capacity. Figure 7.8b illustrates a marginal cost curve that's constant up to a certain level of output, denoted Q_2, at which point it jumps to a new level at which it then stays constant for another range of output. This represents a producer that faces an initial financial outlay after which its variable cost is constant until capacity is reached, at which point it's required to make a second outlay, after which variable cost is once again constant. Consider, for example, a small coach company for which each major outlay reflects the purchasing of an additional vehicle. The producer maximises profits, beyond that of simply equating marginal cost with marginal revenue, by selling Q_1 units at price P_1 – the standard profit maximisation condition – and then selling the excess capacity, $Q_2 - Q_1$, at price P_2, which from the demand curve is the maximum consumers are willing to buy it for. This is why you can get last-minute ticket deals for many airline and bus services.

3 **Third-degree price discrimination**. This is the final price discrimination strategy, in which a monopoly separates its market into different segments according to the demand characteristics of the consumers in each. It then sets an optimal price, given by marginal cost being equal to marginal revenue, for each segment. This is illustrated in Figure 7.8c. The consumers in segment B have a relatively price-elastic demand for the product whereas those in segment C have much more price-inelastic demand (see Section 5.6). By equating marginal cost with marginal revenue for each segment, the producer charges a higher price to segment C consumers since their demand is relatively insensitive to price changes, and a lower price in segment B, where demand is much more sensitive to price changes. The consumers in segment A lie in between those in the other segments and so are charged a moderate price.

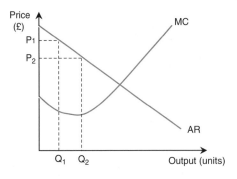

Figure 7.8a First-degree price discrimination

Figure 7.8b Second-degree price discrimination

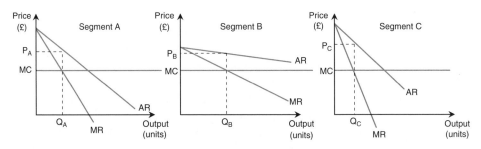

Figure 7.8c Third-degree price discrimination (note: $P_c > P_A > P_c$)

There are two ways that a monopoly can divide its market into segments so that it can employ third-degree price discrimination. First, it can divide the market into distinct groups that then have to prove their identity – for example, cinemas that charge students concessionary prices if they can prove they're in education. This is a **segregation** strategy. Alternatively, it can employ a **self-selection** strategy, which involves it creating a set of conditions that incentivise different consumers to reveal themselves. A good example of this is airlines that charge higher fares for flights on Fridays and Mondays in order to cause those in employment – who are likely to be characterised by more price-inelastic demands – to reveal themselves and to pay the higher fares.

7.5 monopolistic competition

The market structure of **monopolistic competition** was devised separately, but concurrently, by Joan Robinson (see Section 14.7) and Edward Chamberlin in the middle of the twentieth century. Developing effectively the same model at the same time perhaps inevitably caused them to dislike one another: Joan Robinson apparently remarked that Edward Chamberlin would award Ph.D.s to students as long as they found fault with her work.

Monopolistic competition lies in between the structures of pure monopoly and perfect competition in every sense. It's a market in which there are many producers, all supplying similar but non-homogeneous products. There are barriers to entry and exit but they aren't completely prohibitive and so there's a constant fluidity to the market as producers come in and out (see Section 7.4). The barriers are strong enough, though, to prevent the instantaneous entrance of new producers in response to abnormal profit in the market. This means that, while monopolistically competitive producers are able to enjoy abnormal profits in the short run, they cannot do the same in the long run because new producers eventually enter the market and increase competition.

The diagram for a single monopolistically competitive producer in the short run is identical to that for a pure monopoly, as illustrated in Figure 7.7a. As mentioned above, a producer under monopolistic competition sells a product that is in some way different from those of the other producers and so it faces a downward-sloping average revenue (demand) curve (see Section 6.2). It also benefits from barriers to entry, enabling it to earn abnormal profit.

New producers observe the abnormal profit and so gradually enter the market in the hope of getting a share of it. This erodes the share of the market that existing producers command, thereby causing the average revenue (demand) curve for each existing producer to shift inwards, driving down the price it's able to charge. Additional producers continue to enter the market until only normal profits are earned – until its average revenue is equal to its average cost at the profit-maximising output (see Section 6.3). This is the long run equilibrium in monopolistic competition, which is illustrated in Figure 7.9a by the average revenue curve of a monopolistically competitive producer being tangential to its average cost curve: each producer sells Q_{MC} units at a price P_{MC}.

monopolistic competition and perfect competition compared

Let's again make the unrealistic assumption that the cost and revenue curves under monopolistic competition are the same as they are under perfect competition. This allows us to compare the two structures and to assess the implications of monopolistic competition for welfare. Consider Figure 7.9b and Section 7.3:

1. Perhaps unsurprisingly, the price charged by a monopolistically competitive producer is higher, and the output it produces and sells lower, than by those in perfect competition: $P_{MC} > P_{PC}$ and $Q_{MC} < Q_{PC}$.

2. A producer in monopolistic competition isn't productively efficient because the competition it faces isn't as fierce as that in perfect competition, weakening its incentive to minimise its costs. Figure 7.9b shows the monopolistically competitive producer isn't operating at the minimum point on its average cost curve.

3. By charging a price higher than that under perfect competition, a monopolistically competitive producer is allocatively inefficient: the price it charges is higher than its marginal cost at the output level it produces and sells. This means consumers are over-charged and so are consuming an inefficiently low amount of the product.

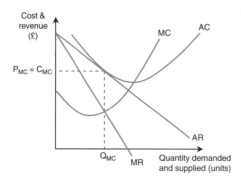

Figure 7.9a A producer in monopolistic competition

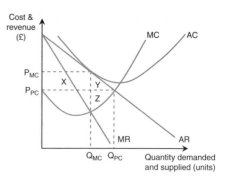

Figure 7.9b Monopolistic competition and perfect competition compared

④ Compared with the producer surplus under perfect competition, a monopolistically competitive producer forgoes surplus represented by area Z in Figure 7.9b because it's selling a lower level of output. However, by charging a higher price it also gains surplus, represented by area X. As area X is larger than area Z its welfare is clearly larger as a result. It's rational for a monopolistically competitive producer to sell less output but at a higher price than it would if it was perfectly competitive, but the producer's gain comes at the expense of consumers, who experience a reduction in consumer surplus of areas X and Y. Overall, monopolistic competition fails to attain Pareto efficiency because total market welfare isn't maximised: each producer causes a deadweight welfare loss to society of Y and Z.

The products that perfectly competitive producers sell are homogeneous, which means that the only way they can compete is through price competition. Producers in monopolistic competition do engage in price competition and in the long run they are unable to charge a price greater than that which brings normal profits; but as their products aren't homogeneous they also engage in brand competition. This involves each producer trying to differentiate its product from those of competitors in an attempt to establish a **niche market monopoly** within the wider market. If a producer does this successfully, it's able to use the resulting market power to charge a price that brings it abnormal profit in the short run, which it enjoys until other producers are able to respond and enter the market, thereby increasing competition and reducing profit levels to that of only normal profit.

7.6 oligopoly

The final market structure we need to look at is that of **oligopoly**. An oligopolistic market is characterised by a few large, dominant producers, and so lies towards the uncompetitive end of the spectrum of competition (see Section 7.1). Products sold under conditions of oligopoly are highly differentiated and significant barriers to entry exist that prevent the entry of most potential competitors (see Section 7.4). The primary characteristic of oligopoly, though, is that of producers' **interdependent decision-making**. In the other market structures each producer can be analysed in isolation, but this isn't the case in oligopoly because there are so few producers that their decisions are made only after careful consideration about how them competitors will respond.

If one producer in an oligopolistic market reduces its price, its competitors are likely to follow suit, sparking a **price war** in which each struggles to gain a market advantage. On the other hand, if a single oligopolistic producer. increases its price, its competitors are likely to keep their prices constant in an attempt to lure consumers away from it. In oligopoly, then, producers are reluctant to alter their prices and so there's a high degree of **price stickiness**. There can be significant changes in the costs producers face without them changing their prices.

To represent this characteristic of such markets, American economist Paul Sweezy developed the **kinked-demand curve** diagram shown in Figure 7.10a, which illustrates a single oligopolistic producer. As its name suggests, the heart of this diagram is an average revenue curve that's kinked, with a price-elastic upper section and a price-inelastic lower section. We saw in Section 6.2 that the marginal revenue curve is always twice as steep as a straight-line average revenue curve, and so the kink may cause a discontinuity – a vertical section – in the oligopoly marginal revenue curve.

The different elasticities of the two sections of the average revenue curve are crucial to explain oligopoly behaviour. As an oligopoly producer faces elastic demand above the prevailing price, it doesn't want to increase its price because doing so reduces its revenue (see Section 6.2); but because it faces inelastic demand below the prevailing price, it doesn't want to reduce its price either, for exactly the same reason. This shows that oligopoly prices are sticky. In fact, if we assume a producer's marginal cost curve cuts through the vertical section of its marginal revenue curve, then its marginal cost curve is able to shift up and down over the entire range of that vertical section without it leading to any change in the price it will charge. For example, in Figure 7.10a the marginal cost curve can shift from MC_1 to MC_2, MC_3 or to any point in between without causing the producer to change price from P_1. This is because in each case P_1 is the price that causes consumers to buy the level of output at which the producer's marginal cost is equal to its marginal revenue: the profit-maximisation condition (see Section 6.3).

oligopoly and perfect competition compared

Figure 7.10a effectively illustrates price stickiness but it fails to tell us anything else about oligopoly markets. For this we need to assume there's a single marginal cost curve and to incorporate its corresponding average cost curve into the diagram. This is done in Figure 7.10b. We can now compare oligopoly to the ideal structure of perfect competition (see Section 7.3)

1 As there are only a few producers in oligopoly, each of which sells products that are highly differentiated, they're able to exert degrees of market power. Perhaps unsurprisingly, then, the price charged by an oligopolistic producer exceeds that charged in perfect competition, $P_O > P_{PC}$, and the corresponding output produced and sold is less than that in perfect competition, $Q_O < Q_{PC}$.

2 As the oligopoly price exceeds that of perfect competition, an oligopolistic producer fails to attain allocative efficiency: its price exceeds its marginal cost at the level of output it produces and sells, which is shown in Figure 7.10b.

3 An oligopolistic producer also fails to attain productive efficiency, meaning it doesn't operate at the lowest point on its average cost curve, because the competition it faces isn't strong enough to induce it to minimise its costs.

4 Being characterised by allocative and productive inefficiency, an oligopoly market is necessarily Pareto inefficient. Each oligopolistic producer uses its market power to increase its welfare. From Figure 7.10b we see that producer surplus is increased compared with that in perfect competition by area X minus area Z. As with the other imperfectly competitive market structures, this comes at the expense of consumer welfare – consumer surplus contracts by area X – and of total social welfare, which is reduced by areas Y and Z, the deadweight welfare loss of oligopoly. Consumers can be made better off without reducing the welfare of producers simply by eliminating the deadweight welfare loss.

the Hotelling model

As there are only a few producers in an oligopoly market, each seeks to obtain a degree of market power by making its products appear different from those

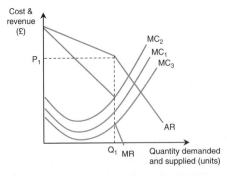

Figure 7.10a *A producer under oligopoly*

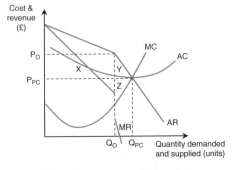

Figure 7.10b *Oligopoly and perfect competition compared*

of its competitors. However, a model developed by Harold Hotelling demonstrates the tendency over time for the degree of such differentiation to contract. In other words, it's likely that the characteristics of the products supplied to the market converge over time.

We can examine the Hotelling model by considering the behaviour of beer sellers at a music festival. Suppose thousands of hot and thirsty fans are gathered on the stretch of beach that surrounds the main stage of the festival, that they're uniformly spread out across the sand and that they have no preference about the beer they drink. Let's also suppose there are two beer sellers, A and B, who locate their stalls on the beach as illustrated in Figure 7.11.

As the fans are indifferent about the two different types of beer being sold, they simply make their purchases from the nearest stall. Seller A receives all the custom from the fans to the left of his position and half of that from those to his right, whilst seller B receives all the custom from his right and the remaining half of the custom from his left. Seller B is clearly in the better location and so it's natural for seller A to move his location to the right, increasing his custom as he does so. Seller B responds by moving his location further towards the left in order to increase his custom as well. The two converge, and settle, in the centre.

Now suppose a third beer seller, arriving late at the festival, sets up her stall. One of the sellers always has to be in between the others as a result. This is clearly a disadvantageous position to be in and so the central seller jumps over one of the others to seize the share of the market to that side. This puts the seller who has been jumped over at the disadvantage, and so s/he too jumps to one of the sides. In this situation there's continual movement amongst the sellers and fans find themselves chasing the sellers around the beach for the duration of the festival. In more economic terms, the market fails to settle at an equilibrium state. This situation is unique to a market with three sellers, though, and adding further sellers once again leads to steady states being attained.

Hotelling's model is applicable to oligopoly in two ways:

1 Depending on the way in which consumers are dispersed, it implies there may be convergence in the actual geographical location of producers. This is noticeable with petrol stations: you can drive for miles and miles without coming across one, and then two or three appear within the same stretch of road.

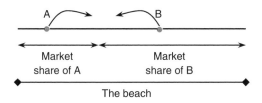

Figure 7.11 Hotelling's location model with two producers

❷ It has a deeper implication in terms of product differentiation. If the beach in Figure 7.11 is taken to represent the spectrum of consumer tastes, over time it's likely that the degree to which products differ declines as producers seek to capture the custom of the more moderate consumers. This implication is strengthened by the real-life observation that consumer tastes are not uniformly distributed, but tend to be clustered around the moderate options (consumer tastes as a whole tend not to be extreme). We see an example of this in action with political parties. Over time, major political parties tend to converge in terms of their policies as they try to capture the 'middle ground'.

7.7 summary

> The prices and quantities of products bought and sold are determined by the interaction of consumers and producers, and so of demand and supply, in markets.
> Market welfare is represented by consumer and producer surplus. Pareto efficiency refers to the maximisation of this total welfare.
> Perfect competition is the market structure against which real markets are compared because it leads to Pareto efficiency. The strong assumptions needed to be satisfied for perfect competition to exist are unrealistic, though.
> Pure monopoly is the market structure in which there's only a single producer. It lies at the opposite end of the spectrum of competition to perfect competition.
> Price discrimination is the monopoly strategy of selling identical products to different consumers for different prices. It increases producer surplus at the expense of consumer surplus.
> The market structures of monopolistic competition and oligopoly lie in between those of perfect competition and pure monopoly on the spectrum of competition.

8 when the interaction goes wrong

We saw in Section 7.3 that perfect competition is the ideal form of market structure because it leads to productive, allocative and Pareto efficiency. However, we also saw that it doesn't exist in the real world because the conditions a market needs to satisfy to be perfectly competitive are simply too demanding. Real-world markets are characterised by some degree of **market power**: most are monopolistically competitive, others are oligopolies and those remaining are monopolies. In all these cases producers employ their market power to maximise their own welfare at the expense of consumers, setting prices higher and selling quantities lower than in the ideal situation. Market power, then, is the first form of **market failure** – of the market not performing as well as we would ideally like it to.

Key term: market failure

Market failure refers to situations in which the free market – a market in which the government doesn't interfere – fails to achieve the desired outcomes of productive, allocative and Pareto efficiency. In other words, it refers to situations in which markets deviate from the model of perfect competition. There are six primary forms of market failure: market power, externalities, merit and demerit goods, asymmetric information and public goods.

The purpose of this chapter is to examine four types of market failure, investigating why they occur and what – if anything – can be done about them. In effect, we examine why the interaction between consumers and producers often fails to result in satisfactory outcomes when these economic actors are left to their own devices. As the definition of market failure shows, there are other forms of market failure as well: you should look these up (see Chapter 15).

Proponents of government intervention argue it's the responsibility of the government to introduce policies to correct market failure. Such intervention may sound uncontroversial and positive, but rarely is it simple in real life. Often when the government intervenes in a particular market it inadvertently introduces distortions into other markets, causing them to deviate even further from the perfectly competitive model. In reality, policy-makers usually have to content themselves with living and working in the world of the **second best**, aiming to establish the best sub-optimal outcome.

8.1 market power

We examined the three general types of market characterised by market power – pure monopoly, monopolistic competition, and oligopoly – and the welfare consequences of each in Chapter 7: we don't revisit that here. What we do examine here are the policies the government can implement to try to correct these effects, of which there are also three: deregulation of potentially competitive markets, competition policy, and regulation of natural monopolies.

deregulation of potentially competitive markets

Deregulation is the weakening of existing government controls over a market – such as patents and licences (see Section 7.4) – to allow it to become more competitive. This is usually accompanied by **privatisation** – the transfer of business ownership from the state to private individuals – but the two don't necessarily go together.

The deregulation process is best understood through an example: the 1986 deregulation of the UK bus market outside London. Before 1986 this market was heavily regulated by the state and was composed of four sectors:

❶ Large state-owned corporations that together provided over half of all local bus miles.

❷ Seven public transport companies that operated in the seven largest metropolitan areas, each of which was controlled by its local county council: these accounted for a quarter of local bus miles.

❸ Municipal bus companies that operated in forty-four of the larger cities and accounted for approximately 12 per cent of local bus miles.

❹ Small private companies operating commercial routes in rural areas or subsidised services in metropolitan areas. These accounted for the remaining local bus miles.

It was recognised in 1984 that the market was characterised by wide differences in costs and levels of efficiency between operators, and extensive cross-subsidisation (see Section 7.4). The British Transport Act (1985), which was officially implemented on 26 October 1986, privatised and deregulated the bus market in England and Wales (but not in London) by introducing three main changes.

(a) Government controls on the size of the bus market were greatly relaxed, allowing companies to operate virtually any service, at fares of their own choosing, by simply giving the local authorities forty-two days notice.

(b) State-owned companies were reorganised as separate entities. Seventy-two National Bus Company subsidiaries were sold off in England and Wales between 1986 and 1988; and the public transport committees and municipal companies were made independent from local authorities and could no longer rely on public subsidies (see Section 8.2). These operators had to become efficient to survive.

(c) The market was divided into two sectors: the **commercial sector** composed of services profitable for private operators to provide, and the **tender sector** composed of unprofitable but socially beneficial services requiring subsidisation. The second of these involved private operators bidding for services put up for tender by local authorities in return for financial support. This competition in the tendering process was intended to minimise public expenditure in the market.

Each of these three strands promoted competition in a market that had, until then, been highly uncompetitive. Similar accounts can be told of the privatisation and deregulation of the British telecommunications and power industries, and of other state-owned companies around the world.

competition policy

For markets already characterised by little regulation, competition can be promoted through **competition policy**, legislation specifically intended to promote competition, making anti-competitive behaviour illegal. The competition policy of the European Commission is based upon five general policies.

1 Encouraging competition.

2 Controlling government support for producers so competitors have a fair shot.

3 Restricting anti-competitive behaviour such as collusion and predatory pricing (see Section 7.4).

4 Controlling mergers and acquisitions to ensure the resulting, larger companies are in the interest of better performing markets.

5 Co-operating with other governments and international organisations to promote competition globally.

European policy is also firmly founded on the concept of **subsidiarity**, meaning that policies are to be enforced in individual member countries wherever possible, leaving the European Commission to intervene only in situations that extend beyond the political boundaries of a single country.

regulation of natural monopolies

Unfortunately, competition isn't possible in all markets. Those in which only a single producer can possibly survive are known as **natural monopolies**.

Key term: natural monopoly

A natural monopoly is a market that's able to sustain only a single producer, usually because the initial start up costs – also known as **capital costs** – are so high the producer needs to receive the entire revenue from the market just to cover them. Any competition at all within such a market reduces the revenue of each producer to beneath that required for it to make normal profit (see Section 6.3), leading ↘

entrepreneurs to close down production. In some natural monopolies the entire market revenue isn't even sufficient to enable a single producer to make normal profit and so government subsidisation is required if there's to be any supply. Railway networks are usually natural monopolies.

Deregulation and competition policy are not appropriate for natural monopolies because they would allow the unfettered abuse of market power. Instead, the government has to turn to two alternative strategies:

❶ **Nationalisation**, whereby production is taken into state-ownership so that the government can, in theory, operate it in the best interests of society.
❷ **Regulation**, whereby production is left in the hands of a privately owned monopoly which is then subjected to specified restrictions.

Past performances of nationalised enterprises have been highly criticised – former British Prime Minister Margaret Thatcher referred to them as 'lame-ducks' – and so emphasis has more recently been placed on regulation. There exists a whole literature on this policy – and in some degree courses whole units are devoted to it – but essentially it involves subjecting natural monopolies to strict pricing restrictions that approximate, as best as possible, the conditions necessary for them to earn only normal profits. To do this requires the government to estimate the efficient cost curves of these companies, which is problematic since the companies themselves are inevitably reluctant to reveal them honestly. Making price restrictions too severe leads to inefficiently large subsidies or to the closing-down of production, but making them too lenient results in the abuse of market power and the earning of abnormal profits. Regulation of natural monopolies, although clearly important and well intentioned, is a minefield. Examples of bodies in the UK designed to impose such regulation include the Water Services Regulation Authority (Ofwat), the Office of the Gas and Electricity Markets (Ofgem: the regulator of energy producers) and the Strategic Rail Authority (the rail regulator).

8.2 merit and demerit goods

The second form of market failure is that of **merit** and **demerit goods**. Merit goods are those that are more beneficial than consumers realise, and so are consumed less than they would be if consumers were fully informed. Demerit goods, on the other hand, are those that are more harmful than consumers realise, and so are consumed more than they would be if consumers were fully informed. A merit or demerit good, then, is a form of market failure because there's an inefficient level of consumption.

Consider a merit good: mouthwash may be a good example. If consumers realised just how beneficial using mouthwash is, they would be willing to buy the volumes of mouthwash at each price shown by the market demand

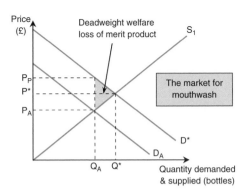

Figure 8.1a Merit good

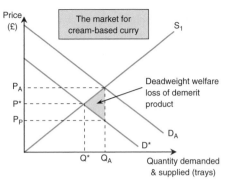

Figure 8.1b Demerit good

curve D* in Figure 8.1a. In equilibrium, then, Q* bottles would be bought and sold. However, because they fail to realise the extent of these benefits they're actually willing to buy only the volumes shown by the market demand curve D_A. This means that the actual equilibrium quantity bought and sold in the market is Q_A bottles. As a result of the informational failure there's under-consumption of mouthwash – the difference between Q* and Q_A bottles. Now consider the Q_Ath bottle. Consumers would be willing and able to pay P_P for this single bottle if they were fully informed of its benefits (from demand curve D*) and producers would be willing and able to produce and sell it for P_A (from the supply curve). If that bottle was produced and consumed society would be better off to the extent of P_P-P_A. But it isn't and so this surplus is lost (see Section 7.2). The same principle applies for each bottle up to the Q*th bottle, at which the market supply curve intersects the market demand curve were consumers fully informed. The shaded area, then, is the deadweight welfare loss to society of the information failure in the market for mouthwash. The under-consumption of mouthwash, which leads to dental problems, represents an inefficient allocation of resources.

Figure 8.1b illustrates the case of a demerit good, such as cream-based (and so highly fattening, albeit very tasty) curry. Consumers may be unaware of just how harmful such curries, if eaten regularly, can be to their health: cholesterol and obesity are two possible effects. The volumes of such curries consumers are actually willing to buy at each price are shown by the market demand curve D_A, but if consumers were fully informed about the health effects of these curries they would be willing to buy only those shown by the market demand curve D*. Q_A trays of these curries are actually bought and sold in the market, which is over-consumption from a social welfare perspective: the social welfare maximising quantity is only Q* trays (where D* = S_1). In line with the analysis of Figure 8.1a, then, the shaded area represents the deadweight welfare loss to society caused by the demerit good.

There are three possible policies the government can adopt to correct market failures such as these:

1. **Information provision.** The government can address the information failure directly by informing consumers of the true benefits and dangers of merit and demerit goods through the media or education. For example, the health benefits of drinking milk have in the past been emphasised in television adverts in the UK, school pupils are continually educated about the need to use contraception, and the potentially negative health effects of smoking cigarettes are clearly labelled on cigarette packets.

2. **Taxation and subsidisation.** The government can change the prices of these products in order to manipulate the quantity bought and sold, reducing the prices of merit goods through subsidisation and increasing those of demerit goods through taxation. Again, in the past milk has been heavily subsidised by the UK government and has been provided free of charge to children in primary education. Cigarettes, on the other hand, continue to be heavily taxed.

3. **Legislation.** The government can introduce laws forcing actors to behave efficiently. It can make the consumption of demerit goods illegal, as it has done in the case of certain drugs. Similarly, it can enforce the consumption of merit goods – for example, the inclusion of fluoride in toothpaste.

taxation and subsidisation: demand and supply analysis

There are two types of taxation: **direct taxes**, which are levied directly on consumers, and **indirect taxes**, which are first levied on producers and are then (to some degree) passed on to consumers in the form of higher prices. The first of these, such as income tax, simply reduces the disposable income of consumers, and so reduces their ability to pay for products and shifts the market demand curves for these products inwards to the left (see Section 5.5). The analysis of indirect taxation is slightly more complicated and is illustrated in Figure 8.2a.

Consider Figure 8.2a, which shows the effect of an indirect tax being levied on a demerit good: remember that the intention is to reduce the consumption

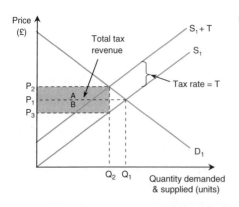

Figure 8.2a Indirect taxation

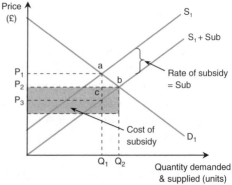

Figure 8.2b Subsidisation

of the demerit good. As an indirect tax is levied on producers, it causes the market supply curve (see Section 6.4) to shift from S_1 to S_1+T, where T is the amount producers have to pay the government for each unit of the product it sells: this is the **tax rate**. The tax causes the price to rise from P_1 to P_2 and so the quantity produced and sold to fall from Q_1 to Q_2.

As is demonstrated in the diagram, the tax rate is not necessarily the same as the increase in the price of the product: it isn't $P_2 - P_1$. This is because the producer doesn't necessarily pass on the entirety of the tax to consumers. The tax rate is represented by the vertical distance between the original and resulting supply curves: $P_2 - P_3$. The total tax revenue received by the government is simply this rate multiplied by the number of units produced and sold – $T \times Q_2$ – which is represented by the shaded area. As the entirety of the tax rate hasn't been passed onto consumers in this case, part of the tax revenue is paid by consumers and part by producers. Consumers pay the amount given by the increase in market price multiplied by the number of units they buy – $Q_2 \times (P_2 - P_1)$ or area A. Producers pay the amount given by the effective reduction in producer price multiplied by the number of units they produce and sell – $Q_2 \times (P_1 - P_3)$ or area B. It's the own-price elasticity of demand (see Section 5.6) that determines the proportion of the tax borne by each group of actors. For perfectly price-inelastic products, producers pass the entire tax rate on to consumers because they know they don't lose any custom from doing so: quantity demanded is completely insensitive to changes in price. For perfectly price-elastic products, on the other hand, producers pay the entire tax rate themselves because they know any increase in price reduces the quantity demanded to zero units.

The own-price elasticity of demand also determines the total tax revenue received by the government from an indirect tax. The government is freer to levy a significant indirect tax on producers of a price-inelastic product because the quantity demanded of it is relatively unaffected. A significant tax rate, coupled with an insignificant reduction in the quantity bought, means the government enjoys significant tax revenue. This is the reason why cigarette and alcohol tax revenues compose such an important part of the public budget.

In real life, demerit goods tend to be addictive and so price-inelastic: consider alcohol, cigarettes, drugs and fatty foods, for instance. It may not be the case, then, that consumption of these products is driven by imperfect information. Consumers are probably well aware of their harmful effects but continue to consume them out of habit. It is not clear how successful indirect taxes are in reducing such consumption, but it is possible that a higher price deters new consumers from developing the habit in the first place, thereby representing a longer-term solution.

Now consider Figure 8.2b, which illustrates the effects of the government introducing a **subsidy** for a merit good: this time remember that the intention is to increase the consumption of the merit good. The effects of a subsidy are effectively the reverse of those of an indirect tax. A subsidy is a transfer of money from the government to producers for each unit of a product they make and sell. The effect is to increase supply: at every market price producers are now willing and able to supply more, and so the market supply curve shifts outwards from S_1 to $S_1 +$ Sub, causing the market price to fall from P_1 to P_2 and the quantity produced and sold in the market to rise from Q_1 to Q_2.

The rate of the subsidy – the amount the government pays to producers for each unit produced and sold – is given by the vertical distance between the original and resulting supply curves $P_1 - P_3$, which is denoted by Sub. The total amount the government is required to pay to affect the market quantity in this way is given by the resulting quantity sold multiplied by the subsidy rate, $Q_2 \times (P_1 - P_3)$, which is the shaded area. The welfare effects (see Section 7.2) of the subsidy are to increase consumer surplus by the area bordered by P_1-a-b-P_2 and producer surplus by that bordered by P_2-b-c-P_3. However, this needs to be compared with government expenditure, and in this case government expenditure exceeds generated welfare by the area bordered by a-b-c.

In fact, unless the demand curve is perfectly price-inelastic and the supply curve is perfectly price-elastic, government expenditure always exceeds additional welfare. The government must finance its expenditure by raising revenue from taxation in other markets, and so the implication is that welfare lost in the markets from which revenue is raised may exceed the additional welfare generated in the subsidised market. This is the problem of the second best. Governments, in trying to correct inefficiencies in one market, introduce additional inefficiencies to other markets and so have to choose the best sub-optimal overall result. The ideal is to finance subsidisation of merit goods by taxation of demerit goods, but even then there are knock-on effects in other markets. An indirect tax, by reducing the purchasing power of a consumers' income, is likely to cause income and substitution effects (see Section 5.5) that impact on other markets.

command and control policies: demand and supply analysis

Alternatively, the government can move a market towards greater efficiency through **command and control policies**: regulations that have to be obeyed by law. Policies such as these take many forms:

1. **Stipulated standards**: minimum standards that products must meet. For example, the often repeated proposal that certain drugs should be legalised so that the government can enforce standards about what substances such drugs comprise.

2. **Quotas**: maximum quantities that can be produced. For example, regulations determining the amount of fish trawlers are allowed to catch, which are designed to protect fish-stocks. Prohibition is effectively a quota of zero.

3. **Price controls**: maximum or minimum prices that can be charged. For example, regulations in local taxi markets determining the fares operators are allowed to charge, thereby protecting consumer welfare.

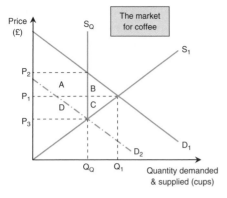

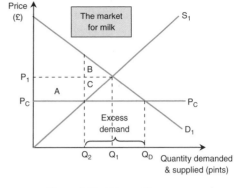

Figure 8.3a Production quota   Figure 8.3b Price ceiling

Consider Figure 8.3a, which illustrates the effects of a production quota in a market for a demerit good such as coffee. The free market establishes an equilibrium price of P_1 at which Q_1 cups are bought and sold. Let's assume that the government has estimated the efficient quantity to be Q_Q cups, and so judges Q_1 cups to be an inefficiently high quantity. The government seeks to eliminate this inefficiency by imposing a quota on producers, stipulating that only Q_Q cups can be produced and sold. This appears to be a perfect solution, but in fact it has serious welfare effects. Since only Q_Q cups of coffee are now supplied to the market (the supply curve is vertical at Q_Q), consumers compete with one another to acquire the available cups, forcing the price of coffee upwards to P_2 for every cup. Producers view this with delight as their surplus increases by area A minus area C – a welfare increase that's at the expense of consumers, who lose surplus equal to areas A and B. The problem with the quota solution, then, is that it causes an inefficient redistribution of welfare from consumers to producers. If the government corrects the information failure directly instead, the market demand curve would shift from D_1 to D_2, establishing the efficient quantity of coffee produced and sold but in a way that consumer welfare increases by area D minus area B and producer welfare falls by areas D and C. Employing a quota as a solution leads to the welfare effects being reversed, at least to some degree.

Now consider Figure 8.3b, which illustrates a **price ceiling** – a legally stipulated maximum price – for a merit good such as milk. The law of demand says that as the price of a product falls, more of it is consumed. Surely, then, enforcing a maximum price of milk, lower than that established by the free market, increases the quantity bought and sold? Figure 8.3b demonstrates that this is not the case. The free market price of milk is P_1, at which Q_1 pints are bought and sold: this is a level of consumption the government deems is too low for health reasons. To increase consumption to the efficient level of Q_D pints, the government introduces a price ceiling at price P_C. The quantity demanded is successfully increased to Q_D pints but the quantity supplied is restricted to only Q_2 pints: suppliers are unwilling to supply more than this at the lower price. The price ceiling causes excess demand to emerge, possibly manifesting itself as queues of people inside supermarkets demanding milk. It also causes the welfare of producers to fall by areas A and C, although consumer surplus is increased by area A minus area B.

The government can also set limits on how low prices can be. These are known as **price floors**. A price floor is simply the opposite of a price ceiling. The government sets a price, let us call it P_F, beneath which the market price cannot fall, perhaps because it wants to ensure producer welfare is protected. A price floor is only effective if it's set at a level higher than the market equilibrium price. If it's lower than that in equilibrium, it simply doesn't have any effect and the market clears as usual. The problem is that at a price higher than that in equilibrium, producers produce and sell more on the market than consumers buy, creating **excess supply** – stocks of final products that cannot be sold. The only way the government can maintain the price floor is by buying up these surplus stocks. If it doesn't do so the market mechanism causes the price to fall. The best example of a price floor is the **Common Agricultural Policy** of the European Union, which stipulates minimum prices for agricultural produce. Farmers' incomes are secured but there are mountains of vegetables and cheese, and lakes of milk and wine, that are wasted – and at a time when multitudes are starving in poor countries.

BOX 8.1: **Public economics**

Phil Jones, University of Bath

Public economics considers the way governments influence the allocation of resources and the distribution of income. There are three perspectives:

1 Normative public economics. Economic theory can be applied to predict how individuals respond to taxes, subsidies, regulations and government expenditures. The analysis focuses on the impact that policy instruments exert on individuals' budget constraints and on how individuals then respond to these new constraints. Economic theory is also applied to comment on the way policy instruments affect the welfare of the community. The gains of those who gain are compared with the losses of those who lose. Cost benefit analysis, for example, compares the 'willingness to pay' of those who benefit from an expenditure project with the costs to those who lose. Taxes, subsidies, regulations and expenditures are efficient if they maximise the net benefit of the community, but efficiency is usually only one criterion. When other criteria (e.g. equity) are relevant, it may be necessary to trade off efficiency for equity in order to maximise social welfare.

2 Positive public economics. While economic theory can be applied to prescribe what governments should do, it can also be applied to predict what governments will do. Just as microeconomic theory can be applied to predict the behaviour of consumers, producers and employees (with reference to their objectives and budget constraints), it can also be applied to predict the behaviour of voters,

politicians and bureaucrats (with reference to a different set of objectives and constraints). If these actors pursue their own interests, governments are unlikely to be as benign as some economists believe when they make policy prescriptions. Normative public economics often commends intervention to correct market failure, but public choice economists are acutely aware of failings in collective decision-making processes. Positive public economics also considers the costs that arise if there's government failure.

❸ Behavioural public economics. Economists are sensitive to growing evidence that behaviour differs systematically from that predicted by neoclassical models. Economists are reassessing how individuals respond to taxes, subsidies, regulations and government expenditures. They are also considering evidence that behaviour is sometimes explained with reference to intrinsic motivation: individuals are often willing to trade off preferred outcomes for preferred action. Behavioural public economics assesses the role of the government when individuals are unable to assess outcomes 'rationally' and when individuals state preference for policies they deem intrinsically 'fair' or 'just'.

A number of texts illustrate these approaches, for example:

> R. A. Musgrave, *Public Finance* (*Cambridge, MA: Harvard University Press, 1959*).
> J. Hindricks and G. D. Myles, *Intermediate Public Economics* (Cambridge, MA: MIT Press, 2006).
> J. Cullis and P. Jones, *Public Finance and Public Choice* (Oxford: Oxford University Press, 2009).

8.3 externalities

Key term: externality

An externality is a cost or benefit imposed on one person as a result of an economic decision made by somebody else in which the effect on the first person is not considered. The decision-makers involved only take their own private costs and benefits into account, and so fail to think about the effects on others. It can also be interpreted as a product for which a market doesn't exist and so whose optimal amount cannot be achieved.

Externalities are the third, and arguably the most interesting, form of market failure that we look at here. They take one of two forms: an **external cost**, in which someone inadvertently suffers because of a decision made by someone else, or an **external benefit**, in which someone's welfare inadvertently increases because of a decision made by someone else.

Let's first consider an external cost. Suppose that an owner of a classic sports car is deciding how many miles to drive one Sunday afternoon. The costs he has to pay to drive include those of petrol, the wear and tear caused to his vehicle and the time taken. These are his **private costs**. We can assume that the marginal costs (see Section 6.1) of the first two are constant for each mile driven: the additional cost of driving the twentieth mile is the same as that of driving the fiftieth in terms of petrol use and wear and tear. The marginal cost of the time spent driving, on the other hand, should be considered to be gradually increasing as the distance travelled increases: the driver probably places an increasing value on time that can be spent doing other things as he drives further. If these costs are combined the driver's **marginal private cost** (MPC) curve gradually increases as he drives more miles. However, by driving his car the driver inadvertently emits carbon dioxide and other pollutants into the atmosphere, causes wear and tear to the road surfaces, and adds to the level of traffic and congestion on the roads. These are the **external costs** he causes, which probably become increasingly severe the more miles he drives. Adding the external costs to the private costs gives us the social cost of his driving, which includes all costs to society. The **marginal social cost** (MSC) curve, then, is derived by adding the marginal external cost curve to the marginal private cost curve.

We now need to consider the benefits involved in the driver's decision about how many miles to drive. For simplicity, let's assume he enjoys the entire **social benefit** – the total benefit to the whole of society – from driving his car (this means that no one else benefits from his driving). Let's also assume the **marginal social benefit** – the additional benefit that he enjoys from every additional mile driven – falls as the number of miles he drives increases. We assume this because his enjoyment is probably characterised by **diminishing marginal utility**: each additional mile driven provides him with an ever falling amount of additional utility (see Section 5.1). The **marginal benefit curve** (MPB = MSB), then, is downward-sloping.

Figure 8.4 combines this into a negative externality diagram. The driver doesn't consider the external cost he imposes on others and so chooses to drive the distance that equates his marginal private cost with his marginal private benefit: Q_p. The reason for this is precisely the same as that directing a producer to equate its marginal cost with its marginal revenue: it maximises the benefit enjoyed (see Section 6.3). However, because of the external costs generated, this distance is inefficiently long. The socially optimal distance, considering all the costs and benefits involved, is Q^* miles. This is the distance at which total social benefit is maximised. Every mile greater than Q^* is associated with a marginal social cost that exceeds the marginal social benefit. This means the shaded area in Figure 8.4 represents a welfare loss to society. This is the **negative externality**.

Let's now analyse an external benefit. Consider an isolated rural village in which there's considerable unemployment, and suppose a food manufacturer decides to locate a new production plant in the locality that will only employ people from the village. Let's assume the private costs to the company, and to society as a whole, are simply those from production, meaning we're ignoring any potential pollution. The marginal private and social cost

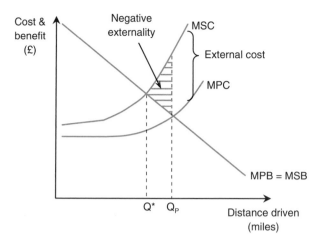

Figure 8.4 *External cost*

(MPC = MSC) curve takes on the form of a typical marginal cost curve (see Section 6.1). The private benefit to the company is that of revenue, and so the marginal private benefit (MPB) curve is simply the company's marginal revenue curve (see Section 6.2). However, the company's production brings considerable benefits to society over and above those of revenue: it reduces unemployment in the local village, thereby helping to ameliorate the poverty and social distress experienced there. The marginal social benefit (MSB) curve, then, positively deviates from the marginal private benefit curve, the difference being these external benefits.

These three curves are combined in Figure 8.5. It's unclear whether the external benefits increase at an increasing or diminishing rate as production expands – does the village enjoy a greater or smaller additional benefit when

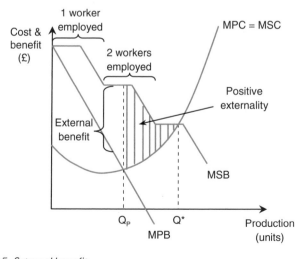

Figure 8.5 *External benefit*

the final unemployed person receives a job compared with the situation when the first was hired? Let's assume the marginal social benefit curve takes on a downward-sloping 'stepped' curve, with each additional step representing the additional social benefit from the hiring of an additional person.

As the company seeks to maximise its profit it produces an output of Q_p: this is the output level at which its marginal private cost is equal to its marginal revenue (see Section 6.3 for the profit-maximisation condition). From a social point of view, though, this is underproduction because this quantity fails to consider the additional social benefits of production. Q^* is the socially optimal level of output, being the output level at which marginal social cost is equal to marginal social benefit, and so an additional worker should be employed. For every unit of output between Q_p and Q^* the marginal social benefit is greater than the marginal social cost. Each of these units is associated with additional benefit to society that's lost because of the private decision-making of the company. The shaded area it forms represents the total social welfare lost as a result. This is the value of the **positive externality**.

externalities as missing markets

As well as modelling externalities as situations in which private and social costs (or benefits) diverge, we can also model them as situations in which there are missing markets. In Section 7.3 we saw how a perfectly competitive market leads to Pareto efficiency. There's no reason why this shouldn't be the same in a market for an externality, if it existed. The problem is that markets don't exist for externalities such as the disturbance caused by a neighbour playing his music loudly in the early hours or the enjoyment caused by another neighbour making his front garden look nice. An absent market means an absent price, which leads to an inefficient level of production or consumption.

Consider two students enjoying the sun on the balcony of their university bar. Student A is talking loudly to a friend whilst Student B is trying to enjoy a book. They both have money and a desire to enjoy their break. The welfare of each is increased by being given more money, with which additional drinks can be purchased, but the welfare of Student A can be increased by being able to talk more whilst that of Student B can be increased by reducing the amount the other talks. These preferences are represented in Figure 8.6 as sets of well-behaved indifference curves (see Section 5.1). The indifference curves of Student A (dashed curves) are rotated by 180 degrees and then laid on top of those of Student B (solid curves): this creates an **Edgeworth box**, named after its creator Francis Ysidro Edgeworth.

Figure 8.6 looks more complicated than it is. The horizontal axis represents the total amount of money possessed by the two students, and the vertical axis represents the total amount of time that can either be consumed by Student A talking or by Student B enjoying peace and quiet (a given moment in time cannot be enjoyed both by Student A talking and Student B enjoying peace and quiet – only one or the other can occur). Now suppose the initial endowment

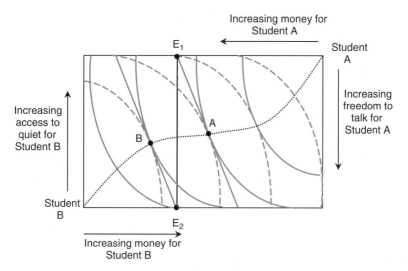

Figure 8.6 Edgeworth box analysis of missing markets

of money and time is represented by E_1. In other words, Student B has control of the time and so is initially able to enjoy it all as peace and quiet. If this were the case, and a market existed, Student A will buy time from Student B, moving the market to point A. This is an equilibrium point because the indifference curves of the two students are tangential, meaning their marginal rates of substitution between time and money are equal (see Section 5.1). With this condition holding, there's no way of reallocating time and money to increase the utility of both students, and so they won't agree to any further trade. For example, Student A would benefit from more time to talk, but this would move Student B onto an indifference curve that gives him a lower utility, and so he would refuse the trade.

Alternatively, suppose that E_2 actually represents the initial endowment, meaning the control of the time available lies in the hands of Student A. If this were the case, the two will trade until point B is established: Student B will buy time from Student A. Again, point B is an equilibrium point because the two indifference curves are tangential at that point and so there's no further mutually beneficial trade.

The dotted line connecting each student's null bundle represents all the points at which the indifference curves of the students are tangential. These are all the points of Pareto efficiency (see Section 1.1) in the market at which equilibrium could be attained. Which one of these points is actually established depends on the initial endowment. The sloped lines connecting the endowments to the final equilibrium points represent the relative values (prices) of time and money that govern the trading that occurs.

This shows the importance of the existence of both markets and clear property rights. If the property rights (initial endowments) regarding the time on the balcony are clear, and if there's a market in which the external costs of noise can be traded, the two students will establish a Pareto efficient outcome through bargaining. However, if either the property rights aren't clearly laid out, or if there's no such market in which to trade, Pareto efficiency cannot be attained and the externality will persist. In this case the talking continues for an inefficiently long time from each student's point of view because Student A fails to consider how Student B is being affected, and Student B is unable to bargain effectively with Student A. In reality, it's likely that neither of these conditions will in fact hold. Consider, for example, road congestion. There's generally no ownership of road space, nor is there a market in which it can be traded – although both of these could feasibly be created – and so individual drivers such as the person represented by Figure 8.4 travel too many miles from a social perspective.

Climate change is perhaps the biggest externality in the economy. By emitting greenhouse gases into the atmosphere we're building up costs that future generations have to pay: we're imposing an external cost on future generations that's becoming increasingly large. We do this because we consider only our own private costs and benefits, and not those of future generations. Another possible reason for the build-up of greenhouse gases is that there's no market for such emissions that future generations can engage in to ensure the optimal amount is emitted today. Issues such as these are examined in environmental economics (see Box 8.2).

BOX 8.2: **Environmental Economics**

Anil Markandya, University of Bath

Environmental economics is the study of the linkages between the natural environment and the economy. Much of the core of economic theory was developed without paying attention to the fact that our economic system is underpinned by complex ecosystems and if we abuse those systems we are likely to have an underperforming economy. It has been in the last half century or so that this imbalance has started to be restored, with the early work of a number of outstanding economists, including Harold Hotelling and Kenneth Boulding in the USA and, more recently, of Kenneth Arrow, David Pearce, Karl-Göran Mäler and a number of others in Europe.

The key aspects of environmental economics can be stated quite simply. The first is that when environmental goods and services (meaning things such as air, water and other natural resources) are undervalued, they are overused and the resulting allocations of resources are sub-optimal. This is tied to the theory of externalities (which focuses on the fact that markets do not exist for all goods and services that are of value), and has been elaborated in environmental economics as the basis of a number of policy interventions to correct for these missing markets. This takes us to the second area of environmental economics, which looks at a range of interventions, including institutional reforms, market-based instruments, command and control policies, better information and others as means for

---

including environmental factors in day-to-day decision-making in the economic sphere.

The subject has had a major increase in interest in the context of climate change, which has been described by Lord Stern as the 'world's biggest externality'. For hundreds of years we have emitted greenhouse gases such as carbon dioxide without taking account of the impact they were having on our climate and the consequences of those impacts. Now we are faced with a crisis of climate change and actions have to be implemented urgently. The difficulty is that we are also dealing with a global public good: no one country's emissions have a big enough impact on its environment for it to take major action. The issue of how to arrive at international agreements in this context brings together environmental economics and game theory and is an active area of research.

More generally, environmental economics is changing the way we think of development and growth. Early growth theorists thought of future living standards as being capable of improvement without limit. With the onset of environmental consideration we have come to recognise that there may be limits to this: at least in terms of the areas where we can increase our consumption of goods and services. We have also to recognise that a sustainable world will look very different from one that simply replicates current practices but on a larger scale. The ways in which constraints on consumption in some areas can combine with incentives to develop new and more effective ways of using resources is a growing area of research under the broad umbrella of environmental economics.

Excellent introductory texts on environmental economics include:

> A. Markandya and J. Richardson (eds.), *Readings in Environmental Economics* (London: Earthscan, 1992).
> A. Markandya, P. Harou, V. Cistulli and L. Bellu, *Environmental Economics for Sustainable Growth* (Cheltenham: Edward Elgar, 2002).
> N. Hanley, J. F. Shogren and B. White, *Environmental Economics in Theory and Practice* (Basingstoke: Palgrave Macmillan, 1997).

Key term: game theory

Game theory is a fascinating field of microeconomics in which the strategic interaction between actors is examined. It usually forms part of the microeconomics units in the second and third years of a degree (see Chapter 15 for excellent introductory texts).

8.4 summary

> Market failure refers to situations in which the free market fails to achieve Pareto efficiency.
> Market power refers to the market failure caused by there being too little competition in a market.
> A merit good is a product that consumers fail to realise the full benefits of and that is under-consumed from an efficiency standpoint.

> A demerit good is a product that consumers fail to realise the full harm of and that is over-consumed from an efficiency standpoint.

> An externality is a cost or benefit imposed on one individual because of a decision made by somebody who did not consider how his/her decision would affect the first individual. It can be modelled through private and social costs and benefits or through missing markets.

> Other failures include those caused by asymmetric information and public goods.

introducing larger-scale analysis: the macroeconomic world

3

the next four chapters

In Chapters 5–8 we analysed the behaviour of individual actors and what results when they interact with one another in individual markets: what I refer to as smaller-scale analysis. We now put them all together to examine the functioning of the economy as a whole. We approach economics in a way that makes individual actors and markets blend into the bigger picture. This is larger-scale analysis. This is **macroeconomics**.

Key term: macroeconomics

Macroeconomics is the study of the economy as a whole: the bigger picture. The purpose of studying macroeconomics is for us to understand what determines how wealthy an economy is, and how that wealth can be increased; what causes the two main economic problems of unemployment and inflation, and how they can be reduced; and how economies interact with one another in the global marketplace and the benefits they derive from doing so.

Introducing the bigger things is the purpose of the following four chapters. Working through them will enable you to read and understand the economic issues featured in any financial newspaper. It will also enable you to engage in current economic debates. For example, how wise is it for the government to be cutting its expenditure when the economy has just come out of recession? In what follows, then, we:

1. Introduce the economy and examine what determines its size and how this can be measured (Chapter 9).
2. Develop and use the tools of demand and supply analysis, but at the level of the whole economy rather than at that of a market (Chapter 10).
3. Investigate the causes and consequences of unemployment and inflation, and what the government can do to reduce them, as well as the role of money (Chapter 11).
4. Place the economy into its international setting, assessing why one economy trades with another, what it trades and whether or not doing so is beneficial (Chapter 12).

As with the previous chapters about microeconomics, the intention is not for these four chapters to take the place of a textbook. It's still important for you to use the books recommended by your macroeconomics lecturers because your exams will be based largely on them. The purpose of the following four chapters is simply to introduce you to macroeconomics in an accessible way, to introduce all the key terms and techniques that you will come across as you study it, and to explain why it's so important.

its importance

There are many important economic issues that microeconomics doesn't help us understand, issues of an economy-wide nature. For example, what determines how wealthy a country is, and does an expansion in this wealth represent an improvement in the standard of living of its population? Why do economies seem to experience cycles, going from situations in which they're growing rapidly and have low unemployment to those in which they're perhaps even shrinking and have masses of people claiming unemployment benefits? Why do economists talk about inflation so much, and what are the effects of countries trading with one another: is this something to be encouraged or constrained? These issues are just as important for the quality of peoples' lives as those examined in microeconomics. In fact, unemployment perhaps damages more lives, and more seriously, in developed countries than any of the issues examined in the previous four chapters. However, they require a different approach if they are to be understood – one that considers the economy as a whole rather than the behaviour and interaction of economic actors – and different types of policies are needed to address them. This is what macroeconomics is all about and why it's just as important and exciting as microeconomics.

9 the size of the economy

As we've already seen, the purpose of studying macroeconomics is for us to understand how the economy as a whole functions and how the government can intervene to make it function better. The first step towards this goal is for us to examine what we actually mean by 'the economy' and what factors determine its size. This is the focus of this chapter.

9.1 a two-economy circular flow

Let's start by examining the model known as the **circular flow of income and expenditure**, a model of how money circulates around the economy. This will help us see what the economy is and what factors are active within in. William Phillips – of **Phillips curve** fame (see Section 11.4) – developed a physical example of this model, in which money is represented by water that flows through a series of tubes and reservoirs representing the workings of the economy. Here we make do with a diagram.

Figure 9.1 is a relatively sophisticated version of the circular flow, including two separate economies interacting with one another in the global marketplace. Consider first the left-hand panel of the diagram, which represents economy A. The model simplifies reality to include only three key microeconomic actors (households, producers and the government) and three key markets (product markets, financial markets and factor markets). As mentioned throughout this book, the purpose of an economic model such as this is to make the analysis as simple as possible whilst including all the elements from reality important for addressing the question at hand: to get the balance between parsimony and realism right (see Section 4.4). We use the circular flow to help us understand what an economy is and how its components interact with one another. You should judge whether or not this particular model gets the balance right.

Before we analyse the model, we can clearly see the difference between microeconomics and macroeconomics from this diagram. Microeconomics focuses on each of the three key actors and markets separately, whereas macroeconomics steps back and considers them all as a whole. Although in reality markets aren't necessarily physical places, in the circular flow they take the form of places that are independent of actors so the flows of money – which are represented by arrows – are more easily seen. In the product markets, house-

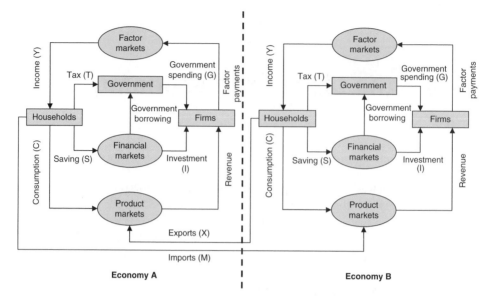

Figure 9.1 *A two-economy circular flow of income and expenditure*

holds buy products from producers, whilst in the factor markets producers buy the factors of production (see Section 1.1) from households.

Let's start with the households in economy A. They're referred to as households rather than consumers because in this model they not only consume products, they also own and supply the four factors of production. By supplying the factors of production to producers through the factor markets they earn income (Y), shown by the arrow going towards them. They then allocate this income to four activities: consumption of domestically produced products (C), consumption of products produced in economy B (M), saving in the financial markets (S), and tax paid to the government (T). There's nothing else they can do with their income and so Equation 9.1 must be satisfied.

$$Y = C + M + S + T \qquad\qquad \text{(Equation 9.1)}$$

The proportions of extra income allocated to each of these activities are known as the **marginal propensities**.

Key term: marginal propensity

Marginal propensity refers to the proportion of extra income allocated to a particular use. The **marginal propensity to consume** (mpc) refers to the proportion of extra income spent on the consumption of domestic products; the **marginal propensity to** ↘

import (mpm) is the proportion of extra income spent on buying products from other economies; the **marginal propensity to save** (mps) is the proportion of extra income saved; and the **marginal tax rate** (mtr) – effectively the marginal propensity to pay tax – is the proportion of extra income given to the government in tax. They're calculated using the general formula in Equation 9.2, in which Δ means 'change in', C denotes the amount spent on domestic consumption and Y stands for income. The marginal propensities necessarily sum to one as all extra income must go towards one of these four things.

$$\text{Marginal propensity} = \frac{\Delta \text{ Use}}{\Delta \text{ Income}}, \text{ for example,mpc} = \frac{\Delta C}{\Delta Y} \qquad (\text{Equation 9.2})$$

The proportions of total income allocated to each of these activities are known as the **average propensities**.

Key term: average propensity

Average propensity refers to the proportion of total income assigned to a particular use. The proportion of total income spent on domestic products is known as the **average propensity to consume** (apc); the proportion of total income saved is the **average propensity to save** (aps); the proportion of total income spent on products from other economies is the **average propensity to import** (apm); and the proportion of total income given to the government in tax is the **average tax rate** (atr). An average propensity is calculated using the general formula in Equation 9.3, in which total amount saved is denoted by S and total income by Y. They again necessarily sum to one.

$$\text{Average propensity} = \frac{\text{Use}}{\text{Income}}, \text{ for example, aps} = \frac{S}{Y} \qquad (\text{Equation 9.3})$$

In the circular flow, the money households spend on domestic consumption flows through the product markets to producers in the form of revenue, which is then spent in three ways. Producers pay some of it to owners and entrepreneurs as profit, some of it to the owners of the other factors of production as their **factor payments** – labour is paid wages and the owners of capital and land are paid rent – and the rest to suppliers of **intermediate products** for their inputs, who then spend their revenue in the same three ways. Eventually, all revenue is returned through the factor markets back to the households because they ultimately own all factors of production.

This clearly isn't the whole story, though, because, as we've already mentioned, some of the income households receive is saved in financial markets (S), some is paid to the government in tax (T), and some is spent on imports (M) and so flows out of the domestic economy and into economy B. These represent **leakages** from the circular flow, and they reduce the amount of money flowing round the economy. However, for each of these leakages there's an associated **injection** into the circular flow. Financial markets invest money in producers (I), the government spends money through the public sector (G), and economy B purchases exports from economy A (X). These injections increase the amount of money flowing round the economy.

The amount of money circulating round the circular flow represents the size of the economy. In other words, it represents how wealthy the economy is. In this very simple model, then, whether economy A experiences **economic growth** – meaning an increase in its size and wealth – depends entirely upon the balance of its leakages and injections. The economy shrinks if the amount leaking out of it exceeds the amount being injected into it, and grows if its leakages are less than its injections. Returning to Phillips's physical representation of this model, if more water is siphoned out of the system than is directed into it, the total volume of water in the system inevitably falls and vice versa.

The focus of our description so far has been on economy A. Exactly the same can be said of economy B as well. The two economies are connected through their **international trade** with one another (see Chapter 12). Consumers in economy A buy products produced in economy B (imports for economy A) whilst those in economy B buy products produced in economy A (exports for economy A). This interaction has important implications for economic policy in each economy.

fiscal policy, GDP and international trade

Despite its simplicity, the circular flow in Figure 9.1 is surprisingly useful for our analysis. Let's use it to examine **fiscal policy**.

Key term: fiscal policy

Fiscal policy is the use of taxation and spending by the government to influence the size of the economy. **Expansionary fiscal policy** refers to the government either increasing its spending or reducing taxation so the amount of money flowing round the circular flow is increased, and **contractionary fiscal policy** refers to it reducing its spending or increasing taxation, with the result that the amount of money in the circular flow is reduced.

Let's assume the marginal propensities take the values shown in Table 9.1. We assume the economies are identical apart from in one respect: consumers in economy A buy imports from economy B, but those in economy B spend the equivalent amount on more domestic consumption.

Now suppose the government in economy A injects £100 billion into the domestic economy whilst keeping everything else in the model constant: this is an example of **expansionary fiscal policy**. (Please note: the assumption that everything else is kept constant or remains the same is known as the **ceteris paribus** assumption.) The government can, for example, inject this money

Table 9.1 Theoretical marginal propensities

Marginal Propensity	Economy A	Economy B
mpc	0.5	0.6
mps	0.2	0.2
mpm	0.1	0
mtr	0.2	0.2

by building a new airport and the infrastructure improvements required for its citizens to access it. The money it spends goes straight to the producers involved in the project. It then eventually makes its way through the circular flow to households in the form of income. Out of this extra income households save £20 billion (their mps is 0.2), pay £20 billion back to the government in tax (their mtr is 0.2), spend £10 billion on products from economy B (their mpm is 0.1) and spend £50 billion on domestic products (their mpc is 0.5). This £50 billion on domestic consumption then flows through the product markets to domestic producers, and again eventually ends up back with households – not necessarily the same households as before – as income. The cycle is then repeated. These households spend half of this extra £50 billion income in the form of domestic consumption and direct the remaining £25 billion towards the financial markets, the government and economy B. This extra £25 billion of domestic consumption again flows to producers – not necessarily the same producers as before – in the form of revenue, and so the cycles continue, each time getting smaller and smaller until the total effect is dissipated and the economy settles at a new size: but what size is this? To answer this we need to introduce a new term: **gross domestic product** (GDP).

Key term: gross domestic product (GDP)

GDP is a measure of the size of an economy, measuring the value of all that's produced in that economy over a twelve-month period. There are two ways of calculating GDP: the **income** and **expenditure approaches**. As the names suggest, the income approach measures the total amount of income received by households over a twelve-month period, and the expenditure approach measures the total amount of revenue received by producers over an equal period. From the circular flow in Figure 9.1 we can see the two approaches are identical because every pound of revenue received by producers eventually makes its way back to households as their income. There are other measures of an economy's size, such as **gross national product** (GNP) and **net national product** (NNP), which you should look into, but here we focus on GDP as it's the most common measure used.

Consider what happens to the GDP of economy A as the government injects £100 billion into it. Let us use the expenditure approach.

Immediately, producers receive an additional £100 billion. They then receive a further additional £50 billion in the second cycle of the process, and a further £25 billion in the third cycle: remember that in each cycle different producers can receive the additional revenue, although this doesn't necessarily have to be the case. Just from these first three cycles of the process the GDP of the economy has increased by £175 billion: GDP measures the total amount of expenditure producers receive. The process continues until the ripple effects die out and the economy settles at a new size. To determine the overall effect of an injection on the size of the economy we need to calculate the **Keynes–Kahn multiplier** of Equation 9.4: first developed by Richard Kahn (see Section 14.7) in the first half of the twentieth century but then employed by his friend and former teacher John Maynard Keynes (see Section 14.6).

$$\text{multiplier} = \frac{1}{1-\text{mpc}} \qquad \text{(Equation 9.4)}$$

In our example here, the mpc is 0.5 and so the multiplier is 2. We can now determine the overall effect by multiplying the magnitude of the injection by the multiplier: in this case, £100 billion by 2, meaning the GDP of economy A expands overall by £200 billion. This is the **multiplier effect**, which demonstrates just how effective fiscal policy can be at stimulating the economy.

Key term: the multiplier effect

An economy's GDP increases because of an injection of money into it, but it actually increases by more than the size of the initial injection. This is the multiplier effect. Although the logic is precisely the same, the equation used to calculate the multiplier effect of changes in government spending – which is shown in Equation 9.4 – is slightly different from that used to calculate the effect of changes in taxation: you should look up the taxation multiplier as well.

Let's now compare this effect to that of exactly the same fiscal policy in economy B. Here, the mpc is 0.6, the multiplier is 2.5 and so a £100 billion injection into this economy causes its GDP to rise by £250 billion. This highlights some very important points about the effectiveness of fiscal policy, and, indeed, of any other injection into the economy:

① **It's dependent upon households' marginal propensity to leak**, that is, to save, import and pay tax. The greater the combined marginal propensity to leak, the less effective any injection is upon the level of GDP. From this we can see that in a recession – when more and more people are losing their jobs, and households increase their marginal propensities to save in case they lose their jobs – the effectiveness of fiscal policy is reduced, making it harder for the economy to recover.

❷ **It's partly determined by inter-linkages with other economies.** In the early part of 2009 the US government put before Congress a proposal to inject $800 billion into the American economy. Attached to the proposal was the condition that this money could only be spent on American products, which was understandable given our analysis above: the intention was to keep as much of the money flowing round the American economy as possible, maximising the multiplier effect on American GDP. However, the policy meant that other economies were to be excluded from its benefits, which they would otherwise experience through the increased demand for their exports. This raised the fear they would retaliate with other **protectionist** measures, meaning they would no longer buy American-made products. Such retaliation would reduce the amount of money flowing into the American economy from exports both immediately and in the future, inevitably harming the American economy. The analysis of political decision-making such as this forms the field of **public choice**: see Box 9.1.

BOX 9.1: Public choice

Toke Aidt, University of Cambridge

Public choice – sometimes called political economy (which is also what economics as a whole was known as until the early twentieth century, see Chapter 13) or political economics – is the economic study of non-market decisions, that is, decisions made within the context of a political decision-making process rather than through a competitive market. Understanding how non-market decisions are reached is important for a number of reasons.

Most important, perhaps, is the fact that in many developed economies more than half society's resources are spent on public services, social insurance and various welfare programmes. This is a non-market decision made by elected politicians and appointed bureaucrats, often under the strong influence of special interest groups. Moreover, the share of GDP controlled by the state has increased exponentially over the last 150 years. By applying the standard methodology of economics – the notion of rationality combined with rigorous statistical testing – public choice is studying how this came to be.

Another important reason why the systematic study of non-market decisions is important is that it provides vital insights into how specific political decision-making processes actually work and whether they can be expected to produce socially desirable outcomes. A good example of this is the study of the properties of different voting rules. Does it matter, for example, whether a society's election system is based on the principle of proportional representation (as is the case in many continental European countries) or on majority rule (as with the first-past-the-post system used in the United Kingdom)? Recent research into this question demonstrates clearly the answer is yes and the choice of election rule can, in fact, explain quite well why some societies have a larger welfare state than others.

The focus of public choice is primarily **positive** in that the objective of study is to understand how non-market decisions are *actually* reached as opposed to the **normative** question of what decisions *should* be reached. Yet public choice does have a normative as well as a positive aim. In contrast to welfare economics that probes the question of what constitutes socially optimal policy (e.g., the optimal income tax or optimal environmental regulation), public choice treats the policy choice as an *outcome* of a non-market decision-making process. The normative aspect, therefore, comes in only at the constitutional level when one starts comparing different ways of organising non-market decision-making processes. Going back to the example with the election rule, positive public choice analysis demonstrates that proportional representation leads to higher government spending and taxation than majority rule. So, if there were reasons why it might be optimal for a society to have a small government rather than a large one, public choice analysis would lead to the conclusion that the optimal election system is majority rule.

Three very good texts for those interested in learning more about the public choice approach: are:

> D. Mueller, *Public Choice III* (Cambridge: Cambridge University Press, 2003).
> A. Hillman, *Public Finance and Public Policy. Responsibilities and Limitations of Government* (Cambridge: Cambridge University Press, 2003).
> J.M. Buchanan and R.A. Musgrave, *Public Finance and Public Choice: Two Contrasting Visions of the State* (Cambridge, MA: MIT Press, 1999).

9.2 economic size and standard of living

Moving away from the circular flow, let's consider the GDP measure in more detail. We've seen above that GDP is a measure of the size of an economy, of the amount of money flowing round it in a given year. However, it's also widely used as a measure of the **standard of living** experienced by actors within the economy: a population living in an economy with a high GDP is often assumed to have a better standard of living than a population living in an economy with a low GDP. You will see this implied in newspapers and in politicians' speeches asserting the need for economic growth. Here we look at four reasons why GDP is often a poor measure of living standards.

❶ **It doesn't indicate what can be purchased with the money measured.** Consider an economy whose GDP increases by 10 per cent between 2000 and 2009 solely because of a 10 per cent increase in the prices of its produce. Clearly the standard of living in the economy hasn't necessarily increased because even though the amount of money flowing round the economy has increased, the amount of output the economy actually produces is unchanged and its citizens cannot buy any more physical produce in 2009 than they could nine years earlier. This first problem arises because the GDP calculated is in fact **nominal GDP**, meaning it's the value of what's produced in terms of current monetary values. To overcome this problem, it's necessary to calculate **real GDP**, valuing the output of the economy in terms of the same prices in both periods, which we call **constant prices**. Continuing the example from above, real GDP in 2009 can be calculated using the prices that prevailed in 2000. This calculation means the GDPs in the two years can be directly compared, which in this case shows us real GDP is unchanged.

② **It fails to account for the size of the population.** Consider two economies with identical GDPs but in one of which lives a population three times larger than that in the other. Clearly, the households in the smaller population are likely to enjoy higher standards of living as they have higher average incomes. There's a simple adjustment that can be made to correct for this problem: the calculation of **GDP per capita**, which is simply average GDP per head. This is calculated by dividing total GDP by the population size.

③ **It fails to take account of how the income is distributed across the economy.** Taking an extreme example, imagine a small economy with a population of approximately 2 million people and GDP of £900 million in 1997. Some £400 million of this goes straight to the ruling family and is saved in bank accounts overseas. This leaves the rest of the population with GDP per capita of approximately £250. Now suppose that five years later, following a successful coup led by a benevolent military general, real GDP – using 1997 prices – amounted to only £800 million, but £700 million of it is now enjoyed by the mass of the population. Total real GDP has fallen, but real GDP per capita has risen to £350. Clearly, the way in which GDP is distributed across a population is an important determinant of its standard of living.

The **Lorenz curve** is an important diagram for analysing income inequality. Two Lorenz curves are illustrated in Figure 9.2a. These diagrams are constructed by lining up the population along the horizontal axis so that individuals with the lowest incomes are closest to the origin and those with the highest incomes are furthest away. Their cumulative income, as a proportion of the economy's total, is then measured up the vertical axis. Plotting the proportion of income enjoyed by each proportion of the population gives us the Lorenz curve. For example, Figure 9.2a shows the poorest 55 per cent of the population of economy A receive only 20 per cent of the economy's total GDP. We then need to add the **line of equality**, which exists by definition – zero per cent of the population must receive zero per cent of the total income and the entire population must receive the entirety of the income – but which also represents an economy that has a perfectly even distribution of income. Income inequality in an economy is represented by the degree to which its Lorenz curve lies beneath this line. As such, economy A in Figure 9.2a has a more unequal income distribution than economy B.

This all seems very simple, but now consider Figure 9.2b. The poorest citizens in economy B receive a greater proportion of their economy's GDP than do the corresponding citizens in economy A, but the difference in over-all inequality is difficult to assess. To make this comparison more concrete, we need to calculate the **Gini coefficient**, which is essentially the ratio of the area between the line of equality and the Lorenz curve of an economy to the complete area underneath the line of equality. A Gini coefficient of one repre-sents an economy that's perfectly unequal – a single member of the population receives all the income – and a Gini coefficient of zero represents an economy with perfect equality, that is, one represented by the line of equality. Of course, neither of these extreme cases exists. However, it may still be the case that the two economies in Figure 9.2b have identical Gini coefficients and so all we can say is the degree of inequality is the same in both, but to the benefit of different members of the populations. In 2005 the Gini coefficient of America was just under 0.47, whilst the average across the EU was 0.31. In 2007–2008 that of the UK was 0.34.

④ **It fails to reflect that standard of living is influenced by a whole range of non-income factors,** such as the population's access to quality health care, its social freedom – the right to vote, to live a life free from discrimi-nation and to be geographically and occupationally mobile, for instance – and the condition of the natural environment. Factors such as these are crucial determinants of living standards, which don't necessarily increase with GDP. For example, it has been shown that as GDP rises, environmen-tal degradation increases as well, until a certain level of income is reached at which the population begins to spend money on improving the environ-ment. However, Partha Dasgupta, a leading development economist, has demonstrated that income levels are highly correlated with a range of these factors – literacy rates, life expectancy and infant mortality for instance. It's perhaps reasonable to accept changes in GDP as an indication of changes

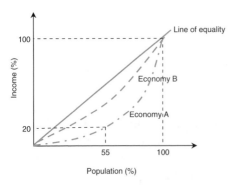

Figure 9.2a *Unambiguous Lorenz curve analysis*

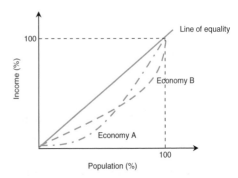

Figure 9.2b *Ambiguous Lorenz curve analysis*

in standard of living when the changes are significant, but when only small changes are considered, what's happening to these other factors are likely to be more important.

economic growth and development

Economic growth simply refers to an expansion of an economy's GDP. As the analysis above suggests, this is an important part of **economic development** but it certainly isn't the whole story: there are many other factors that determine living standards within an economy and its level of development. Together, then, these things form the focus of **development economics** – see Box 9.2.

BOX 9.2: **Development economics**

Oliver Morrissey, University of Nottingham

Development economics combines two issues: first, the analysis of the process of economic development, in particular the ways in which it is distinct from economic growth; and second, the application of economic analysis to enhance our understanding of characteristics of developing countries. In general, standard textbook economics cannot be applied to developing countries; often, different models are required to capture distinct features of poor countries. For example, as formal or wage employment covers a small proportion of the labour force, standard notions of unemployment are not appropriate for understanding the nature of informal labour markets.

More specifically, development economics comprises three main strands:

1. Growth and development. While the study of growth involves attempting to identify the factors that determine how countries can increase output and income (and why some fail to do so), development recognises the need to also consider the relationship with human welfare (such as health, education and poverty). An example of this is the ongoing research into why countries in sub-Saharan Africa have had low growth rates, causing them to fall behind the rest of the world and making it very difficult to reduce the high levels of poverty there.

2. Microeconomic analysis of markets and households in low-income countries. For most households in rich countries adults work to earn money and then spend this on consumption and saving. Farm households in poor countries make production and consumption decisions together and so, in economic terms, they are more complicated. Is it better to grow what they can eat, or grow cash crops (such as tea or coffee) to sell and use the income to buy food? Should they send children to school or is it more important for children to contribute to work on the farm and in the household? These are not decisions faced by the rich, but the poor face them every day.

---

③ Understanding distinct macroeconomic problems. For example, in developed countries inflation is considered to be a feature of monetary policy, and so central bank decisions on money supply and interest rates can influence the rate of inflation. In poor countries the majority of people engage in day-to-day cash transactions; interest rates do not influence them since they neither save nor borrow in formal financial markets. How, then, can monetary policy influence inflation there?

The problems of developing countries are at the heart of global economic concerns. Reducing global poverty requires growth in poor countries, but also human development (increasing access to health and education). Achieving growth and development requires us to understand how individuals and households act and how markets function (or which do not function) in poor countries. Development economics addresses these problems.

Two very good texts on development economics are listed below. The second is more advanced and more technical than the first.

> D. Perkins, S. Radelet and D. Lindauer, *Economics of Development* (New York: Norton, 2006)

> A. Thirlwall, *Economics of Development* (Basingstoke: Palgrave Macmillan, 2011).

9.3 international comparisons of GDP

We see from our analysis above that GDP is often used as a measure of a population's standard of living, but that care is needed when we use GDP in this way. Following on from this, GDP is also used to compare the sizes of different economies: an economy with a greater GDP than another is often assumed to be larger or more productive. However, care is also needed when making these comparisons because of the **hidden** and **underground economies**, both of which exist to some degree in every economy.

Key term: the hidden economy

The hidden economy refers to all activities undertaken in the economy that do not involve money and so go unreported. Developing countries are likely to have relatively large hidden economies compared with developed countries because of the major role played by subsistence agriculture. Output that is then sold contributes to GDP, whereas that privately grown for direct consumption does not.

Key term: the underground economy

The underground economy refers to activities undertaken in the economy for money that are purposely not reported to the authorities in order to avoid taxation. These activities are legal in all respects, apart from not being reported. The underground ⊿

economy doesn't include trade in illegal substances: such trade is referred to as the **black economy**. An example of the underground economy is a plumber who repairs his neighbour's shower for cash so s/he doesn't need to report it, thereby avoiding income tax. This activity doesn't contribute to GDP, whereas if it was reported it would do so.

Two economies may have identical GDPs and so may seem to be of the same size. However, if one of them comprises much larger hidden and underground economies than the other, it actually produces greater output.

purchasing power parity

We've already seen that GDP isn't a perfect measure of welfare because it fails to reflect the purchasing power of a population. This is also an important reason why it's difficult to compare GDPs across economies. Consider two economies with identical GDPs – measured using their own current prices – but where one has lower prices than the other. The economy with the lower prices must have produced a greater output during the twelve-month period than the other, and so must be the larger economy.

When comparing the sizes of two or more economies, we can overcome the problem caused by there being a different price level in each economy by calculating their GDPs using the same price level for each economy. Any differences in GDPs measured in this way then solely represent differences in the output levels produced in these economies. A related concept is that of **purchasing power parity**, which we examine in Section 12.5.

9.4 determination of output in the long run: the classical model

We've seen that the size of an economy is measured as the monetary value of its output over a twelve-month period – given by its GDP – and that an economy's growth depends on the balance between its leakages and injections. We now need to examine how this size is determined in the first place, which means turning to the two main models of output determination, one of which examines the economy in the short run and the other in the long run. Following the chronological order in which they were developed, we take the long run model here and the short run model in the next section.

The long run model is also known as the **classical model of output determination**. At the heart of this model are the assumptions that everything is able to adjust flexibly and that actors respond to changes efficiently. It's these assumptions that make it a model of the long run: there are no fixed factors of production (see Section 6.1).

the amount of expenditure

The first step of the model is to examine the level of total expenditure (E) in the economy. This is usually composed of four parts: domestic **consumption**

(C), **investment** (I), **government spending** (G) and **net exports** (the total amount spent on exports minus that spent on imports, X – M). However, for simplicity let's assume the economy is **closed**, meaning it doesn't engage in international trade at all. This means expenditure is given by Equation 9.5. We now need to understand what determines the amount of each of these three components.

$$E = C + I + G \qquad \text{(Equation 9.5)}$$

Key term: consumption

Consumption refers to the total amount that domestic consumers spend on **consumption goods** produced by domestic producers. Consumption goods, in turn, are products intended for immediate consumption and enjoyment. For example, bottles of milk and packets of cereal are usually consumption goods.

Key term: investment

Investment refers to the total amount spent on investment goods – also known as **capital goods** – within the economy. Investment goods are products not bought for immediate enjoyment but for a return at some point in the future. For example, shares in a business and expensive pieces of artwork bought purely because they increase in value over time are both investment goods.

Let's assume the amount of domestic consumption is a function of consumers' disposable income, which is the income they're left with after taxation is deducted. Mathematically, we express this as $C = C(Y–T)$, where Y is income and T is the total amount taken in tax. However, we need to be precise about this **consumption function**. Consumers have to consume a certain amount of basic necessities such as water and warmth to survive irrespective of their disposable income, and then, as their disposable income increases they're likely to consume more. From these two observations we can write the consumption function as in Equation 9.6, in which α is the necessary, or **autonomous**, expenditure consumers spend even if they have no disposable income; β is the marginal propensity to consume out of disposable income (see Section 9.1), and Y_d is disposable income.

$$C = \alpha + \beta Y_d \qquad \text{(Equation 9.6)}$$

This more precise consumption function is illustrated in Figure 9.3a. The marginal propensity to consume out of disposable income, β, is the gradient of the function: it's the amount by which consumers increase their expenditure when they receive an additional £1 of disposable income. Any consumption

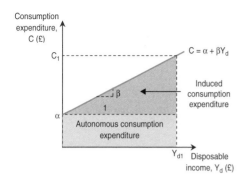

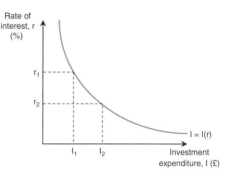

Figure 9.3a Consumption function

Figure 9.3b Investment function

expenditure over and above the autonomous amount is known as **induced consumption** expenditure. The diagram shows that when disposable income is Y_{d1}, total consumption expenditure is C_1, of which α is autonomous and βY_d is induced.

Other forms of the consumption function have been proposed, some of which are examined in Box 9.3 along with the derivation of the marginal propensity to consume from a consumption function and the difference between the marginal propensity to consume in the short and long run.

BOX 9.3: **More on consumption functions**

The consumption function is vitally important in macroeconomics because it shows how the level of consumption in the economy is determined and how it changes due to changes in the income level. Only by understanding this function can we understand how the economy functions and how effective government policies can be.

The Keynesian consumption function

The consumption function of Equation 9.6 is the **Keynesian consumption function**: although it represents the work of the classical economists it was John Maynard Keynes (see Section 14.6) who formalised it in this way. The principle is that the consumption in the economy is a function of total disposable income: as disposable income in the economy rises, consumption rises as well.

The marginal propensity to consume out of disposable income – the proportion of extra disposable income spent on consumption – in this function is given by β. This can be verified by partially differentiating the function with respect to disposable income:

$$\text{mpc} = \frac{\partial C}{\partial Y_d} = \frac{\partial \left(\alpha + \beta\, Y_d \right)}{\partial Y_d} = \beta$$

This marginal propensity gives the gradient of the linear consumption function, as shown in Figure 9.3a.

The average propensity to consume out of disposable income is given by dividing total consumption by total disposable income:

$$apc = \frac{C}{Y_d} = \frac{\alpha + \beta Y_d}{Y_d} = \frac{1}{Y_d}\alpha + \beta$$

The average propensity to consume out of disposable income gives the gradient of the line between the relevant point on the consumption function and the origin. To see this, consider Figure 9.3a: the average propensity to consume out of disposable income at a level of disposable income Y_{d1} is the slope of the line from that point on the consumption function to the origin.

alternative consumption functions

The Keynesian consumption function appeared at first to explain the data well. However, Nobel Prize winning economist Simon Kuznets noticed a problem. The Keynesian consumption function suggests that, as disposable income rises, the average propensity to consume out of disposable income falls. The data shows this to be the case during short periods of time, but over the longer term average propensity to consume is surprisingly constant: the average propensity to consume in the 1880s was very similar to that in the 1930s despite large increases in disposable income. Two main alternative consumption functions have been proposed to explain this, both by other Nobel Prize winning economists.

The first is the **life-cycle hypothesis** of Franco Modigliani, which says that individuals spread their consumption evenly over their entire life-time, taking account of their wealth (the value of everything they own) as well as their income (the value of what they receive in a given period). Up until retirement, individuals save rather than consume some of what they earn, building up their wealth which they then spend in retirement to maintain their consumption levels. This explains the Kuznets problem because, in the short term, as disposable income increases we move up the consumption function and average propensity falls; but, over a longer period, it's wealth that increases, causing the whole consumption function to shift upwards, with the result that the average propensity to consume remains constant.

The second is the **permanent-income hypothesis** of Milton Friedman (see Section 14.9). According to this, an individual's income is composed of two parts: **permanent income**, which is the average income the individual expects to receive over time, and **transitory income**, which is income that individuals are surprised to receive. Friedman conjectured that individuals base their consumption decisions on their permanent income only: Keynes used the wrong variable. Over a short period of time, increases in income are likely to be from increased transitory income. Individuals don't change their consumption much in response to this, and so the average propensity to consume out of disposable income falls: consumption hasn't changed but disposable income has increased. Over a longer period of time, though, increases in income are likely to be from increased permanent income. Individuals respond to this by increasing the amount they spend and keeping their average propensity to consume out of disposable income constant.

marginal propensity to consume in the short and long runs

Consider the following consumption function, which says that consumption today (in period t) is determined by the level of autonomous consumption (α), the current level of disposable income (Y_{dt}) and the amount spent on consumption in the last period (C_{t-1}).

$$C_t = \alpha + \beta_1 Y_{dt} + \beta_2 C_{t-1} \qquad \text{(Equation B9.3.1)}$$

You should be able to interpret and use a function such as this. The marginal propensity to consume out of current disposable income is simply β_1 – which you can derive by partially differentiating the consumption function with respect to current disposable income – and the average propensity to consume out of current disposable income is derived by dividing current consumption by current disposable income. These are the short run figures because they consider only the current time period.

However, you may also be asked to calculate the long run marginal propensity to consume out of disposable income. To do this, you need to remove the time subscripts because in the long run all the effects over time are taken into account. This gives Equation B9.3.2.

$$C = \alpha + \beta_1 Y_d + \beta_2 C \qquad \text{(Equation B9.3.2)}$$

You now need to rearrange it and find the marginal propensity to consume in the same way as before, which is done in Equations B9.3.3 and B9.3.4.

$$C - \beta_2 C = \alpha + \beta_1 Y_d$$

$$(1 - \beta_2)C = \alpha + \beta_1 Y_d \qquad \text{(Equation B9.3.3)}$$

$$C = \frac{\alpha - \beta_1 Y_d}{(1 - \beta_2)} = \frac{\alpha}{1 - \beta_2} + \frac{\beta_1}{1 - \beta_2} Y_d$$

$$\text{mpc} = \frac{\partial C}{\partial Y_d} = \frac{\beta_1}{1 - \beta_2} \qquad \text{(Equation B9.3.4)}$$

Consider, for example, the consumption function $C_t = 100 + 0.3 Y_{dt} + 0.15 C_{t-1}$. The marginal propensity to consume out of disposable income in the short run is 0.3, and that in the long run is 0.3/0.85, which is approximately 0.35.

Let's now examine the amount of investment in the economy. We assume investment expenditure is a negative function of the **interest rate** (r), which we express mathematically as $I = I(r)$ and illustrate as in Figure 9.3b.

The interest rate is effectively the price of borrowing money. Actors who make investments usually have to borrow the money they invest, and so as the interest rate increases it's more expensive for them to borrow and they therefore invest less; and as the interest rate falls it's less expensive for them to borrow, and so they invest more. Figure 9.3b shows precisely this. At an interest rate of r_1 actors within the economy invest an amount I_1. When the interest rate falls to r_2 investment expenditure increases to I_2.

Finally, let's look at **government spending**: the amount the government spends in the economy, usually on the public sector. We tend to ignore how the government decides how much to spend: we just assume the amount is given somehow (the field of public choice examines the question as to how government decisions are actually made: see Box 9.1). If government spending exceeds tax revenue, $G > T$, the government is said to be running a **budget deficit**: it's spending more than it receives. If government spending is less than tax revenue, $G < T$, it has a **budget surplus**: it's spending less than it receives. And in the special case that government spending is equal to tax revenue, $G = T$, we say the government has a **balanced budget**.

We're now able to make the expenditure equation above more precise, which we do in Equation 9.7. Please note that government spending isn't determined by anything in the model. This is because of our assumption that it's just given somehow: we say it's determined exogenously, meaning it's set outside the model. We're now also in a position to examine the complete classical model of output determination. However, there are two different ways we can do this. We can look at it through the output market or through the market for loanable funds. Let's do each in turn.

$$E = C(Y-T) + I(r) + G \qquad \text{(Equation 9.7)}$$

the output market

Now we've examined what determines the amount of expenditure in the economy, the next step is to look at what determines the amount produced in the economy. Here we simply assume that output – which we also denote by Y because output and income are the same, as shown by the circular flow (see Section 9.1)– is a function of the amount of labour (L) and the amount of capital (K) employed by producers. If producers expand the amount of either labour or capital they use, output also expands. We express this as the **production function** in Equation 9.8.

$$Y = F(K, L) \qquad \text{(Equation 9.8)}$$

Classical economics is all about market clearing, and this situation is no exception. It must be the case that the value of output produced equals the amount of expenditure in the economy, Y = E. In other words, everything produced in the economy is consumed through the combined effects of consumption, investment and government spending. This is precisely what the circular flow for a closed economy also suggests. If we assume the amounts of government spending, taxation, capital and labour in the economy are exogenously determined – which we represent mathematically by placing bars on top of them – we can express this equality as Equation 9.9, which is simplified to Equation 9.10.

$$E = C(\overline{Y}-\overline{T}) + I(r) + \overline{G} = f(\overline{L}, \overline{K}) = \overline{Y} \qquad \text{(Equation 9.9)}$$

$$\overline{Y} = C(\overline{Y}-\overline{T}) + I(r) + \overline{G} \qquad \text{(Equation 9.10)}$$

As the amounts of labour and capital are exogenously given, the resulting level of output must be as well since it's determined by the production function (which is why Y has a bar over it as well). The only variable that isn't exogenously determined in the equation is the interest rate, and therefore the amount of investment expenditure. It's this that adjusts upwards and downwards to bring the output market into equilibrium, where Y = E.

Consider Figure 9.4, which simply illustrates Equation 9.10. The amount of output produced doesn't vary with the rate of interest and so is a vertical line at $\overline{Y}$. This level of output is determined by the amounts of labour and capital used by producers, and those amounts are set outside our model. The level of expenditure, though, is a negative function of the interest rate and so is represented by a downward sloping curve. This is because expenditure is composed partially by investment expenditure, which is negatively determined by the interest rate. At an interest rate r_1, then, expenditure in the economy is only

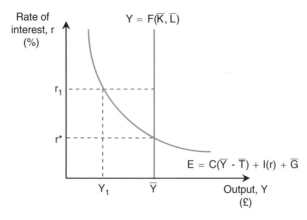

Figure 9.4 *The output market*

sufficient to consume output Y_1. The amount of output produced, though, is $\overline{Y}$, meaning there's excess production. The interest rate falls to r^* (the reason for which is explored below), causing investment expenditure to rise until the level of total expenditure is equal to an output of $\overline{Y}$.

In this model of output determination, the production function and the volumes of the factors of production employed determine the amount of output produced in the economy. The rate of interest then adjusts so that the amount of expenditure is such that the output market is in equilibrium, and all output produced is consumed.

Consider possible changes in the economy:

1. **Technological progress that improves the efficiency of the production function.** This means that, given the same amounts of capital and labour as before, more output is now produced. This is shown in Figure 9.4 by the vertical output curve shifting outwards to the right. The effect of technological progress, then, is that output expands and the interest rate falls. There has to be a reduction in the interest rate because investment expenditure must rise to take up some of the increased output: the rest is taken up by increased consumption as households receive higher incomes from increased production.

2. **An increase in taxation.** This would cause the expenditure curve in Figure 9.4 to shift downwards because consumption expenditure contracts due to a lower level of disposable income. The amount of output is unaffected because the production function and the volumes of labour and capital don't change. The only effect of such fiscal tightening in this model is to reduce the interest rate so the increase in investment expenditure exactly offsets the reduction in consumption spending.

the market for loanable funds

The weakness of examining the classical model through the output market is that it fails to give any explanation as to why the interest rate adjusts to equilibrate the market. We can overcome this weakness by examining the model through the **market for loanable funds**: the market in which borrowers borrow money from lenders. First, let's rearrange Equation 9.10 so the amount of investment is its focus, as in Equation 9.11.

$$I(r) = \overline{Y} - C(\overline{Y} - \overline{T}) - \overline{G} \qquad\qquad (Equation\ 9.11)$$

The right-hand side of Equation 9.11 is an expression for **national saving**: the total amount of money saved in the economy, which is the sum of **private saving** and **public saving**. If we assume households either spend or save all their disposable income, private saving is simply disposable income minus consumption expenditure, $Y - T - C$. Public saving, on the other hand, is the amount of tax revenue the government does not spend: the extent to which the budget is in surplus, $T - G$. Adding these two types of saving together gives the level of national saving, $Y - T - C + T - G = Y - C - G$, which is the right-hand side of Equation 9.11.

Equation 9.11 simply states the amount of national saving must be equal to the amount of investment expenditure – all saving is invested – which can be expressed more simply as $\overline{S} = I(r)$ and illustrated in Figure 9.5. We express national saving as being exogenously determined – and so having a bar above it – because it's determined by the amounts of output, consumption and government spending and they're all exogenously determined themselves. Figure 9.5 shows that, with an interest rate r_1, national saving $(\overline{S})$ is in excess of investment (I). This means that lenders have more money than borrowers want to

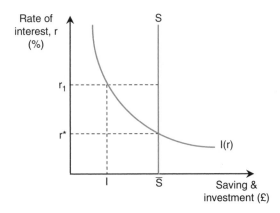

Figure 9.5 The market for loanable funds

borrow, and so lenders reduce the interest rate they charge in order to entice borrowers to borrow more. The interest rate falls until r* at which all saving is borrowed and invested. Conversely, an interest rate lower than r* means more money is demanded by borrowers than lenders possess. People trying to borrow and invest in this situation compete with one another for the available money, driving up the interest rate they pay as they do so. In both cases the interest rate settles at its equilibrium rate, r*, at which there's neither excess supply of, nor excess demand for, funds.

If we assume the amount of output is determined by the production function, the volumes of labour and capital available in the economy are fixed, and the amount of government expenditure is somehow exogenously determined, then it is interaction between borrowers and lenders in the market for loanable funds that determines the interest rate and the amount of investment.

Consider now the effect of an increase in government spending in the classical model. Equation 9.13 demonstrates that such a policy change causes national saving to contract. In Figure 9.5 this would cause an inward shift of the vertical national savings line, increasing the interest rate and reducing the amount of investment. As we assume the level of output is fixed, the amount of investment must fall by precisely the same amount the government increases its expenditure. This model clearly shows how government spending perfectly **crowds out** private investment, leaving the level of output unchanged. From this we see how government spending is actually ineffective in this model.

Key term: crowding out

Crowding out is the idea that the expansionary effect of an increase in government spending on GDP is cancelled out by a reduction in investment because increased expenditure causes an increase in the interest rate. **Perfect crowding out** refers to fiscal policy having absolutely no expansionary effect on GDP because of its contractionary effect on investment.

It was by referring to this model that officials in the UK Treasury rejected Keynes's calls for the government to stimulate the economy through increased government spending in order to increase output and employment during the Great Depression of the 1930s. Clearly, they argued, such action simply causes the interest rate to rise and so the level of investment to fall, making government intervention impotent. Furthermore, they argued, the model shows that the economy always produces the amount of output determined by its factors of production – that is, the maximum amount of output it can produce – which means that government intervention is unnecessary as well as being ineffective. This argument became known as the **Treasury view** and was the focus of much of Keynes's work, to which we now turn.

9.5   determination of output in the short run: the Keynesian model

Working during the Great Depression of the 1930s, John Maynard Keynes (see Sections 13.4 and 14.6) became increasingly dissatisfied with the classical model, which couldn't explain how the high unemployment in the economy at the time could exist and persist as it did. As we saw above, classical wisdom suggests the economy always produces the amount of output that requires all its factors of production to be employed, but the reality of the 1930s showed this wasn't how the economy actually functions.

Keynes's response to this discrepancy between economic theory and reality was to argue that focusing on the long run – in which markets clear and factors of production are fully employed – was futile because the economy might never reach the long run, and if it did it would take so long as to be irrelevant to those living at the time: 'in the long run we are all dead' is his most famous phrase. Instead, he argued, economists should focus on the short run: a period of time during which markets are unlikely to clear, the economy might become stuck in a sub-optimal state and in which unemployment might be high and persistent. The purpose of this section is to examine what has become known as the **Keynesian model of output determination** and to examine how Keynes's work implies that output is determined in the economy.

The General Theory of Employment, Interest and Money was the culmination of Keynes's work, in which he developed a more realistic and effective framework for macroeconomic analysis. This book was an immediate success, forming the basis of the **Keynesian revolution** (see Section 13.4) that shifted the focus of economic analysis from the long run to the short run and developed macroeconomics as a separate field of study (until that time analysis of economy-wide issues was effectively microeconomic in nature). As with many influential texts, though, it isn't an easy read, and so its fundamental points were assimilated into a more digestible form by Sir John Hicks (see Section 14.8). This is the **IS-LM model**, which we explore here, and which is one of the most eloquent models in economics. It comprises two markets – the product market and the money market – which are brought into simultaneous equilibrium by the interest rate.

Before we examine this model, it's important to remember that, although it's the leading interpretation of *The General Theory* – and is often taught as though Keynes developed it himself – it is only a single interpretation among many. Keynes did not develop IS-LM analysis himself and many Keynesian scholars suggest other interpretations and simplifying frameworks – for example, that by Lorie Tarshis – are in fact better representations of Keynes's work (see Box 9.4).

BOX 9.4: **The shameful treatment of Lorie Tarshis**

Unfortunately, most economists have never come across the work of Lorie Tarshis. The reason for this isn't only an interesting example of how the subject has developed, it's also an important reason why this book – and all books used by universities across the world – contain what they do.

Lorie was born in Toronto in 1911. After graduating from university there, in 1932 he moved to Cambridge to read the Economics Tripos – the economics degree at the University of Cambridge – over two years and to then study for a Ph.D. During his time at Cambridge he attended the lectures in which Keynes presented *The General Theory* and he engaged in the work of the Cambridge Circus (see Section 14.7) that was so influential in the Keynesian revolution: in his Ph.D. thesis he connected the work on imperfect competition by Joan Robinson and that on the short run by Richard Kahn, on the one hand, with that of Keynes in *The General Theory*, on the other.

After fighting in Italy during the Second World War, Lorie took up a post at Stanford University. Having witnessed first-hand the development of the ideas behind the Keynesian revolution, he set out his interpretation of Keynes's work in his first textbook, *The Elements of Economics* (1947). But this was the time of the red scare in America, and the powerful anti-communist movement targeted the work of Keynes and advised universities across the country not to buy Tarshis's book, even though Tarshis made it clear it wasn't a political work. By the time the storm had passed, Paul Samuelson's alternative book had been widely adopted, setting the convention of learning Keynes's work through the Keynesian Cross and IS-LM models. Had it not been for the political intervention, the book you're reading now may well have contained Tarshis's interpretation of Keynes – which Keynesian economists argue is a much better and truer interpretation – rather than that of Hicks and Samuelson.

This isn't the end of the effects, though. Keynesian economists argue that by focusing on the IS-LM approach, the Phillips curve (see Section 11.4) was inappropriately integrated into what became known as Keynesian economics: even though it bore no resemblance to Keynes's work at all. When the Phillips curve failed in the 1970s, monetarist and new classical economists (see Sections 13.3 and 13.5) argued that Keynesian economics had failed and neoclassical economics took over as the dominant school of economics once again, and so it's that we all learn today. Had Tarshis's work been allowed to flourish, Keynesian economists contend that the Phillips curve wouldn't have received so much attention and that Keynesian economics would have been able to explain what happened in the 1970s. The whole nature of our subject could now be very different as a result.

Lorie died in Toronto on 4 October 1993. His work has largely been forgotten: a sad development in the history of our subject. If you're interested in finding out more about Lorie's life and work, you should read Geoff Harcourt's article in the *Economic Journal* of September 1995.

the product market

The first part of the IS-LM model is the product market, which represents the production and trade of output in the economy. Equilibrium in this market is represented by the **IS curve**, which is derived from two constituent models: the **investment function** and the **Keynesian Cross diagram**.

① The investment function is the same as that in the classical model, showing the relationship between the amount of investment – by which I mean expenditure on capital or investment goods – in the economy and the interest rate. As we saw above, an interest rate rise causes total investment in the economy to fall, and an interest rate fall causes it to rise (see Figure 9.3b).

② The Keynesian Cross diagram, developed by Paul Samuelson as an interpretation of Keynes's original analysis, is illustrated in Figure 9.6. It starts with the expenditure function from the classical model (see Equation 9.9, which says overall expenditure is simply the sum of consumption, investment and government spending), but it plots the graph of this function with expenditure measured along the vertical axis rather than the interest rate. To this is added a 45° line, showing the equilibrium level of expenditure in the economy: the level of expenditure at which output is stable because everything that is produced is purchased (output is equal to expenditure). In Figure 9.6, then, with expenditure of E_1, the equilibrium level of output is Y_1. To see this, consider a level of output less than this, such as Y_2. At such a level of output, expenditure exceeds output: expenditure is E_2 but that necessary to pay for the output produced is only E'. Producers, sensing an opportunity to earn greater revenue, respond to situations such as this by what is grandiosely known as **unplanned inventory de-accumulation**, simply meaning they sell their spare product stocks. If their inventories are insufficient to satisfy the excess demand, they also expand their production, necessarily employing more factors of production to do so and driving output upwards to Y_1. Conversely, at levels of output above Y_1, expenditure is less than output. Producers are unable to sell all their output and so engage in **unplanned inventory accumulation** – meaning they place surplus stocks in storage – and they reduce their production. Output falls until it's at Y_1: the level at which the product market is in equilibrium and output is stable.

Combining the investment function and the Keynesian Cross diagram leads to the IS curve, which shows the point of equilibrium in the product market for every possible interest rate. Figure 9.7 illustrates precisely this derivation, placing the investment function in panel b and the Keynesian Cross in panel a. Consider, for example, an interest rate r_1. At this rate, investment is equal to I_1 (from Figure 9.7b) and expenditure – given a level of tax revenue of T_1 and a level of government spending of G_1 – is represented by the expenditure curve

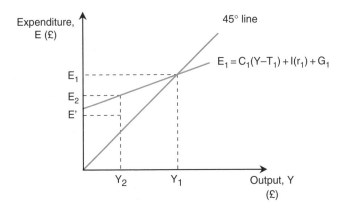

Figure 9.6 *The Keynesian Cross*

E_1 in Figure 9.7a. Given this expenditure curve, then, Figure 9.7a shows that the product market is in equilibrium at an interest rate r_1 if there's an output Y_1. The IS curve simply summarises this result, plotting the point with interest rate r_1 and output Y_1 as a point of equilibrium in the product market. Now consider a rise in the interest rate to r_2. The investment curve in Figure 9.7b shows this rise in the interest rate causes investment to fall to I_2, which then impacts the Keynesian Cross by shifting the expenditure curve downwards to E_2, assuming tax revenue and government spending are unchanged. At this lower level of expenditure, the product market is in equilibrium at the lower output Y_2. The IS curve plots the point with interest rate r_2 and output Y_2 as another point of equilibrium in the product market. Repeating this exercise for every interest rate leads to the derivation of the downward-sloping IS curve shown in Figure 9.7c.

You may find the direction of causation diagram in Figure 9.8 helpful when analysing the IS curve. You start with an interest rate change and assess how the amount of investment changes as a result (from the investment function). You then assess how this change affects the amount of expenditure

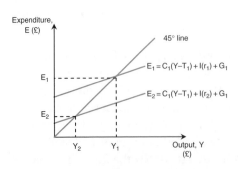

Figure 9.7a *The Keynesian Cross again*

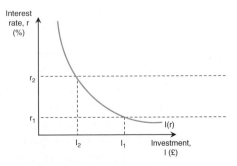

Figure 9.7b *The investment function again*

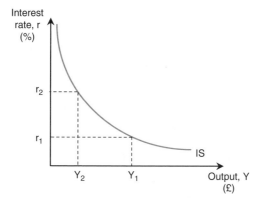

Figure 9.7c The IS curve

and so the equilibrium amount of output in the economy (from the Keynesian Cross diagram). This allows you to see the output effect of a change in the interest rate.

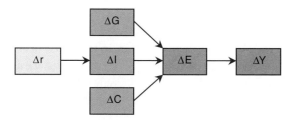

Figure 9.8 Analysing the IS curve

Whenever the interest rate changes there's a movement along the IS curve, from one combination of interest rate and output to another. You can also analyse changes in the other elements of expenditure (consumption and government spending) by holding the interest rate constant and then following the effects of the change through the diagram. These other changes cause the IS curve to shift, meaning the interest rate is unchanged but there's a new equilibrium output.

the money market

Let's now turn to the money market, which involves the real supply of and demand for money in the economy. This leads to the second component of the IS-LM model: the LM curve. Equilibrium in this market is simply the point at which the real supply of money in the economy is equal to the demand for it. This is illustrated in Figure 9.9a. As the diagram shows, the interaction of this demand and supply determines the interest rate in the economy, which is effectively the price of holding money rather than saving it in a bank to earn a financial return (see the definition of the interest rate on page 170).

It's assumed in the IS-LM model that the **real money supply** – the amount of money in the economy measured in current prices (M) divided by the **price level** in the economy (P) – is exogenously determined by the government, and so is fixed. This is shown in Figure 9.9a as the vertical line denoted (M/P).

Key term: the nominal and real money supply

The money supply refers to the amount of money in the economy, which can be assumed to be determined by the government. There are two specific types of the money supply. The first is the **nominal money supply**, which is the amount of money in the economy measured in terms of current money, meaning it's simply the number of units of the domestic currency flowing round the economy's circular flow of income. The second is the **real money supply**, which is a measure of what the money in the economy can buy – its actual value. The real money supply is calculated by dividing the nominal money supply by the **price level** in the economy, where the price level is the average price across the economy.

The demand for money, on the other hand, is represented by the **liquidity preference curve** (LP). This demand refers to the desire of actors in the economy to hold their wealth as cash rather than as assets that earn them a financial return. In other words, it refers to the preference that people have for liquidity (cash is completely liquid, meaning that it can be used immediately, whereas other assets are often less liquid, meaning it takes time for people to be able to use the wealth they represent) – the demand for money and liquidity preference mean the same thing. Keynes conjectured the demand for money is composed of three parts.

1. **Transactionary demand for money**. The first reason why economic actors want to hold money is to buy products. This motive for holding money is a positive function of income: as actors enjoy greater income they desire greater consumption and so need to possess larger amounts of money.

2. **Speculative demand for money**. The second reason why actors want to hold money is to make a return on investments. This demand for money is a negative function of the interest rate: at higher interest rates money earns more from being saved in banks rather than being held, meaning that the cost of holding money for speculative purposes is greater and so less money is demanded for this reason.

3. **Precautionary demand for money**. Parents often tell their children to make sure they always have some money put aside for a rainy day: money they can use in an emergency. Despite the typical dismissal that follows such advice,

actors actually do just this: the precautionary reason for holding money. This demand is unaffected by changes in either income or the interest rate.

These three motives for demanding money together comprise Keynes's theory of liquidity preference, and lead to the downward-sloping liquidity preference curve in Figure 9.9a, denoted by LP. It's downward-sloping because of the negative relationship between the speculative demand for money and the interest rate, and is also a function of the level of income in the economy. The intersection of this and the real money supply determines the equilibrium interest rate in this model of the economy (for the same reasons as price determination in Section 7.1). Notice how the interest rate is determined differently in this model than it is in the classical model of Section 9.4

The LM curve simply illustrates the relationship between the equilibrium interest rate and the level of income (or output, as they're the same). To see how it's derived, look at Figure 9.9a. Consider the level of output Y_1. With income equal to this, the liquidity preference curve is given by LP_1 and as the real money supply is given by M/P the equilibrium interest rate is r_1. The LM curve in Figure 9.9b plots the point with output Y_1 and interest rate r_1 as a point of equilibrium in the money market. Returning to Figure 9.9a, now consider an increase in output to Y_2. Economic actors enjoy greater income and so demand more money for transactionary reasons, meaning the liquidity preference curve shifts upwards to LP_2: actors want to hold more money at every rate of interest. The real money supply hasn't changed and so the equilibrium interest rate rises to r_2. The LM curve in Figure 9.9b plots a second point, with output Y_2 and interest rate r_2, as another point of equilibrium in the money market. By repeating this exercise for all possible levels of income, we can derive the whole LM curve shown in Figure 9.9b.

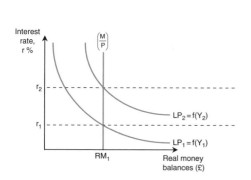

Figure 9.9a Money market

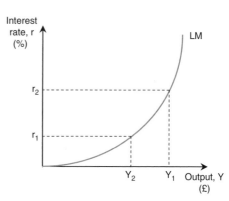

Figure 9.9b LM curve

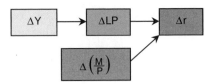

Figure 9.10 *Analysing the LM curve*

As with IS curve analysis, you may find the direction of causation diagram in Figure 9.10 helpful when analysing the LM curve. Holding the real money supply constant, you start with a change in the level of output or income and assess how it first affects liquidity preference and then the equilibrium interest rate.

Changes in the level of output or income simply cause movements along the LM curve. You can also analyse changes in the real money supply, which involves holding liquidity preference constant whilst shifting the vertical real money supply curve inwards (for a contraction of the real money supply) or outwards (for an expansion of the real money supply). These changes cause the interest rate to change whilst the level of income remains constant, and so cause the LM curve to shift.

the complete model

We can now complete the IS-LM model and use it to analyse a number of situations. The model is very clever – in fact I think it's the most impressive model you come across in your first year – but it isn't easy to fully understand all the steps involved. Please work through the examples below carefully, using all three diagrams involved in the IS curve (Figure 9.7), both of those involved in the LM curve (Figure 9.9) and the final diagram in which the IS and LM curves are brought together, as in Figure 9.11a.

Equilibrium in the economy as a whole is given by the intersection of the IS and LM curves. This is the combination of interest rate and output level at which the economy is stable and is under no pressure to change. To see why this is so, let's formally define the meaning of these curves:

Key term: the IS curve

The IS curve maps out all combinations of interest rate and level of output at which the product market is in equilibrium. In other words, it shows all combinations of interest rate and level of output at which there's no excess supply or excess demand for output in the economy: everything produced is purchased either through consumption expenditure, investment expenditure or government expenditure. It's in the product market that the level of output is determined.

Given these definitions, the point at which the IS and LM curves intersect is the single combination of interest rate and output level at which both the product and money markets are in equilibrium at the same time. As both markets are in equilibrium separately, there's no pressure on either the interest rate or the level of output to change and so the whole economy is stable. This is what it means for the economy to be in equilibrium in this model.

Consider again Figure 9.11a and suppose the initial equilibrium in the economy is at an interest rate r_1 and an output level Y_1: the existing IS and LM curves are those subscripted with the number one. We can now use this model to analyse the effects of a number of changes, each of which involves us going through a number of steps. We analyse two such changes here.

1 **A change in the real money supply.** Consider the LM diagram again, and assume the government expands the nominal money supply (M), in effect by simply releasing more units of currency into the economy.

Step 1: **Consider the effect in the money market.** The real money supply shifts outwards to the right because we haven't yet seen the effect this change has on the price level and so for now we assume the price

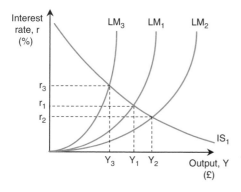

Figure 9.11a IS-LM analysis when LM changes

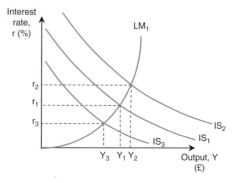

Figure 9.11b IS-LM analysis when IS changes

level doesn't change. The liquidity preference curve is unaffected, and so remains at LP_1. The outward shift of the real money supply causes the interest rate to fall, which implies the LM curve as a whole shifts outwards – there's now a lower interest rate at output Y_1 – which we show in Figure 9.11a as the LM curve shifting from LM_1 to LM_2.

Step 2: **Consider the knock-on effect in the product market**. The reduced interest rate causes investment to rise, which in turn causes overall expenditure to rise: as shown by an upward shift in the expenditure curve in the Keynesian Cross. Producers respond to this by expanding their production, causing output to increase and us to move down the IS curve: at a lower interest rate there's greater output.

Step 3: **Consider the secondary effects in the money market**. As output increases, actors have more money and so liquidity preference expands because they demand more money for transactionary reasons. As the LP curve shifts upwards, the interest rate rises again: above the rate determined in step 1 but below the rate it was initially.

Step 4: **Consider the overall effect**. As Figure 9.11a shows, the interest rate falls to r_2 and output expands to Y_2: an expansion of the money supply causes the interest rate to fall and output to expand. However, the interest rate doesn't fall as much as the effect in the money market alone suggests because there's an increase in output that partially offsets it.

Notice the circularity of the logic above. The interest rate is determined in the money market by the intersection of the real money supply and liquidity preference. Liquidity preference, though, is determined by the level of output and so, indirectly, the interest rate is also determined by the level of output. At the same time, the level of output is determined in the product market by the level of overall expenditure, which is partly determined by the level of investment. The level of investment is in turn determined by the interest rate, and so, indirectly, the level of output is also determined by the interest rate. The economy is in equilibrium, then, when the level of income leads to the interest rate necessary for that level of income to be established.

The direction of causation diagram in Figure 9.12 shows this circularity and may be helpful for you when using the IS-LM model for analysis. In the diagram, the key parts that must interact in a perfectly circular way for the economy to be in equilibrium are linked by solid arrows, but it's possible to analyse the effects of changes in any of the variables. You can start the analysis at any point in the diagram.

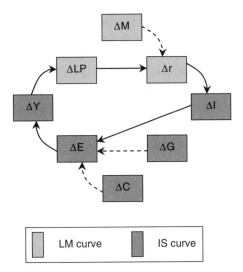

Figure 9.12   IS-LM analysis

Key term: monetary policy

Monetary policy refers to the government expanding or contracting the size of the nominal money supply in order to alter the interest rate, and the levels of investment, expenditure and output in the economy. Expansionary monetary policy refers to an increase in the money supply, which – ceteris paribus – causes the interest rate to fall, and investment, expenditure and output to rise. Contractionary monetary policy refers to a reduction in the money supply, which – ceteris paribus – causes the interest rate to rise, and investment, expenditure and output to fall.

2 **A change in government spending.** We now follow the process in Figure 9.12 to analyse the effects of an increase in government spending.

Step 1:   **Consider the effect in the product market.** The increase in government spending causes overall expenditure to rise, and so the expenditure curve in the Keynesian Cross shifts upwards. Producers respond by expanding their production, meaning output expands. We don't yet know the effect on the interest rate so we assume for now it stays constant. There's now greater output for the same interest rate, implying the IS curve shifts outwards from IS_1 to IS_2 in Figure 9.11b.

Step 2:   **Consider the knock-on effect in the money market.** The increase in output means actors have higher incomes and so demand more money for transactionary reasons. The liquidity preference curve in the money market shifts upwards, and as the real money supply hasn't changed, the interest rate rises. This is shown by the movement up the LM curve in Figure 9.11b.

Step 3: **Consider the secondary effect in the product market.** The increase in the interest rate causes investment in the product market to fall, leading the expenditure curve in the Keynesian Cross to fall again: but not all the way back to where it was initially. Output falls again as a result.

Step 4: **Consider the overall effect.** The overall effect is shown in Figure 9.11b. The IS curve shifts outwards from IS_1 to IS_2, which causes a movement up the LM curve. The economy settles at a new equilibrium, with interest rate r_2 and output Y_2, at which the new interest rate leads to the level of income necessary to establish that precise interest rate, and which causes smooth circularity in Figure 9.12.

It was noted above that the Treasury view derived from the classical model of output determination said government spending is completely ineffective: any increase in government spending simply causes a perfectly offsetting amount of investment because it forces up the interest rate. In other words, there's perfect crowding out of investment. IS-LM analysis shows this isn't the case. An increase in government spending causes the interest rate to rise and this does cause investment to fall, but the crowding out isn't complete and so output expands as a result. Fiscal policy can be effective, which is why Keynes argued vehemently against the Treasury view.

Most modern textbooks – and the subheadings in this chapter – suggest that Keynesian models such as the IS-LM model are useful for analyisng the short run and that they complement the classical analysis of the long run. This isn't how Keynes intended his analysis to be understood, though. Keynes argued that the long run is irrelevant because the economy never actually gets there. As such, the only useful analysis is that of the short run, and so the two approaches are substitutes for one another rather than complements.

9.6 summary

> Macroeconomics is the study of the economy as a whole. It involves, in particular, the study of what determines the size of an economy, what causes unemployment and inflation, how economies interact with each other, and how these can all be improved.

> GDP measures the size of an economy as the total amount of income or expenditure within a given economy over a twelve-month period. Care needs to be taken when using GDP as a measure of standard of living and as a way of comparing the sizes of different countries.

> The classical model of output determination is often referred to as a model of how the size of an economy is determined in the long run. It predicts that government spending is futile because of perfect crowding out.

> The IS-LM model is often referred to as the Keynesian and short run model of output determination. It predicts government spending is an effective way of expanding the size of an economy.

demand and supply but on a bigger scale

In Chapter 9 we examined what determines the amount of output produced in the economy using two models – the classical and Keynesian models of output determination. Both of these models involve the interest rate as the key to how the economy adjusts to equilibrium, and both of them ignore the role of the price level (the price level didn't feature in any significant way during our analysis in Chapter 9). In fact, in the classical model output isn't affected by money at all – it's determined solely by the physical quantities of the factors of production and the production function. It is then the interest rate in the classical model (which is determined by the supply of, and demand for, loanable funds) that determines the level of expenditure through investment so that everything produced is consumed. There are two distinct parts to the economy in the classical model: the **real economy**, which involves physical quantities of things and determines the amount of output, and the **monetary economy**, which involves money and determines the interest rate – and never do the two affect one another. This is known as the **classical dichotomy**.

Key term: the price level

The price level refers to the average price of all products in the economy. An increase in the price level is known as **inflation**, whilst **deflation** refers to a reduction (see Section 11.3).

This chapter examines how the price level in the economy influences the amount of output produced, which involves developing and analysing the model of aggregate demand and supply. The following chapter uses this analysis to explore the key problems of unemployment and inflation.

John Maynard Keynes (see Section 14.6) was acutely aware of the **fallacy of composition**, which simply says if something is true for the parts of a body it isn't necessarily true for the body as a whole: the total isn't simply the sum of the parts. Being aware of this, he introduced the concepts of **aggregate demand** and **aggregate supply** in order to analyse the whole economy as an entity in its own right, separate from the actors within it. This marked the birth of macroeconomics as a distinct sub-discipline of economics, the approach that places the focus on the economy as a whole rather than on the actors within it.

10.1 aggregate demand

Key term: the aggregate demand curve

Keynes introduced the notion of aggregate demand (AD) to refer to the total amount of demand for all products in the economy. The aggregate demand curve illustrates the relationship between this total demand and the price level. It's a downward-sloping curve: a reduction in the price level is associated with an expansion of aggregate demand, and an increase in the price level is associated with a reduction of aggregate demand.

We can derive the aggregate demand curve using our IS-LM analysis of Section 9.5 simply by altering the price level that features in the money market. Consider Figures 10.1a and 10.1b. Initially the price level is P_1 and so the real money supply is M/P_1: we assume the nominal money supply is exogenously set by the government at M. As output is Y_1, liquidity preference at each interest rate is given by the liquidity preference curve LP_1, and so the equilibrium interest rate is r_1. The initial LM curve, then, is LM_1, which includes the existing equilibrium combination of interest rate r_1 and output Y_1. Now consider a reduction in the price level from P_1 to P_2. If we assume that the nominal money supply remains constant at M, the reduction in the price level causes the real money supply to rise to M/P_2. If we also assume output remains at Y_1, this causes a movement along the LP_1 curve. As the demand for money hasn't changed but the real money supply has increased, the interest rate falls from r_1 to r_2. With unchanged income, this causes the LM curve to shift outwards to LM_2. Precisely the same happens again if there's another reduction in the price level to P_3: the interest rate falls to r_3 and as output remains at Y_1, the LM curve shifts outwards to LM_3. From this we see that a reduction in the price level causes, ceteris paribus, the LM curve to shift outwards. The converse is also true: an increase in the price level causes, ceteris paribus, the LM curve to shift inwards.

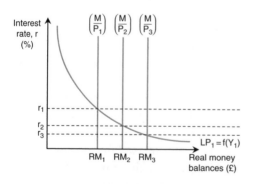

Figure 10.1a Price level changes

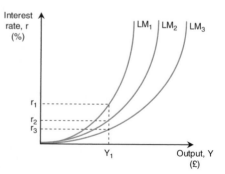

Figure 10.1b LM curve

Figures 10.2a and 10.2b complete our derivation of the aggregate demand curve. The first of these panels illustrates the full IS-LM analysis of price level changes. Initially, the price level is P_1 and so the LM curve is given by LM_1: in the figure it's labelled such that LM_1 is a function of P_1. Combining this with the existing IS curve, IS_1, leads to the economy being in equilibrium at interest rate r_1 and output Y_1. Suppose there's now a reduction in the price level to P_2, causing the LM curve to shift outwards to LM_2, as in Figure 10.1a. The effect of this is to cause the interest rate to fall, which in turn causes investment and output to rise, as represented by a movement down the IS curve. As output expands, the liquidity preference curve shifts outwards because actors demand more money for transactionary reasons (see Section 9.5). This prevents the interest rate from falling as much as it does in Figure 10.1b, which keeps output unchanged. The interest rate settles at r_2, at which the resulting output Y_2 is such that an interest rate of r_2 is established in the money market: the circularity of the IS-LM model we see in Section 9.5 is achieved. Overall, then, the fall in the price level causes the interest rate to fall to r_2 and, more importantly for the derivation of the aggregate demand curve, the level of output to rise to Y_2.

Consider now a second reduction in the price level from P_2 to P_3. This causes the LM curve to shift outwards again, this time to LM_3. The interest rate falls once more, causing investment and output to rise as shown by a further movement down the IS curve. The increased output prevents the interest rate from falling as much as it would if income remained unchanged, and the economy settles at a new equilibrium with interest rate r_3 and output Y_3. Again, the overall result of the fall in the price level is a reduction in the interest rate and an expansion of output.

Figure 10.2b plots this overall relationship between the price level and the level of output, which is equal to expenditure because of equilibrium in the Keynesian Cross diagram (see Section 9.5). At a price level P_1, IS-LM analysis demonstrates expenditure and output are Y_1. A reduction in the price level to P_2 causes output to increase to Y_2, and a further reduction in the price level to P_3 causes it to increase to Y_3. This relationship is the aggregate demand curve.

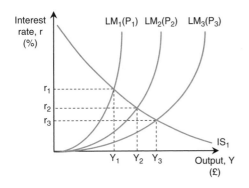

Figure 10.2a Price level changes

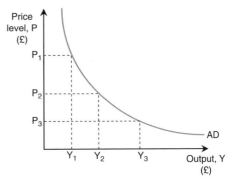

Figure 10.2b Aggregate demand

From this we see the aggregate demand curve shows us the output level that's equal to the total expenditure in the economy at every given price level: for every price level it shows the level of output at which the IS-LM model is in equilibrium. This is summarised in Equation 10.1, in which Y(P) is the level of equilibrium output that's a function of the price level, E is the total amount of expenditure in the economy, and C, I, G, X and M are the levels of private consumption, investment, government spending, exports and imports, respectively.

$$Y(P) = E = C+I+G+X-M \qquad \text{(Equation 10.1)}$$

10.2 aggregate supply

To complete the model we now need to examine aggregate supply.

Key term: the aggregate supply curve

Aggregate supply refers to the total output of an economy. The aggregate supply curve shows the relationship between this total output and the price level. It's an upward-sloping curve, meaning that as the price level increases output tends to expand, and as the price level falls output tends to fall.

In the long run, once the economy has adjusted in every way it needs to and there isn't any further pressure on output to change, the economy produces the **natural level of output**, Y^*. This level of output is determined by the amounts of the factors of production in the economy and the available technology reflected in the production function: it's the level of output produced in the classical model of Section 9.4 and to which the economy tends towards over time. The **long run aggregate supply** (LRAS) curve, then, is a vertical line at output Y^*.

In the short run, though, the level of output produced in the economy may deviate from this natural level. The **short run aggregate supply** (SRAS) curve is given by the general formula of Equation 10.2, which shows that it's because of actors' expectations that output may not be at the natural level. In particular, it's the expected price level (P^e) which is important. When actors expect a price level different from what the price level actually is (P) output isn't at its natural level. When they underestimate the price level $(P^e < P)$ aggregate supply exceeds the natural level $(Y > Y^*)$, and when they overestimate it $(P^e > P)$ aggregate supply is less than the natural level $(Y < Y^*)$. The long run is reached when their expectations have adjusted to be correct $(P^e = P)$, which means the natural level of output is produced $(Y = Y^*)$.

$$Y = Y^* + a(P-P^e), \text{ where } a > 0 \qquad \text{(Equation 10.2)}$$

A number of explanations have been proposed by economists as to why output may deviate from its natural level in the way Equation 10.2 suggests.

These are the theories of the short run supply curve. We examine only one of them here: the **sticky-wage model**, which says it's the inflexibility of the **nominal wage rate** that causes the expected price level to deviate from the actual price level, and so causes output to deviate from its natural level.

Key terms: the nominal and real wage rates

The nominal wage rate is the amount workers are paid in purely monetary terms. It takes no account of the price level in the economy. The real wage rate, on the other hand, is a measure of what workers can actually buy with the money they're paid. It's calculated by dividing the nominal wage rate by the price level. Consider, for example, a producer that paid its workers £6 per hour in 1990, when the average price level was P_1. In 2010 it pays its workers an hourly rate of £10 and the average price level is P_2, double what it had been twenty years earlier: $P_2 = 2P_1$. The nominal wage rate this producer pays has increased over the period, from £6 to £10. However, the real wage rate it pays has actually fallen: $(£6/P_1) > (£10/2P_1)$ which can be simplified to $(£6/P_1) > (£5/P_1)$.

We need to make three assumptions for the sticky-wage model:

1 The amount of output produced by producers (Y) is solely determined by the amounts of labour (L) and capital (K) they employ, and the amount of capital is fixed, making it a short run model (see Section 6.1). We can express this mathematically as the production function in Equation 9.8.

2 The amount of workers employed is determined by the demand for labour (D_L), which is in turn determined by the real wage rate (w): the nominal wage rate (W) divided by the actual price level (P). We express this mathematically as $w = W/P$ and $D_L = f(w)$. An increase in the real wage rate reduces the amount of labour producers demand, meaning the amount of labour employed and the amount of output produced both fall. A reduction in the real wage rate increases the amount of labour demanded, causing the amount of labour employed and the amount of output produced to expand.

3 Employment contracts are determined before the actual price level is revealed. Workers and producers negotiate with one another, agreeing the real wage rate that workers will ideally be paid. This is called the **target real wage** (w^t). Given expectations about what the price level will be during the lifetime of the employment contracts (P^e), the nominal wage rate is determined and written into the contracts. The nominal wage is set so that when it's divided by the expected price level, the target real wage is realised. This is shown in Equation 10.3, which, when rearranged, shows us the nominal wage is given by the target real wage multiplied by the expected price level: Equation 10.4.

$$w^t = \frac{W}{P^e}$$
(Equation 10.3)

$$W = w^t \times P^e \qquad \text{(Equation 10.4)}$$

Once the actual price level becomes known – which happens after the contracts have been signed and the workers have started work – producers are able to calculate the actual real wage rate they're paying workers by dividing the contracted nominal wage rate by the actual price level: Equation 10.5.

$$w = \frac{W}{P} = \frac{w^t \times P^e}{P} \qquad \text{(Equation 10.5)}$$

$$w = w^t \times \frac{P^e}{P} \qquad \text{(Equation 10.6)}$$

There are three possible situations: the actual price level can exceed that which had been expected, it can be less than that which had been expected, or it can be equal to that which had been expected.

When the actual price level exceeds that which had been expected $(P > P^e)$, we see from Equation 10.6 that the actual real wage is less than that which both workers and producers had intended: $w < w^t$. From the second assumption above, this induces producers to hire more labour than they were expecting to, and this – from the first assumption – means output increases beyond the level at which expectations are realised. Output exceeds its natural level: $Y > Y^*$.

When the actual price level is less than that which had been expected $(P < P^e)$, we see from Equation 10.6 that the actual real wage is greater than that which had been intended: $w > w^t$. Producers respond to this by hiring less labour than they were expecting to, which causes output to be less than its natural level: $Y < Y^*$.

Figure 10.3 summarises this in the form of the short run aggregate supply curve. When price expectations are accurate the amount of output produced is equal to the natural level. When the actual price level exceeds that expected the amount of output produced exceeds the natural level. And when the actual price level is less than that expected the amount of output produced is less than the natural level.

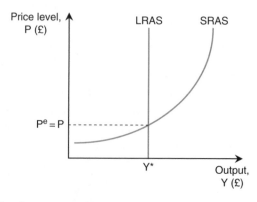

Figure 10.3 The short run aggregate supply curve

It's important to note from this explanation that the reason why the short run aggregate supply curve is upward-sloping – and why short run output can deviate from its natural level – is because the nominal wage rate is fixed or 'sticky'. This stickiness arises because the nominal wage rate is determined based on the price level that workers and producers expect and is then held fixed for a specified period of time: the duration of employment contracts. Unexpected changes in the price level cause the actual real wage rate to deviate from the targeted rate. In turn, this causes the amount of labour that producers employ and the output that is produced to deviate from their target and natural levels. The long run is reached when expectations have fully adjusted and are correct, and so in the long run the natural level of output is always produced.

10.3 the complete model

Putting the aggregate demand and supply curves together completes the model. Just as we can use the IS-LM model to analyse changes in the economy, so we can use the aggregate demand and supply model. Although it's possible to analyse many effects, let's examine the same two effects we analysed in Section 9.5.

1. **An increase in government spending: an example of expansionary fiscal policy.** Consider Figure 10.4. The economy is initially in a position of long run equilibrium at point A. It's producing its natural level of output (Y^*) and the prevailing price level is P^*, which is equal to the expected price level, $P^e = P^*$.

   Short run effect: Government spending is a component of aggregate demand (Equation 10.1) and so an expansion of government spending causes the aggregate demand curve to shift outwards from AD_1 to AD_2. At the prevailing price level P^*, the amount of output produced is Y^* but the amount demanded is now Y_1: there's excess demand in the economy, which inevitably causes producers to increase the prices they charge and the price level to rise. This must mean the price level begins to rise above that which workers and producers had expected and so the real wage rate falls. Producers respond to this by hiring more labour and producing more output (following the logic of Section 10.2). The increase in government spending causes the economy to move from point A to point B, the price level to rise from P^* to P_1, and the output produced to expand from Y^* to Y_2. We call this a short run **inflationary gap**, which is labelled in Figure 10.4.

Key term: inflationary gap

An inflationary gap refers to a situation in which aggregate demand increases, causing the economy to produce more than its natural level of output and the price level to rise. It's a short run effect because in the long run the economy reverts back to producing its natural level of output.

Long run effect: As the actual price level has increased, workers and producers gradually adjust their price expectations upwards, causing the targeted real wage rate during employment negotiations to rise. Gradually, the nominal wage rates producers have to pay increase as a result, and so at every price level they're now willing to produce less output because of higher production costs. This is shown by the short run aggregate supply curve gradually shifting inwards from $SRAS_1$ to $SRAS_2$, which returns the economy to a long run equilibrium position at point C, at which the natural level of output is produced and the prevailing price level is at the higher rate P_2.

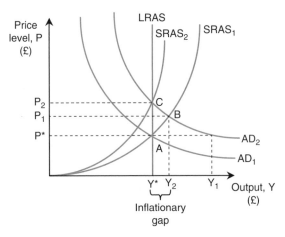

Figure 10.4 Increased government spending in the AD-AS model

Overall effect: An increase in government spending causes a short run expansion of output and employment, but in the long run only increases the prevailing price level.

❷ **A reduction in the real money supply: an example of tightening monetary policy**. Consider Figure 10.5 in which the economy is initially at point A, a position of long run equilibrium in which it produces the natural level of output (Y^*) at a prevailing price level P^*, which is the level workers and producers expect.

Short run effect: From our IS-LM analysis of the money market in Section 9.5, a reduction in the real money supply causes the interest rate to rise, which in turn causes the levels of investment and expenditure to fall at every given price level. The effect of this is that the aggregate demand curve shifts inwards from AD_1 to AD_2. At the price level P^* there's now Y^* being produced but only Y_1 being demanded: there's excess supply in the economy, which inevitably causes producers to reduce the prices they charge and the price level to fall. The price level falls beneath the level expected by workers and producers, causing the real wage rate producers pay to rise. Producers respond to this by reducing the amount of labour they employ and the amount of output they produce. The economy moves from point A to point B, and the levels of output and price fall to Y_1 and P_1 respectively. We call this a **recessionary gap**.

Long run effect: As the actual price level falls, workers and producers adjust their price expectations downwards. This reduces the targeted real wage during labour negotiations, which gradually reduces the nominal wages and production costs producers have to pay, causing them to increase their production at every price level. This is shown by the short run aggregate supply curve shifting outwards from $SRAS_1$ to $SRAS_2$. The economy gradually moves back to a position of long run equilibrium at point C, at which it produces its natural level of output but at the lower price level P_2.

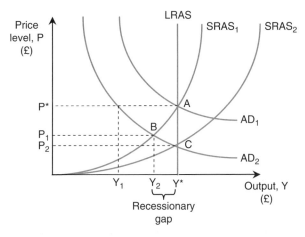

Figure 10.5 Monetary tightening in the AD-AS model

Overall effect: Monetary tightening causes a contraction in output and employment, but only in the short run: in the long run it serves only to reduce the price level.

10.4 the IS-LM and AD-AS models compared

The IS-LM model is useful for examining the effects of economic changes on an economy's short run equilibrium output and interest rate. It only shows the short run effects, though, because we usually have to assume when doing the analysis that the price level doesn't change. The AD-AS model, on the other hand, is useful for analysing the effects of the same changes but on the equilibrium price and output levels in both the short and long runs: we allow the price level to change. Rather than being competing models, they complement one another nicely, and by using them together we can enrich our analysis.

Consider, for example, a reduction in government spending. We analyse the effects of this in Figures 10.6a and 10.6b, assuming the economy is initially in a position of long run equilibrium – points A and A' in the two diagrams – and there aren't any other changes: the ceteris paribus assumption.

❶ Using the IS-LM model (Figure 10.6a) the reduction in government spending from G_1 to G_2 causes a reduction in expenditure and so an inward shift of the IS curve from IS_1 to IS_2 (see Section 9.5). Overall, this causes both the interest rate and output level to fall: the economy moves from point A to point B.

❷ Using the AD-AS model (Figure 10.6b) reveals further insight about the effects of this policy change. As government spending is a component of aggregate demand, its reduction causes the aggregate demand curve to shift inwards from AD_1 to AD_2. The expected price level initially remains at P^* and so there's a movement down the prevailing short run aggregate supply curve $(SRAS_1)$, moving the economy from point A' to point B'. The reduced expenditure causes both the levels of output and price to fall.

❸ In the short run the policy causes a reduction in the interest rate (and so an increase in investment), a reduction in the price level and a reduction in the level of output. As investment is a component of aggregate demand, the aggregate demand curve doesn't shift inwards as far as it would have done had the interest rate not changed. This shows the benefits of combining different models in the analysis of a single event.

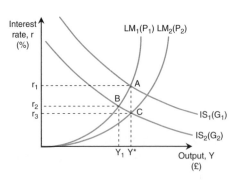

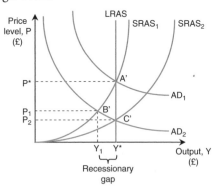

Figure 10.6a Reduction in government spending in the IS-LM model

Figure 10.6b Reduction in government spending in the AD-AS model

❹ As the price level falls below that previously expected, the price expectations of workers and producers gradually adjust downwards, causing the nominal wage rate to be gradually reduced and production costs to fall. The

introducing larger-scale analysis: the macroeconomic world

short run aggregate supply curve gradually shifts outwards from SRAS$_1$ to SRAS$_2$, as shown in Figure 10.6b, which further reduces the price level to P$_2$ and restores production to its natural level, Y*. The economy moves back to a position of long run equilibrium at point C.

⑤ Although the IS-LM model is really a short run model of the economy, in which the price level is held constant, it can be used to illustrate long run effects as well. In this case, if we assume the nominal money supply remains unchanged, the falling price level causes the real money supply to expand. This causes the LM curve to shift outwards from LM$_1$ to LM$_2$ and the economy to move down the new IS curve, IS$_2$, to point C. The interest rate is further reduced and so investment rises, causing output to return to its natural level, Y*.

BOX 10.1: **Business cycles and stabilisers**

The path of an economy's real GDP tends to be cyclical, as shown in Figure B10.1. This is known as the **business cycle**. The upward trend of real GDP demonstrates the economy's tendency to grow over time: economic growth (see Section 9.2).
   We see there are four distinct phases of the business cycle:

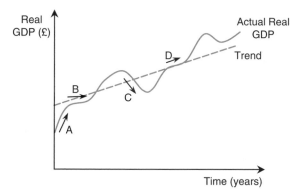

Figure B10.1 *The business cycle*

① Times when the economy is growing rapidly, as in period A in the diagram, during which unemployment is low and declining and the price level is growing.
② Times when both the output and price levels of the economy are growing more slowly, as in period D.
③ Times, such as period B, when the economy is stagnant: the levels of output and price don't change.
④ Times when the economy actually contracts: output shrinks, unemployment increases and the price level falls. Period C in the diagram illustrates such a period.

The first of these are known as **booms**, which can be caused by increases in aggregate demand. They can be analysed using a diagram such as Figure 10.4, which illustrates a positive demand-side shock: aggregate demand expands, causing both the levels of output and price to increase and growth to quicken. Gradually the economy corrects itself and the levels of output and price settle at the trend rate of expansion.

The final periods are known as **busts** or **depressions** and are caused by reductions in aggregate demand. These can be analysed using diagrams such as Figure 10.5 which represents a negative demand-side shock. The negative shock causes the aggregate demand curve to shift inwards, suppressing the price level, causing the output level to contract and leading to an increase in unemployment. Again, the economy eventually corrects itself as lower prices gradually cause production costs to fall and production to expand. The economy settles back to an equilibrium in which it resumes its growth at the trend rate.

In both cases there are pressures within the economy that cause it to correct itself. However, governments can also introduce **automatic stabilisers** to dampen down the initial effects. The welfare state is an example of such a stabiliser. As output falls and unemployment expands in a recession, aggregate demand is prevented from contracting as much as it would do naturally by the unemployed receiving state benefits rather than no income at all. This slows and reduces the fall of aggregate demand. In a boom, on the other hand, incomes increase, which causes aggregate demand to rise. However, aggregate demand isn't allowed to rise as much as it would do naturally because higher incomes are generally subject to higher tax rates, which slow and reduce the expansion of aggregate demand. In both cases the automatic stabilisers serve to keep the path of the economy around its trend.

In severe recessions and booms, governments can also employ **discretionary stabilisers**. By using fiscal and monetary policy, they can counteract the effects of the business cycle that cause the economy to diverge from the trend. However, this isn't as simple as at first it may appear, for a number of reasons:

1. It isn't always apparent what the cause of the shock is, making it difficult to choose the appropriate policy response.
2. Even when the appropriate response is clear, it isn't usually obvious what the extent of the policy should be. There's a danger of injecting too much into the economy during a recession, causing it to lurch from recession straight into a boom; and withdrawing too much from it in a boom, having the reverse effect.
3. Policy is always hindered by time-lags, which make it likely that once a policy response becomes active the economy will have corrected itself (at least partially), meaning the policy actually causes the economy to lurch the other way. There are three time-lags involved:

a. That between when the shock occurs and when the government observes it.

b. That between the observation of the shock and the decision about what should be done.

c. That between the decision being made and its effects actually being felt.

④ Governments are subject to political influence and are prone to making policy decisions in response to this influence rather than in response to the actual economic situation (this is analysed in the field of public choice: see Box 9.1).

Overall, policy-making is a mine-field, leading some economists to promote a laissez-faire stance.

10.5 summary

> The aggregate demand and supply model can be used to analyse price changes and effects in the economy, complementing IS-LM analysis.
> The aggregate demand curve shows the total level of expenditure in the economy at each price level. It's downward-sloping and can be derived from the IS-LM model.
> An aggregate supply curve shows the total amount of output produced in the economy at each price level.
> The short run aggregate supply curve is upward-sloping and can be derived from models such as the sticky-wage model.
> The aggregate demand and supply model can be used to analyse and explain the business cycle.
> The long run aggregate supply curve is vertical at the natural level of output: the level of output determined by the volumes of capital and labour in the economy and the prevailing technology (as reflected in the production function).

11 unemployment, money and inflation

The model of aggregate demand and supply we developed in Chapter 10 is also useful for analysing unemployment and inflation, the two most serious concerns of macroeconomists. The purpose of this chapter is to examine these concerns, looking at their causes, effects and the policies the government can implement to address them.

11.1 unemployment

Unemployment – which can be very generally defined as the number of workers without jobs – is perhaps the most serious problem an economy faces, for a number of reasons:

1 **Wasted resources**. It represents factors of production that aren't being used and so an economy that is not producing as much output as it can. This can be seen in Figure 11.1, which shows a **production possibility frontier**: a curve showing the maximum combinations of products that an economy can produce, which is concave because of **diminishing marginal returns** (see Section 6.1). Combinations A and B are both fully efficient, meaning that if the economy in the diagram is producing either of those combinations of output it is using all its factors of production fully and is producing the most it can from these resources: it's productively efficient (see Section 1.1). Combination C shows a sub-optimal level of production, which

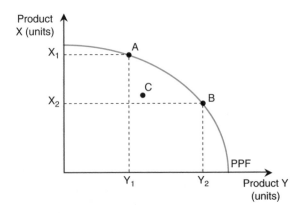

Figure 11.1 A production possibility frontier

can be caused either by the economy not using its resources efficiently or by there being unemployment. Clearly, the economy can do better than this.

② **Further costs**. Developed economies give their unemployed citizens income – unemployment benefits – from which they can live. The more unemployment there is, the more costly these benefits become. Furthermore, unemployment appears to be positively associated with health problems and crime: as it increases, so too do these costs to society.

③ **Personal costs**. Perhaps the most important reason, though, is its effect on individuals and their families. In a society that values people by how successful they are in their careers – which is the case in most developed economies – the unemployed are labelled as failures, which is a hard stigma to bear. Being unemployed often leads to depression and family problems. These personal costs are impossible to quantify properly, but there's no doubt about how significant they are.

unemployment in the aggregate demand and supply model

We can see from the aggregate demand and supply model both the classical and Keynesian views of unemployment. Let's examine each in turn here.

To understand the classical view we need to distinguish between two types of unemployment: **voluntary unemployment** and **involuntary unemployment**. The voluntary unemployed are those who choose not to work at the nominal market wage rate. They don't actually seek jobs because the nominal wage rate on offer isn't sufficient to make them want to do so. The very wealthy and parents who stay at home with their children are good examples of voluntary unemployment: if the nominal wage rate was raised high enough they would choose to work. The involuntary unemployed, on the other hand, are those who want to work at the market nominal wage rate but cannot find jobs. They're actively seeking work but without success.

Now we can turn to the classical view. The classical model of output determination in Section 9.4 suggests the economy always produces the level of output determined by the available amounts of the factors of production – which includes the amount of labour wanting to work – and the prevailing technology as represented by the production function. According to this view, unemployment isn't a serious problem. As long as the economy functions properly and markets are free to adjust to any changes, the economy always employs all its factors of production and there won't be any involuntary unemployment. We saw precisely the same in our analysis of the aggregate demand and supply model in Chapter 10: the natural level of output is always produced in the long run, and any deviations from this in the short run are caused because the nominal wage rate isn't able to adjust to changes in the expected price level. If the nominal wage rate is constantly free to adjust, any changes in the expected price level cause it to change instantly, so that the natural level of output is maintained. Again, there isn't any involuntary unemployment: everyone who wants to work at the nominal market wage rate is employed. Of course there may be voluntary unemployment as some people decide working isn't lucrative enough for them, but this isn't a problem: it's a matter of personal choice.

Consider the microeconomic model of the labour market in Figure 11.2, which illustrates this view in more detail. The total size of the labour force – the total number of individuals within the economy of working age who are physically and mentally able to work – is denoted by FE, the full-employment level of employment. The amount of labour producers in the economy demand at each nominal wage rate is given by the demand for labour curve (D_L). It's downward-sloping because as the nominal wage rate increases, production costs increase and so producers aren't willing and able to produce as much output and to hire as much labour as before. The amount of labour supplied by potential workers in the economy at each nominal wage rate is given by the labour supply curve (S_L). It's upward-sloping because of the reasoning above: as the nominal wage rate increases it becomes increasingly attractive to work and so more individuals choose to work and those already doing so supply more of their time. Putting these two curves together in the standard way shows us the equilibrium nominal wage rate is W^*, at which E^* workers are employed. This leaves FE – E^* workers unemployed, but only voluntarily so: they could find work if they were willing to supply their labour for a lower nominal wage rate.

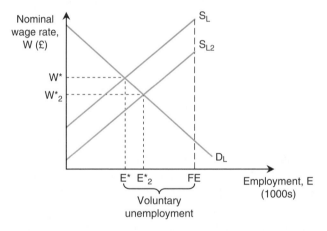

Figure 11.2 *The classical model of unemployment*

Now consider what happens if more individuals decide they want to work at the market nominal wage rate. This causes the labour supply curve to shift outwards to S_{L2} – at each nominal wage rate there's a greater supply of labour – which causes the nominal wage rate to fall to W^*_2 and the amount of labour employed to increase to E^*_2. Again, there isn't any involuntary unemployment: everyone wanting to work at the nominal wage rate being offered is employed. At the level of the whole economy, the natural level of output increases because more factors of production are now available.

If the nominal wage rate is fully flexible – meaning it's able to quickly adjust to changes such as this in the labour market – it simply changes to ensure there isn't any involuntary unemployment, causing the natural level of output to adjust accordingly (and the vertical long run aggregate supply curve to shift – see Section 10.2). Unemployment, then, is only ever a problem if the nominal wage rate isn't flexible – if it's sticky as in the theory of the short run aggregate supply curve in Section 10.2 – because this is when involuntary unemployment can arise. Consider Figure 11.3. The equilibrium nominal wage rate is W^* and the equilibrium amount of employment is E^* as before. However, the actual nominal wage rate prevailing in the labour market isn't able to fall below W', and so producers demand only E_d amount of labour while potential workers supply an amount E_s. There's excess supply of labour which cannot be cleared and which represents the involuntarily unemployed.

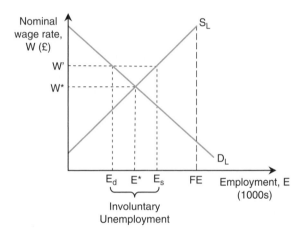

Figure 11.3 Sticky wages in the classical model of unemployment

There are numerous possibilities as to why the nominal wage rate may be sticky like this, including:

1. **Contracts**. Long-lasting employment contracts fix the nominal wage at the agreed rate, preventing it from adjusting freely. This is the basis of our sticky wage model in Section 10.2.

2. **Unions**. Trade unions, seeking to secure the best possible employment terms for their members, can cause the nominal wage to be rigid. They can exert their power of industrial action – such as inducing their members to work to rule or even to stop work altogether – to ensure producers aren't able to reduce the nominal wage rate below a certain level.

3. **Efficiency wages**. Rather than the nominal wage rate being sticky because of the influence of workers or their unions, this explanation suggests they're sticky because of the influence of employers. Worker motivation

and productivity is a positive function of the nominal wage rate – as the wage rate increases, labour productivity rises – and so it's actually beneficial for employers to pay their workers more than the minimum they would work for because the supplement induces them to work harder. It's possible to calculate the optimal supplement to pay, equating the marginal cost of the extra wages to the marginal benefit of the additional productivity. This is the theory of efficiency wages.

④ **Minimum wages**. Finally, the stickiness may originate from the government. If the government judges W^* to be too low for some reason, it can impose a legally binding minimum rate beneath which the nominal wage cannot fall (a price floor: see Section 8.2).

The classical model of unemployment places the blame for involuntary unemployment on labour market rigidities such as these, and asserts the need to dispense with lengthy contracts, unions and minimum wages to enable the market to function freely.

For John Maynard Keynes (see Section 14.6) the classical model did not reflect the economy he saw around him. In the Great Depression of the 1930s there were long queues of people seeking work but unable to secure positions. Many of Keynes's contemporaries drew on the classical model and attributed these queues to the nominal wage rate being too high. All that was needed, they argued, was for the nominal wage rate to be reduced and the labour market would clear, eliminating involuntary unemployment entirely. However, the nominal wage rate fell but the queues only got longer.

Keynes argued that the problem wasn't the nominal wage rate being too high: the problem was a lack of aggregate demand in the economy. Consider again Figure 10.5, which illustrates his argument nicely. He believed that the economy had been struck by a large negative demand shock. The Wall Street Crash of October 1929 had sparked a series of events that culminated in causing the British aggregate demand curve to shift inwards from AD_1 to AD_2 and a large recessionary gap to open up. As aggregate demand fell, producers cut their output – many of them shutting down altogether – and drastically reduced the amount of workers they employed. The price level and the nominal wage rate fell, but the short run aggregate supply curve didn't shift outwards to the right as our analysis on page 95 suggests it would – it was stuck at $SRAS_1$. This is where Keynes would have disagreed with our analysis above. He would have argued that economic output doesn't only deviate from the natural level because of the effects of a sticky nominal wage: it's also possible for the economy to get stuck in a situation of low aggregate demand and supply, and low nominal wages if producers don't believe that aggregate demand is high enough for any additional output they make to be consumed. This is what he claimed had happened in the 1930s. As such, reducing the nominal wage rate further would only worsen the problem: it would mean those lucky enough to have work would receive lower incomes and so would reduce their demand for products, causing aggregate demand to fall further and unemployment to rise even more. Instead, he argued the solution was for the government to spend more and increase aggregate demand itself. This would cause the aggregate demand curve to shift back out-wards to the right towards AD_1, and output and employment to increase.

A similar story can be told about the recent global financial crisis. The fail-ure of the sub-prime mortgage market in America in 2007 sparked a series of events that led to many developed economies being hit by large negative aggre-gate demand shocks, causing aggregate demand to fall and unemployment to rise in these economies. Having learned the lessons of the Great Depression, many governments injected large sums of money into their economies to stim-ulate aggregate demand and to start the recovery. Such action reduced some of the negative effects of the recession, but these economies now find themselves burdened by incredibly large debts. Many governments are now actively trying to reduce these debts by cutting spending and increasing taxation, but the dan-ger is that if they do so too quickly they might reduce aggregate demand too far, thereby worsening the recession.

the natural rate of unemployment

We saw above that the natural level of output is the amount the economy pro-duces if it uses all its factors of production, and is the amount to which it tends in the long run. By 'all its factors of production' we mean it uses all those who want to work, and not necessarily all those able to work: there can be volun-tary unemployment at the natural level of output.

The **natural rate of unemployment** is an important related concept. It's the average rate of involuntary unemployment around which the actual rate fluc-tuates, and can be considered as the steady-state rate to which the economy tends in the long run. The reason any involuntary unemployment exists in the long run is because there's always **frictional unemployment**.

Key term: frictional unemployment

It isn't possible to eliminate involuntary unemployment entirely because there will always be individuals moving between jobs, even when the economy is producing its natural level of output. It's often the case that when an individual leaves one producer and needs to find alternative employment, there's a period of time in between when s/he's involuntary unemployed: s/he doesn't find another job instantaneously even if the labour market is perfectly flexible. This type of unemployment is known as **frictional unemployment**.

Consider the following model of the natural rate of unemployment by Hall, which is outlined in Gregory Mankiw's excellent textbook *Macroeco-nomics* (see Chapter 15). In any one month there's a proportion of the work-force made unemployed but also a proportion of the unemployed who secure employment. Let's denote the first of these by s, the rate of job separation, and the second by f, the rate of job finding. Let's further denote the total labour force by L, the number of individuals in the labour force who are currently employed by E, and the remaining individuals, who are unemployed, by U. It's necessarily the case that $L = U + E$ and the rate of unemployment is U/L.

If the economy is at its natural rate of unemployment, its labour market and so its rate of unemployment must be stable. In other words, at the natural rate of unemployment the number of individuals being made unemployed must be perfectly offset by a corresponding number of individuals moving into employment having been unemployed. Mathematically, then, the natural rate of unemployment implies that $fU = sE$. Using this we can derive an expression for the natural rate of unemployment by working through a number of steps.

Step 1: Start with the condition for the natural rate of unemployment:

$$fU = sE \qquad\qquad\qquad \text{(Equation 11.1)}$$

Step 2: Substitute into it the expression for the number employed:

$$fU = s(L - U) \qquad\qquad\qquad \text{(Equation 11.2)}$$

Step 3: Multiply out the terms in brackets:

$$fU = sL - sU \qquad\qquad\qquad \text{(Equation 11.3)}$$

Step 4: Divide through by the total labour force to obtain the unemployment rate (the amount unemployed as a proportion of the workforce):

$$f\frac{U}{L} = s - s\frac{U}{L} \qquad\qquad\qquad \text{(Equation 11.4)}$$

Step 5: Rearrange and simplify:

$$\frac{U}{L}(f + s) = s \qquad\qquad\qquad \text{(Equation 11.5)}$$

Step 6: Rearrange to derive an expression for U^*, the natural rate of unemployment:

$$U^* = \frac{s}{s + f} \qquad\qquad\qquad \text{(Equation 11.6)}$$

We see from the expression in Equation 11.6 that the natural rate of unemployment is entirely dependent on the rates of job separation and job finding. For example, if 5 per cent of the employed workforce lose their jobs each month ($s = 0.05$) and 15 per cent of those unemployed secure new jobs each month ($f = 0.15$), the natural rate of unemployment is 25 per cent of the labour force. This shows us the natural rate of unemployment is a measure of the amount of frictional unemployment in the economy. In fact, in the long run, when the economy is producing its natural level of output, all involuntary unemployment is frictional. If the government is to reduce this natural rate, it needs to reduce frictional unemployment by either reducing the rate of job separation or increasing the rate of job finding – or both.

One way of increasing the rate of job finding is to reduce **geographical** and **occupational immobility** in the economy. Geographical immobility refers to the situation in which a person is looking for work and is suitable for existing vacancies but is unable to take up a new job because s/he isn't able to change where s/he lives. This could be for a whole host of family, informational and practical reasons. The government can address the second and third of these by providing information about jobs across the whole economy and by establishing schemes such as that in which it buys a person's house – which it then sells on – enabling the initial homeowner to move more quickly and easily. Occupational immobility refers to the situation in which people are looking for work but are unable to change the industry in which they work. This can also be addressed through information provision, but also through the provision of training programmes that give the unemployed the skills they need to take up jobs in a range of different industries.

hysteresis

The final aspect of unemployment that we should examine is that of **hysteresis**. This refers to the situation in which the labour market fails to return to its original position after a shock. To analyse this aspect we need to introduce one final type of unemployment: **structural unemployment**.

Key term: structural unemployment

This is perhaps the most concerning and problematic type of unemployment because of its potentially long-term nature. Structural unemployment is caused by the contraction or expiration of a whole industry. Consider, for example, those who worked in the shipbuilding industry of Northern Ireland. With **de-industrialisation** they found their industry shrinking and, as it did so, they lost their jobs. Effectively, the entire workforce of an industry wasn't only jobless but, possessing no other skills than those required for building ships, completely without any prospects to find alternative employment. Without government help, those made structurally unemployed face an almost impossible task of securing further employment because they're unable to participate in the economy. Other examples are those of coal-miners in South Wales and, more recently, car manufacturers in the Midlands of England.

Unemployment becomes increasingly serious the more it's prolonged, for three reasons:

1. **Stigma**. Producers are reluctant to employ people who have been unemployed for a long time. The fact that someone has been in prolonged unemployment increases the perceived risk of hiring them: what negative characteristic have all other employers seen in them in the past?

② **Skill atrophy.** As the period of time in which an individual is jobless increases, the more their employment skills are likely to diminish. This is known as skill atrophy. The long-term unemployed, then, tend to be less employable, irrespective of any preconceptions on the part of producers.

③ **Psychological effects.** The more rejections an individual receives from producers, the less effort they're likely to put into further applications, as they become increasingly demotivated.

When considered together, these three factors point to the conclusion that the likelihood of attaining employment declines the longer an individual is out of work. The structurally unemployed are likely to be affected by all three of these influences and so can easily find themselves long-term unemployed.

Let's now turn to the notion of unemployment hysteresis. Consider Figure 11.4, which looks far more complicated than it actually is. Initially the economy has a supply of, and demand for, labour of S_{L1} and D_{L1} respectively. The labour market clears at point A, which is at the natural rate of unemployment (E^{*1}) and a nominal wage rate of W_1. For whatever reason, suppose there's now an adverse demand shock, causing a reduction in the demand for labour shown by a shift in the demand for labour curve to D_{L2}. Let's assume the nominal wage rate is sticky and so remains at W_1 for a time. The economy moves to point C and involuntary unemployment opens up to the extent of $E^{*1} - E_2$. The nominal wage rate begins to decline, eventually clearing the market at point B, with a lower level of employment (E^{*2}) and a lower wage rate (W_2).

So far this analysis is the same as that of the classical model above. However, the hysteresis model suggests that if those who lose their jobs initially, those between E^{*1} and E_2, are unemployed for a long time – in other words, if the market clearing process is slow – they become increasingly unemployable for the three reasons above. In effect they become detached from the labour market. This causes the supply of labour to shift inwards from S_{L1} to S_{L2} : the difference being those who have become detached from the labour force and so are effectively no longer part of the labour force, which we denote by DU.

The effect of this is that when the demand for labour recovers, moving back to D_{L1}, the economy is now in the situation in which there's a lower supply of workers. The market-clearing equilibrium is now point D rather than point A. The natural rate of unemployment has increased, the long run level of employment is now E^{*2} and the equilibrium nominal wage rate has increased to W_3. The detached workers are no longer able to participate in the labour market: an amount of unemployment that the market cannot absorb on its own. The economy hasn't returned to its initial state after a shock: this is hysteresis.

As the market is incapable of absorbing the long-term and structurally unemployed, it's the responsibility of the government to do so through supply

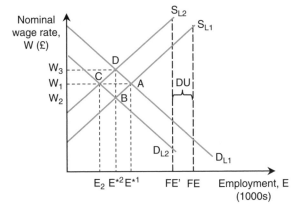

Figure 11.4 Unemployment hysteresis

side policies. These are policies such as the provision of training courses and employment advice that aim to make the unemployed employable once more.

BOX 11.1: **Labour economics**

John Sessions, University of Bath

Labour economics addresses the operation and dynamics of the market for labour. Labour markets function through the interaction of buyers of labour (i.e. employers) and sellers of labour (i.e. employees), and labour economics considers how the behaviour of these two groups impacts upon wages, employment and income. Labour economics therefore embraces a considerable range of phenomena and provides insights into economic and social issues of the utmost importance. It covers topics such as the causes and effects of wage rates, employment, unemployment, labour costs, the number of hours workers supply per week, how hard the work is, hiring and firing, workplace injuries, minimum wages, decisions by individuals as to whether or not they should participate in the labour market, trade unions, strikes, the impact of mandatory contributions, retirement, education and training.

Labour is a factor of production and shares some traits with other factors such as land and capital. It is, however, innately human and thus it is unique in being driven by its own internal utility function – employers need to obtain both the *presence* and *cooperation* of labour in order to create output. And unlike other factors, an excess supply of labour is directly, and often hugely, damaging to human lives.

An excellent introductory labour economics text is:

> C. McConnell, C., S. Brue and D. MacPherson, *Contemporary Labor Economics* (New York: McGraw-Hill, 2007).
> A more advanced text is:

> P. Cahuc and A. Zylberberg, *Labor Economics* (Cambridge, MA: MIT Press, 2008).

11.2 money

Having used the aggregate demand and supply model to examine unemployment, we now use it to examine the second economy-wide cause for concern and focus of economic policy: **inflation**. However, to do this inevitably requires us to understand what money is, and so it's to that we turn first.

money and the money supply

> ## Key term: money
>
> Money is an asset that fulfils three main functions in the economy:
>
> (1) **A medium of exchange**. The primary function of money is to make transactions quick and easy by enabling the value of all products to be measured using a common scale – the number of euros, for instance – and by providing an asset for which they can be exchanged, thereby overcoming the **double coincidence of wants** problem (see Box 11.2).
> (2) **A store of value**. The second function of money is to be an asset in which actors can hold their wealth for buying products in the future: to enable them to inter-temporally reallocate their purchasing power.
> (3) **A unit of account**. The third function of money is to provide a common measurement in which wages, costs, revenues, profit and value can all be measured and compared. This is vital for actors to be able to make economic decisions.

> BOX 11.2: A brief and descriptive history of money
>
> **Stage one: bartering societies**
> Economies in the past were based on **barter**, where one product was directly exchanged for another. But there were two big problems with this system:
>
> **1** The need for a **double coincidence of wants**. Imagine a horse breeder in a barter-based society who wanted a skin of milk. With trade by barter, he had to find a dairy farmer who wanted horses and was willing to exchange milk to obtain them. If this wasn't possible because the dairy farmer had no need for horses, but had a dire thirst for ale, the horse breeder would then have had to find a brewer willing to exchange ale for horses, so that he could then exchange ale for milk with the dairy farmer. If this wasn't possible because the brewer didn't want horses either, but desperately needed new barrels, the dairy farmer would then have had to find a cooper who would exchange barrels for horses, so that he could then exchange barrels for ale with the brewer, and then complete his intended trade with the dairy farmer. If this wasn't possible because the cooper... and so the process could have continued. This is the double coincidence of wants problem: a time-consuming problem that caused trade to be difficult, if not impossible.
>
> **2** **Indivisibility**. However, even if the dairy farmer wanted horses and so trade was immediately possible, how much 'horse' would have been needed for the

milk? Unless the volume of milk had been particularly large, a whole horse would probably have been too much, but 'chopping' a piece off the horse to pay for the milk would have caused the value of the animal to fall to that simply of meat. This was the indivisibility problem, which also made trade by barter difficult, if not impossible.

Stage two: intermediate goods

These two problems eventually led societies to use intermediate goods as a primitive form of money. Different communities employed different goods in this role: precious metals, jewels and even salt were all used (Roman soldiers were often paid in salt). Using items such as these overcame the double coincidence of wants problem because anything could be exchanged for the intermediate good in the knowledge that it could then be used in exchange for something else. In the case above, the horse breeder could give the dairy farmer a certain amount of the intermediate good in exchange for milk and the dairy farmer could in turn use it to purchase the ale he craved. However, using intermediate goods had its own problems.

(a) Scarcity. The intermediate good had to be scarce if it was to be an effective medium of exchange. For example, sand couldn't have been used by a tropical island community because if ever someone had wanted something he would merely have had to make a trip to the beach, scoop up some sand and use it in the exchange. The recipient, knowing there was an endless supply of sand within walking distance would obviously have refused the trade because he could keep hold of the item in question and make his own trip to the beach to obtain the sand.

(b) Divisibility. The intermediate good needed to be characterised by forms of different values if it was to overcome the indivisibility problem. For example, if a certain type of jewel was to be used it needed to be available in different sizes or qualities so that it could be used for different valued exchanges: if it was available in just one value, indivisibility would again be a problem.

(c) Quality assurance. There needed to be an easy and effective way of assessing the quality of the intermediate good. Most – if not all – intermediate goods came in varying qualities, and so if it was left to personal judgement as to whether it was of good enough quality it would have been ineffective as a medium of exchange because buyers and sellers would have disagreed about its quality.

Stage three: valuable coins

To overcome these three problems, societies began to manufacture items specifically for use in trade: coins. These were usually, but not always, manufactured from precious metals – in his famous *Travels*, Marco Polo observed that in parts of Kublai Khan's Mongol Empire coins were made from salt – and were often of different denominations in order to overcome the indivisibility problem. They were also usually engraved with the seal or likeness of the ruler: an official mark of authenticity and trust that overcame the quality assurance problem and ensured the supply of money was controlled by the authorities. These coins were valuable in their own right: isolated communities in Kublai Khan's empire wouldn't just use their coins as money but also as an essential cooking ingredient! Coins overcame all the problems that had arisen with previous forms of money, but suffered from their own problem: the inconvenient necessity for people to store and carry volumes of coins.

Stage four: fiat money

In response to the inconvenience of valuable coins, the wealthy deposited their money in banks in exchange for receipts that proved their ownership. Perhaps inevitably, they began to use these receipts in their transactions: transferring the ownership of the money rather than the money itself. With this, paper money came into use: something that Marco Polo observed had happened in China long before Europeans had conceived the idea. By being exchangeable for valuable material, this money still possessed innate value. A British pound sterling, for example, is so called because it was possible to exchange a unit of it for a pound in weight of sterling silver. Money maintained this characteristic until well into the twentieth century: the United Kingdom was on the **Gold Standard** until the outbreak of the First World War – and then again for a disastrous period in the interwar period – meaning that every British pound was supported by a certain amount of gold within the UK economy. Since the Second World War such ties to valuable materials have been dispensed with, although for a time the currencies of developed economies were pegged to the United States dollar in the **Bretton Woods financial system**. Modern money no longer has innate value and its use as a medium of exchange, store of value and unit of account is solely based on trust: hence the name fiat money. Usually such money functions perfectly well, but when the trust fails there are severe consequences.

Stage five: modern developments

The final stage in this brief description of the development of money was the creation of credit and the introduction of electronic transfers. It is now no longer necessary for people to physically exchange money in transactions, or indeed even to possess sufficient money to cover that required. In value terms, by far the most money transacted is now done so electronically – simply the transfer of digits from one account into another with the trading parties never actually seeing any money – and the widespread use of credit cards allows people to make transactions based on the expectation of being able to pay for them at a later date. These modern developments enable more transactions to be completed and at greater speed than previously, enhancing the ability of economies to grow. However, they bring with them greater dangers. For example, with widespread bank lending, banks only hold a fraction of the total value of their deposits (this fraction is determined by law and is called the **reservation ratio**). As long as trust in the financial sector remains strong, this is a beneficial way of running the sector as it allows the money to be used more widely, thereby generating greater wealth; but when it fails, as it did in East Asia in the early 1990s, banks can be forced to shut down as depositors try to withdraw their funds that the banks simply don't possess. The failure of a single bank can rapidly turn into a string of banking collapses as fear spreads through the population. Countries across East Asia witnessed their financial sectors collapse, which in turn led to widespread bankruptcy, unemployment and a prolonged and severe recession. It was in order to safeguard against this eventuality that the Bank of England prevented the closure of Northern Rock in 2007. Such concerns about the potential dangers of modern money are the ongoing focus of many financial economists.

The **money supply** simply refers to the quantity of money available for actors in the economy to use as they see fit. It's the amount of money flowing round an economy's circular flow of income (see Section 9.1). This supply is usually controlled by an economy's central bank. In the UK it's the Monetary Policy Committee of the Bank of England that controls the supply of pounds sterling, whilst across the Atlantic the Federal Open Market Committee of the Federal Reserve controls the supply of US dollars. Very simply put, committees such as these primarily control their respective money supplies through **open market operations**: the buying and selling of government bonds, which are effectively investments in the government for a specified return. For example, if the Monetary Policy Committee of the Bank of England wants to reduce the supply of sterling it sells government bonds to the public, thereby removing the amount they're sold for from the economy. Conversely, if it wants to expand the UK's money supply it repurchases bonds currently held by the public, thereby injecting sterling into the system.

models of monetary effects

Having looked at what money is and how its supply is generally controlled, we can now move on to analyse how the money supply affects the economy: a question that has been discussed at the very least since the time of the medieval scholars (see Section 13.2).

The classical economists, particularly David Ricardo (see Section 14.2) and Karl Marx (see Section 14.4) promoted a **commodity theory of money**. During their lives money was effectively composed of gold, silver and other precious metals, and so these thinkers argued that the value of money was determined primarily through the cost of its production, or in this case its extraction. Accordingly, the value of money was neutral, meaning it didn't have any real, physical effects: its supply didn't affect the actual amount of output produced. It was just the same as any other commodity.

Such a commodity theory of money is the true classical theory of money. Unfortunately, and somewhat confusingly, John Maynard Keynes (see Section 14.6) referred to the theory subsequently developed by the neoclassical economists as the classical theory of money, a term that has continued to be used in textbooks and academic courses. The neoclassical theory was developed by Simon Newcomb (1885) and Irving Fisher (1911), although it had been proposed in the eighteenth century by the philosopher, historian and social commentator David Hume. It takes the form of the **equation of exchange**, which relates the money supply (M^s), the transactions velocity of money (V), the price level (P) and the number of transactions in the economy (T) in the way expressed as Equation 11.7.

$$M^s \times V = P \times T \qquad \text{(Equation 11.7)}$$

The equation of exchange is actually tautological, meaning it's true by definition. This is because the transactions velocity of money is defined as

Equation 11.8, which says it's the average number of transactions that each unit of money is used for. For example, if the price level is £10, there are 100,000 transactions made in the economy and the money supply is equal to £100,000, each pound sterling must on average be used for ten transactions.

$$V = \frac{P \times T}{M^s} \qquad \text{(Equation 11.8)}$$

Economists often use the slightly different version of the equation of exchange shown by Equation 11.9. The number of transactions is replaced by the total output of the economy. These two variables aren't identical, but are closely related: the more output there is, the more transactions there must be if it's to be consumed. In both versions it's assumed the only purpose of money is to be a medium of exchange: there's no other motive for holding money.

$$M^s \times V = P \times Y \qquad \text{(Equation 11.9)}$$

To make the equation of exchange into a theory of money supply effects we need to introduce two assumptions. First, the velocity of money is approximately constant. Secondly, there's **money neutrality**, meaning changes in the money supply don't affect actual output. The classical economists viewed the economy as having two parts – the real economy in which the level of output is determined, and the money economy in which the price level and the rate of interest are determined – and thought one didn't affect the other. This is known as the **classical dichotomy** and is the same as money neutrality: an assumption the neoclassical economists maintained. With these assumptions the equation of exchange becomes the **quantity theory of money** of Equation 11.10, in which a bar above a variable denotes that it's fixed.

$$M^s \times \overline{V} = P \times \overline{Y} \qquad \text{(Equation 11.10)}$$

The quantity theory of money simply asserts that any change of the money supply causes a proportionally equal change in the general price level. The implication of this is that the monetary authorities can control the price level – and so the rate of inflation – by controlling the money supply. Irving Fisher accepted that this is only a long run theory because the assumption of money neutrality doesn't necessarily hold in the short run: he wasn't as strict about the classical dichotomy as David Hume had been.

A way of understanding the quantity theory of money is to think about buying shoes for a growing child. When the child is small, you buy him a small pair of shoes. As he grows, you buy larger and larger pairs. If you buy the child a pair that's too small, it hurts his feet and prevents him from growing properly. If you buy him a pair that's too big, he finds it difficult to walk in them and may hurt himself. You need to increase the size of his shoes at the same rate at which his feet grow. Precisely the same is true of the economy and its money supply according to the quantity theory. The economy's output is determined by the amounts of the factors of production available and the existing technology that's reflected in the production function. Over time, this output grows as technology improves and so the economy can produce more output from its available resources. It's vitally important that the money supply is increased at the correct speed. Not increasing it enough causes the price level to fall: from Equation 11.10 we see that, if output increases more than the money supply, the price level or the velocity of money must fall, which restricts the economy's growth. However, we also see from Equation 11.10 that increasing the money supply too fast causes the price level to rise – inflation – which causes the value of money to fall and its effectiveness as a medium of exchange, store of value and unit of account to be compromised. The authorities need to increase the money supply at the same rate at which the economy grows.

Economists at the University of Cambridge in the early part of the twentieth century – particularly Alfred Marshall (see Section 14.5), Arthur Pigou and John Maynard Keynes (see Section 14.6) – took a slightly different approach by focusing on the demand for money (M^d) rather than its supply. The **Cambridge equation**, as it has become known, is shown in Equation 11.11, and rearranged to show the demand for real money in Equation 11.12. It's based on the very different assumption that money isn't just used as a medium of exchange: it's also a store of value. In other words, these economists argued that not all income is spent on consumption: a proportion, k, is demanded so that it can be held onto. In 1917 Pigou also introduced the precautionary motive for demanding money.

$$M^d = k \times P \times Y \qquad \text{(Equation 11.11)}$$

$$\left(\frac{M}{P}\right)^d = k \times Y \qquad \text{(Equation 11.12)}$$

The Cambridge economists maintained that the proportion of income people hold onto rather than spend (k) cannot be assumed to be constant: it's determined by the interest rate and the level of wealth. They also argued that uncertainty and confidence can affect this proportion too, and so, if real money demand remains constant, can lead to fluctuations in the total level of output in the economy. These fluctuations are only short-lived, though, because the classical dichotomy and money neutrality hold in the long run.

Keynes went further than this, arguing that the classical dichotomy doesn't hold at all. In his analysis, changes in either real money supply or demand cause changes in the output level via changes in the interest rate. We see this in the IS-LM analysis of Section 9.5.

11.3 inflation

the costs of inflation

Changes in the price level characterise every economy at all times. Usually, when the price level is increasing at say 2 per cent a year, inflation isn't much of a problem at all. In fact, low and stable inflation is taken to be characteristic of a healthy economy as it suggests that aggregate demand is expanding; and it's certainly preferable to the danger of deflation, which Keynes thought is much more dangerous than inflation because deflation causes the economy to be in a vicious contractionary cycle. A lack of aggregate demand causes producers to cut their prices, causing deflation, but unless the level of output demanded increases this causes the revenues of producers to fall and so they either reduce the sizes of their workforces or reduce the wages they pay, leading to a further contraction in aggregate demand, further deflation, and so on.

BOX 11.3: **Inflation and interest rates**

The interest rate is effectively the price of holding onto money as cash rather than saving it. A high interest rate means holding money as cash is costly because it could earn a high financial return if it was saved: a return that's forgone by holding onto it. We examined how the interest rate is determined, and the difference between the classical and Keynesian view of this, in Chapter 9. This analysis fails to distinguish between the two types of interest rate, though. That reported by financial institutions is actually the **nominal interest rate**. For example, if you save £1000 in a bank account offering an annual interest rate of 10 per cent you earn £100 in interest and at the end of the year have £1100. However, this says nothing about what happens to your purchasing power. If the annual inflation rate is 8 per cent, the price level increases by 8 per cent by the end of the year and so the increase in your purchasing power is approximately only 2 per cent. The difference between the nominal interest rate (i) and the inflation rate ($\dot{P}$) is, for small changes in the variables, approximately the **real interest rate** (r) shown in Equation B11.3.1.

$$r = i - \dot{P}$$ (Equation B11.3.1)

Rearranging this expression gives the **Fisher equation** shown in Equation B11.3.2.

$$i = r + \dot{P} \qquad \text{(Equation B11.3.2)}$$

This shows that changes in the nominal interest rate can be caused by changes in either the real interest rate or the inflation rate.

Let's also express the **quantity theory of money** (Equation 11.10) in percentage change form, as in Equation B11.3.3. With the assumptions of constant velocity and money neutrality – which mean the percentage changes of both velocity and output are zero – this shows there's a one-to-one relation between the percentage change in the money supply and the change in the inflation rate, as shown in Equation B11.3.4.

$$\% \Delta M^s + \% \Delta V = \% \Delta P + \% \Delta Y \qquad \text{(Equation B11.3.3)}$$

$$\% \Delta M^s = \% \Delta P \qquad \text{(Equation B11.3.4)}$$

The quantity theory of money says a 1 per cent increase in the money supply causes a 1 per cent increase in the rate of inflation. The Fisher equation says that a 1 per cent increase in the inflation rate causes a 1 per cent increase in the nominal interest rate. Together, then, there's a one-to-one relationship between the inflation rate and the nominal interest rate. This is known as the **Fisher effect**.

There are costs of inflation, which largely depend upon whether the inflation is expected or not. Inflation that's expected and so can be planned for imposes three costs on the economy:

1. **Shoe-leather costs**. Box 11.3 shows the positive, even one-to-one, relationship between the inflation rate and the nominal interest rate. This means that a higher inflation rate leads to a higher nominal interest rate, which increases the return actors receive from saving their money in banks. With high inflation, then, actors want to save their money in a bank for longer and so instead of taking £500 out of the bank at the start of a month they may decide to withdraw £125 each week. High inflation leads to more frequent trips to the bank, costing individuals in terms of time and effort: it wears out their shoe-leather.

2. **Menu costs**. A higher inflation rate means producers have to update the prices they charge more frequently to maintain their profit margins. The costs of this – of printing new price lists and catalogues – are known as menu costs.

3. **Inefficiency of unstable relative prices**. The microeconomic theory of consumption is based on consumers making their consumption decisions by reference to relative prices: it is relative prices that determine the slopes

of budget lines (see Section 5.2). In a situation of high inflation, producers simply cannot keep their price lists continually up to date and so relative prices of products continually change. A product that's relatively expensive compared with the general price level at the start of the period has its relative price cut as the price level rises. This makes it more costly to ensure consumption and production decisions are optimal, reducing the efficiency of the economy.

Inflation that isn't expected is perhaps more serious because it surreptitiously causes redistribution of wealth amongst individuals. There are two primary examples of this:

1 **Between lenders and borrowers**. A loan is usually made on the condition that a specified amount of interest is paid by the borrower, depending on the time it takes for him to repay his debt. This amount of interest is specified in the form of a nominal interest rate, but as we see in Box 11.3 there's a difference between the nominal interest rate and the real interest rate, and it's the real interest rate that's of most concern to the lender and borrower. The inflation rate is approximately the difference between the nominal and real interest rates and so an unexpectedly high inflation rate means the borrower actually pays backs less in real terms than was expected at the time the loan was arranged. Consider, for example, an individual who borrows £1000 from a colleague at work. At the time of the deal the inflation rate is 2 per cent and the Monetary Policy Committee at the Bank of England shows no signs that it will change. Based on this expectation, the loan is agreed on the condition that a 10 per cent nominal interest rate is paid. This means that at the end of the period the borrower is expected to pay back £1100, which means the lender earns approximately an 8 per cent increase in the purchasing power of his £1000. However, during the period the inflation rate unexpectedly increases to 10 per cent. The borrower repays his debt in full, paying £1100 to his colleague, but the £100 earned by the lender is now actually needed to simply maintain his purchasing power: he earns absolutely nothing in real terms. This is an extreme example, but it effectively illustrates the point that unexpected inflation benefits the borrower and hurts the lender.

This example illustrates another way of categorising interest rates: not according to whether they're real or nominal, but according to their expected and realised values. An interest rate specified before an event has occurred is known as the **ex ante** interest rate and is based on what the individuals involved expect to happen during the period in which the event is to occur. The interest rate actually realised after the event is known as the **ex post** interest rate. In the example above, the ex ante real interest rate was approximately 8 per cent whereas the ex post real interest rate was approximately zero.

❷ Harming those with fixed nominal incomes, such as pensioners. Consider a retired individual who receives a fixed nominal income from his pension each month or a disabled individual in receipt of a fixed nominal monthly income from the welfare state. Suppose their incomes have been fixed at £500 per month. Any increase in the inflation rate causes their purchasing power to fall: their nominal incomes remain constant but the prices of the products they buy rise.

All these costs – both of expected and unexpected inflation – become extremely serious when there's **hyperinflation**: an inflation rate in excess of 50 per cent per month, which is more than a hundredfold increase in the price level in the course of a year. Germany experienced such hyperinflation in the 1920s. At the Treaty of Versailles, which marked the end of the First World War, the Allies forced Germany to commit itself to paying them a vast sum of reparations over a number of years. Germany effectively financed its repayments in the early 1920s by printing money, an action known as **seigniorage**. Inflation quickly rose from approximately 10 per cent per month at the start of 1922 to in excess of 10,000 per cent in 1923. There are anecdotes of people having to use wheelbarrows to carry their paper money into towns to buy their groceries, and of thieves tipping the money out and running off with the barrows! Waiters in restaurants and cafés stood on tables, announcing the prices every half an hour because they were changing so quickly. Drinkers in pubs bought all five pints they expected to drink that evening as soon as they took their places at the bar because that was cheaper than buying them as the evening progressed: the sacrifice of warm beer was more than worth it.

the causes of inflation and the policies for solving it

There are two general causes of inflation – **cost-push** and **demand-pull** inflation – which can be examined using our aggregate demand and supply model of Chapter 10. It must be borne in mind when doing this, though, that the aggregate demand and supply model shows changes of the price level rather than changes of the inflation rate, the latter being the rate of change of the former. A change in the price level in this model, then, should be interpreted as a temporary change in the inflation rate to establish the new price level. Second year undergraduate work generally requires you to use the DAD-SAS model, which is a version of the aggregate demand and supply model that looks specifically at inflation.

Let's first examine cost-push inflation by considering Figure 11.5. Suppose the economy is initially at point A, at which it's producing its natural level of output (Y^*) and so is on its long run aggregate supply curve. The economy is in a steady state position as short run aggregate supply is equal to aggregate demand and so there's no pressure on the economy to move from this point. Suppose now the economy experiences a temporary negative supply shock, possibly an increase in the global price of oil. This causes production costs to rise, shifting the short run aggregate supply curve inwards from SRAS$_1$ to SRAS$_2$, and causing the economy to move up the aggregate demand curve to point B. The price level rises from P$_1$ to P$_2$ – representing an increase in inflation – and there's a reduction in output from Y* to Y$_1$. A recessionary gap opens up, denoted by RG.

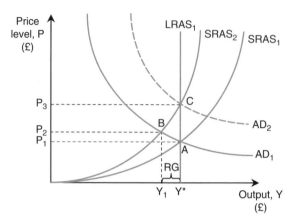

Figure 11.5 Cost-push inflation and monetary accommodation

The extent of the inflationary increase caused by the supply side shock depends on the response of the government: of which there are two possibilities.

❶ **Allow the economy to correct itself.** The price level has increased and so there's initially upward pressure on the nominal wage rate (as in our analysis in Section 10.2), but the unemployment caused by the recessionary gap eventually asserts a stronger downward pressure on the nominal wage rate – the unemployed offer themselves for work at lower nominal wage rates – causing production costs to fall and the short run aggregate supply curve to shift outwards again to SRAS$_1$. The economy slowly returns to its long run steady state at point A. The problem with this is it can be a slow process, during which the unemployment causes the population to suffer, provoking political unrest.

❷ **Monetary accommodation.** To avoid the suffering and political unrest of allowing the economy to correct itself, the government is inevitably tempted to eliminate the recessionary gap more quickly. It can do this through **monetary accommodation**: increasing the money supply in response to the increased costs. As we see in our analysis of the complete aggregate demand and supply model in Section 10.3, expanding the money supply causes the aggregate demand curve to shift outwards from AD$_1$ to AD$_2$, moving the economy to the long run steady state at point C. The recessionary gap is eliminated and the economy is restored to its natural level of output more quickly, but at the expense of further inflation: the price level increases further to P$_3$.

This analysis has been for a single supply shock, but the economy can also be subject to repeated shocks. By accommodating these shocks the government creates an inflationary spiral in which the price level increases rapidly. The only way of halting the spiral is to choose not to accommodate a shock and to allow the economy to correct itself, albeit to a higher steady-state price level than that which existed initially: to go 'cold turkey'.

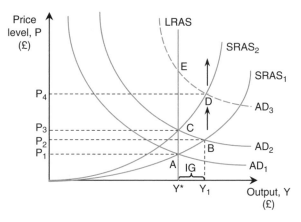

Figure 11.6 Demand-pull inflation and monetary validation

Let's now consider Figure 11.6, which represents demand-pull inflation. Suppose the economy is initially at point A again, producing its natural level of output (Y^*), where short run aggregate supply is equal to aggregate demand. Now suppose there's a positive demand shock: perhaps a sudden and significant escalation of government spending to fund unexpected military operations abroad. This causes aggregate demand to increase, shifting the aggregate demand curve from AD_1 to AD_2. The economy moves to point B, the price level increases from P_1 to P_2 – inflation – and output expands from Y^* to Y_1, opening up an inflationary gap (IG).

Once again, the extent of the inflationary increase depends on the government's response: and there are again two possibilities:

❶ Allow the economy to correct itself. The government can stand back and do nothing, causing the economy to eventually move from point B to point C: the increased price level gradually causes the costs of producers to rise, shifting the short run aggregate supply curve from $SRAS_1$ to $SRAS_2$. The inflationary gap closes and the price level increases to P_3. However, this process necessarily involves a contraction of output and so the government is inevitably tempted to maintain the inflationary gap – an economy that produces a high level of output is politically popular, whereas any contraction in output is politically damaging to the government.

❷ Monetary validation. The government can try to maintain the inflationary gap by expanding the money supply: when the money supply is expanded in response to an inflationary gap it's called **monetary validation** rather than accommodation. As we see above, such validation shifts the aggregate demand curve further to the right, to AD_3, moving the economy to point D instead of to point C. This increases the price level once again, to P_4: a further spurt of inflation. At point D the government is faced with the same decision again: does it allow the economy to correct itself through a movement to point E, or does it employ further monetary validation? Very easily – and quickly – the economy can find itself in an inflationary spiral, with each subsequent monetary validation causing the price level to increase at an increasing rate. Such a spiral can only be broken by the government resisting the temptation to further validate the shock, allowing the economy to correct itself.

In the 1970s Milton Friedman (see Section 14.9) famously said inflation is 'always and everywhere a monetary phenomenon'. By this he meant it's fuelled only by the government expanding the money supply too quickly. Remember our illustration of the quantity theory of money in Section 11.2 – which Friedman was resurrecting by saying this – of buying shoes for a child: expanding the money supply too quickly compared with the rate at which the economy is growing inevitably causes inflation. Friedman wasn't saying that inflation is only caused by the government expanding the money supply too quickly: the analysis above shows that inflation can be initially caused by both supply and demand shocks. Rather, he was saying that inflation is only sustained if it's either accommodated or validated by expansionary monetary policy. If the economy is allowed to correct itself, the inflation initially caused by a demand or supply shock will be relatively short lived. The problem is that 'relatively short lived' can actually be a long and painful period.

11.4 inflation, unemployment and expectations

In 1958, William Phillips, a professor at the London School of Economics, discovered a remarkably uniform, negative relationship between the rate of wage inflation and the rate of unemployment in the UK over a period of a hundred years – a relationship illustrated in Figure 11.7a. In the 1960s Robert Solow and Paul Samuelson showed the relationship to hold more generally between the rates of inflation and unemployment, which led to the conventional **Phillips curve** displayed in Figure 11.7b.

Key term: the Phillips curve

The Phillips curve shows a negative association between the rates of inflation and unemployment of an economy.

The implication of the Phillips curve is that the government can choose which combination of inflation and unemployment prevails in the economy. If

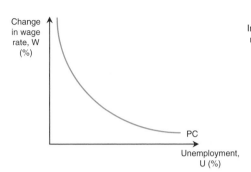

Figure 11.7a *The original Phillips curve relationship*

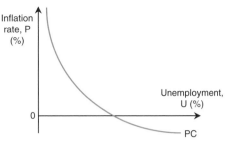

Figure 11.7b *The conventional Phillips curve*

it thinks the inflation rate is too high it can reduce it, but at the cost of greater unemployment. Likewise, if it thinks unemployment is too severe it can reduce it, but at the cost of greater inflation.

By integrating the Phillips curve relationship into our analysis of the previous section, we can enrich our conclusions. To do so, though, we need to transform the conventional Phillips curve. Instead of measuring the unemployment rate on the horizontal axis we need to plot the relationship in terms of the economy's output level, which creates the mirror image of the curve in Figure 11.7b. The combined model is displayed in Figure 11.8. The upper panel shows both a recessionary and inflationary gap, caused by the aggregate demand curve shifting to AD_1 and AD_2 respectively. The lower panel displays the horizontally inverted Phillips curve, which shows the change in the price level caused by a recessionary gap is less than that caused by an inflationary gap of equal size. The inflation caused by the inflationary gap, denoted by $\dot{P}_2$, is larger in absolute terms than the deflation caused by the recessionary gap, denoted by $\dot{P}_1$. This is one reason why economists tend to focus on inflation: it can become a serious problem quickly.

We can now include the role of inflationary expectations into the analysis: the level of inflation that actors within the economy expect to prevail. To do this we first need to construct **expectations-augmented Phillips curves**, which represent the short run relationship between inflation and unemployment given a particular rate of inflation expectations within the economy: they're also known as **short run Phillips curves**. Consider Figure 11.9, which shows three expectations-augmented Phillips curves (EPCs). Each of these Phillips curves is shifted vertically by the level of expected inflation it represents. In other words, each expectations-augmented Phillips curve is associated with a given expected rate of inflation. EPC_1, for example, represents the trade-off between inflation and unemployment when individuals within the economy expect the rate of inflation to be zero; EPC_2 represents this trade-off when expected inflation is $\dot{P}_1$; and EPC_2 represents this trade-off when expected inflation is $\dot{P}_2$.

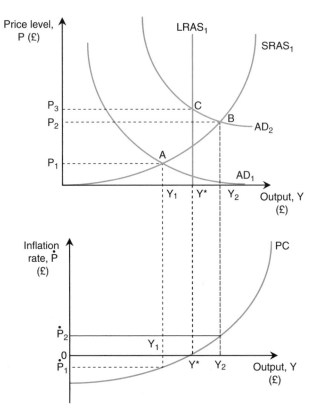

Figure 11.8 AD, AS and the Phillips curve

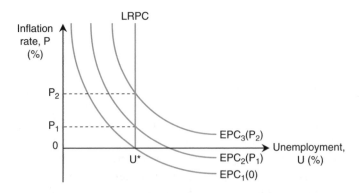

Figure 11.9 Expectations-augmented Phillips curve analysis and NAIRU

The unemployment rate at which the zero inflation expectations-augmented Phillips curve (EPC_1) is equal to zero is called the **non-accelerating inflation rate of unemployment** (**NAIRU**). The points on all expectations-augmented Phillips curves associated with this unemployment rate form the **long run Phillips curve** (**LRPC**). At this level of unemployment the expected level of inflation is equal to the actual inflation rate and so there's no pressure on the economy to move from this point: what actors expect actually happens and so producers and households are happy with their decisions as they are. This is long run equilibrium in Phillips curve analysis. At every point that isn't on the long run Phillips curve, though, the actual rate of inflation isn't what actors expect. Actors change their expectations to account for this difference, moving the economy to a new expectations-augmented Phillips curve and a point on the long run Phillips curve at which the NAIRU is established. The inflation rate may increase or fall in the process, but at NAIRU it ceases to change.

The final step in the analysis is a consideration of how expectations are actually formed. There are two general theories on this:

❶ **Adaptive expectations.** This is where the expected rate of inflation is slowly adjusted until it's the same as that which actually prevails in the economy.

❷ **Rational expectations.** This is where the rate of inflation expected in the next period adjusts instantaneously in response to changes in the economy today. This theory is at the heart of Robert Lucas's (see Section 14.13) new classical economics and much of modern macroeconomics.

We can now complete our analysis of inflation. Figure 11.10a simply reproduces the inflationary gap diagram using our aggregate demand and supply analysis from above. This demonstrates the level effects of such a demand-side shock. Figure 11.10b displays an expectations-augmented Phillips curve analysis of the same demand-side shock.

Suppose the economy is initially at point A, which is a steady-state long run position. The economy is producing its natural level of output (Y^*), which coincides with the NAIRU (U^*). Individuals in the economy expect the inflation rate to be $\dot{P}_1$, an expectation that's realised. Now suppose there's a positive demand shock, causing the aggregate demand curve to shift from AD_1 to AD_2, moving the economy to point B. Output increases to Y_1, opening up an inflationary gap, and the unemployment rate correspondingly falls to U_1: frictional unemployment (see Section 11.1) is reduced. The inflation rate increases to $\dot{P}_2$, raising the price level from P_1 to P_2.

If we assume expectations are formed adaptively, actors continue to expect the inflation rate to be $\dot{P}_1$ and so the economy moves along the prevailing expectations-augmented Phillips curve, EPC_1, to point B – this is the expectations-augmented Phillips curve that represents this expected rate of inflation. Only gradually do their expectations adjust to the higher level, causing the economy to progressively move onto higher expectations-augmented Phillips curves. As expectations adjust, the short run aggregate supply curve shifts inwards: producers expect higher production costs and so plan to reduce the amount they supply at each and every price level. Eventually the economy settles again at point C, at which expectations and the short run supply curve have fully adjusted, and it's in a position of long run equilibrium at the natural rate of output and the NAIRU.

However, if we assume expectations are formed rationally, actors quickly adjust to the demand shock, causing the economy to move to EPC_2. Consequently, the short run aggregate supply curve quickly shifts inwards to $SRAS_2$,

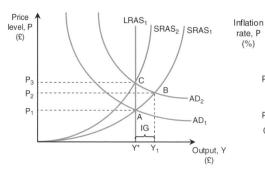

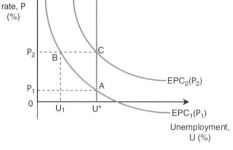

Figure 11.10a *The level effects of an inflationary gap*

Figure 11.10b *The inflationary effects of an inflationary gap*

moving the economy to point C. Any inflationary gap the policy might create is quickly eliminated and so effectively there's only an increase in inflation. This is the message of new classical economics.

We can employ the same analysis to understand the effects of a negative demand shock, which is simply a case of reversing the logic from above. We once again assume the economy is initially in a long run steady state position, at which the prevailing aggregate demand and short run aggregate supply curves intersect on the long run aggregate supply curve. On the expectations side, individuals find the inflation rate they expect is actually realised, meaning the economy is on the long run Phillips curve. The economy is producing its natural level of output, employing a workforce corresponding to the NAIRU to do so.

Now assume there's a negative demand shock, causing the aggregate demand curve to shift downwards. Output contracts, opening up a recessionary gap, and the unemployment rate correspondingly increases. The inflation rate falls, causing the price level to fall. Now, if we assume expectations are formed adaptively, actors continue to hold their current expectations about the inflation rate. The economy moves along the prevailing expectations-augmented Phillips curve, because that curve represents the rate of inflation that is currently expected, to the point that corresponds to the increased level of unemployment and the lower actual inflation rate. Only gradually do their expectations adjust to this lower rate, causing the economy to progressively move onto lower expectations-augmented Phillips curves. As expectations adjust, the short run aggregate supply curve shifts outwards: producers expect lower production costs and so plan to increase the amount of output they supply at each and every price level. Eventually the economy settles at a new long run steady state, at which expectations and short run supply have fully adjusted to the lower inflation rate, and it's in a position of long run equilibrium at the natural rate of output and the NAIRU.

However, if we assume expectations are formed rationally, actors quickly adjust to the demand-side shock, causing the economy to move quickly to this new long run position. Any recessionary gap the policy might create is quickly eliminated and so the only effect of the policy is a reduction in inflation.

The role of expectations in this analysis cannot be exaggerated. The theory of rational expectations effectively implies that any increase in aggregate demand is simply inflationary, failing to increase output and reduce unemployment: even in the short run. This is the position held by new classical economists, who assert that any government attempt to manage the economy is futile. The best the government can hope to do is to control the money supply so inflationary pressures don't build up. The alternative theory of adaptive expectations, on the other hand, maintains there's scope for the government to influence the levels of output and unemployment through demand management policies, albeit in the short run.

We've only looked at positive and negative demand shocks and the effects they have on the price level, inflation, output and unemployment. You should use our model here to analyse the effects of positive and negative supply shocks as well.

BOX 11.4: Money, banking and finance

Bruce Morley, University of Bath

The study of money, banking and finance involves three main areas:

1. The importance of the financial system to the economy through its role in the efficient allocation of resources. For instance Walter Bagehot argued that it played a vital role in encouraging the early industrialisation of England. The financial system is responsible for transferring capital from parts of the economy where it is in surplus (savers) to those areas where it is in deficit (investors). The creation of financial intermediaries is essential as they provide a service that reduces the cost of information collection and transaction costs that the individual borrower or saver has to pay. Financial intermediaries can be divided into banks and financial markets, with the banking system having the critical responsibility for running the payment system, an important part in the conduct of monetary policy and the provision of credit to industry.

2. The importance of money, which acts as a medium of exchange. Money additionally serves as a unit of account, store of value in the absence of inflation and as a standard of deferred payment, which has a vital role in the creation of credit by financial intermediaries.

3. The way in which the financial system affects the whole economy, including investment, foreign exchange markets and economic growth. Other important aspects of finance include the modelling of asset returns, the pricing, diversification and management of risk, the regulation of banks and the efficiency of the financial system, known as the **efficient markets hypothesis** (EMH). The importance of financial development to economic prosperity has become an important issue and is one explanation for countries developing at different speeds. Although the basic functions of the financial system vary little across countries, there are substantial differences in terms of the quality and variety of financial products on offer and the complexity of instruments to price and control risk. Historically, countries have developed either a financial market based economy, such as those of the UK and USA, or a more bank-focused economy, as was the case in Germany, although in recent years these differences have been reduced.

There are a number of helpful books on this subject including:

> P.G.A. Howells and K. Bain, *The Economics of Money, Banking and Finance: A European Text* (Essex: Prentice-Hall, 2005).
> F.S. Mishkin, *The Economics of Money, Banking and Financial Markets* (Boston, MA: Pearson, 2004).

11.5 summary

> The classical view of unemployment is that, as long as markets are free and flexible, involuntary unemployment will be short-lived and so isn't a serious problem. The emphasis, then, is on removing all market rigidities to enable this to happen.

> The Keynesian view of unemployment is that the economy can become stuck in a situation of low aggregate demand and high unemployment, and therefore requires government intervention to correct it.

> Unemployment hysteresis is the idea that unemployment is persistent, meaning the labour market doesn't return to a constant natural rate of unemployment: over time unemployment can become increasingly severe.

> Money fulfils three functions in the economy. It's a medium of exchange, a store of value and a unit of account.

> The neoclassical quantity theory of money suggests that inflation – which is an increase in the price level of an economy – is directly linked to the growth of the money supply.

> The aggregate demand and supply model suggests inflation is caused by either an increase in production costs (cost-push inflation) or an increase in aggregate demand (demand-pull inflation). The extent of the inflationary increase in either case depends on the response of the government: whether it employs monetary accommodation (in the case of cost-push inflation) and monetary validation (in the case of demand-pull inflation) or it allows the economy to correct itself.

> The Phillips curve shows a negative association between the rates of inflation and unemployment in an economy.

12 the economy in its international setting

Apart from in Section 9.1 our analysis of the whole economy – of output, the interest rate, the price level, inflation and unemployment – has been restricted to that of a **closed economy**: one cut off from the rest of the world. Leaving the analysis at this would be hugely unsatisfactory as the way economies relate to one another is clearly such an important aspect of the real world. In this chapter we examine some of the aspects of an **open economy**: an economy that trades with one or more other economies. The purpose here is for us to understand why economies engage in international trade and how the exchange rates on which this trade is based are determined.

12.1 why economies trade

The first question we need to answer is why economies choose to interact and trade with one another. To do this we turn to the work on international trade by eighteenth-century British economist David Ricardo (see Sections 13.2 and 14.2), which is perhaps clearest to examine using an example.

Suppose there are just two economies, let's call them the UK and Australia, and they each possess 1000 units of labour with which they each produce only two products, bottles of cider and wine. The UK needs 4 labour units to produce a bottle of cider but 5 units to produce a bottle of wine. Australia, on the other hand, requires 2 labour units to produce a bottle of cider and only 1 unit to produce a bottle of wine. These labour requirements aren't affected by the amounts of each product the economies produce: we assume there are **constant returns to scale** rather than the diminishing marginal returns we examined in Section 6.1. Suppose also that the wage rate paid in the UK is £5 per labour unit and that in Australia is A$10 per labour unit, where A$ denotes Australian dollar. Given all this, the cost of a bottle of cider in the UK is £20 and in Australia is A$20, and the cost of a bottle of wine in the UK is £25 and in Australia is A$10. This is summarised in Table 12.1.

Consider now the situation in which the economies are closed. There's no trade between them and so they each use half their labour to produce cider and the other half to produce wine. The UK produces 125 bottles of cider and 100 bottles of wine, whilst Australia produces 250 bottles of cider and 500 bottles of wine. Overall, then, the world enjoys 375 bottles of cider and 600 bottles of wine.

Table 12.1 The benefits of trade

Products	UK	Australia	Both
Amount of labour per bottle			
Cider	4	2	-
Wine	5	1	-
Wage rate per unit of labour			
	£5	A$10	-
Cost per bottle			
Cider	£20	A$20	-
Wine	£25	A$10	-
Closed economy production (using half the labour for each)			
Cider	125 bottles	250 bottles	375 bottles
Wine	100 bottles	500 bottles	600 bottles
Perfect specialisation			
Cider	250 bottles	-	250 bottles
Wine	-	1000 bottles	1000 bottles
Imperfect specialisation			
Cider	250 bottles	130 bottles	380 bottles
Wine	-	740 bottles	740 bottles

We see from this that Australia needs fewer labour units than the UK to produce both a bottle of cider and a bottle of wine: it can produce both products more cheaply than the UK. We say Australia has an **absolute advantage** in the production of both cider and wine. However, Australia has a **comparative advantage** in the production of wine, meaning it needs to sacrifice fewer bottles of cider for each bottle of wine it produces than does the UK. For every bottle of wine Australia produces it must reduce its production of cider by half a bottle – it costs one labour unit to produce a bottle of wine but two to produce a bottle of cider – whereas for the UK to produce an extra bottle of wine it must reduce its output of cider by 1¼ bottles of cider. Likewise, the UK has a comparative advantage in cider production: to produce an extra bottle of cider means the UK has to reduce its output of wine by 0.8 bottles, whereas for Australia to produce an extra bottle of cider means it has to reduce its production of wine by two bottles.

David Ricardo suggested that each economy should **specialise** its production according to its comparative advantage. In this example, the UK should specialise in cider production and Australia in wine production. The fifth section of Table 12.1 shows the output produced if the two economies perfectly specialise in this way, that is, if the UK produces only cider and Australia only wine. The outcome is a greater output of wine overall but a smaller output of cider, and so it isn't obvious whether or not specialisation has improved the situation. However, suppose the UK perfectly specialises and so produces only cider, but Australia only imperfectly specialises, producing 130 bottles of cider and 740 bottles of wine. The last section of the table shows there's a clear benefit from this because the world production of both products is enlarged as a result.

The above example indicates there can be a benefit in specialisation – a benefit that Adam Smith (see Sections 13.1 and 14.1) had observed in terms of domestic production earlier than Ricardo – but it doesn't tell us about international trade. With specialisation there's clearly the potential for everyone to be better off because more is produced overall, but for this to be realised there needs to be trade between the two economies.

Consider the situation in which the exchange rate between the two currencies is £1 = A$1: a UK citizen gets A$1 for each of his pounds and an Australian citizen gets £1 for each of his Australian dollars. For a UK consumer to buy a bottle of Australian wine now costs him £10: the bottle costs A$10, which is equivalent to £10 because of the exchange rate. This benefits the consumer because he would have to pay £25 for a bottle of domestic wine. For an Australian consumer to buy a bottle of UK cider costs him A$20, which is the maximum amount he will pay for it because he can buy it domestically for that as well.

Now consider the situation in which the exchange rate is £2.5 = A$1. For a UK consumer to buy a bottle of Australian wine now costs him £25, which is the maximum he will pay for it because he could buy a domestic bottle of wine for that price. For an Australian consumer to buy a bottle of UK cider costs him A$8, which is cheaper than he can buy cider at home.

This shows that as long as the exchange rate is between £1 = A$1 and £2.5 = A$1 the consumers in each country will buy products from the other country: there will be international trade and everyone benefits from lower prices and greater quantities. This is the reason economies engage in international trade.

12.2 the trade balance and the national accounts identity

Having seen the benefits of international trade, the next question to answer is how much do economies trade? This leads us onto the **trade balance**, which we examine here.

We saw in Chapter 9 that the output of a closed economy (Y) is equal to the amount of consumption (C), investment (I) and government spending (G) within it; the amount of consumption is a positive function of disposable income (Y-T); the level of investment is a negative function of the interest rate (r); and government spending can be assumed to be exogenously determined. We summarised this as Equation 9.10, which is reproduced here as Equation 12.1 and which is known as the **national accounts identity**.

$$Y = C(Y - T) + I(r) + \overline{G} \hspace{3cm} \text{(Equation 12.1)}$$

The right-hand side of Equation 12.1 represents domestic expenditure, E^d. We can simplify the identity to $Y = E^d$: output is equal to domestic expenditure. In order for us to begin to examine the economy in its international setting we need to incorporate the two aspects of international trade into this identity:

❶ **Exports.** Some of the domestically produced output is purchased by households in other economies. In other words, some of the domestic output is consumed as exports (X). This represents money flowing into the domestic economy: an injection into its circular flow (see Section 9.1).

❷ **Imports.** Some of the domestic consumption, investment and government expenditure is spent on products produced in other economies: imports (M). This represents money flowing out of the domestic economy: a leakage from its circular flow (see Section 9.1).

National output or income, then, is composed of domestic expenditure, plus export revenue, minus import revenue. This is summarised as Equation 12.2.

$$Y = E^d + X - M \qquad \text{(Equation 12.2)}$$

This immediately leads to an expression for the trade balance – the difference between export revenue and import revenue, also known as the **value of net exports** $(X - M)$ – which is expressed as Equation 12.3. If the trade balance is positive, the value of the economy's exports exceeds that of its imports, which is called a **trade surplus** and represents a net injection into the circular flow. If the trade balance is negative, the value of the economy's exports is less than that of its imports. This is known as a **trade deficit** and represents a net leakage from the circular flow. If the trade balance is zero, the economy has **balanced trade**.

$$Y - E^d = X - M \qquad \text{(Equation 12.3)}$$

Equation 12.3 is also an identity, meaning it's true by definition. It only shows us the effect of the trade balance on national output and income. To understand the trade balance more fully we need to examine the factors that actually determine it.

12.3 the nominal exchange rate

Usually when people discuss the **exchange rate** they're referring to the **nominal exchange rate**.

Key term: the nominal exchange rate

The nominal exchange rate, usually denoted by e, represents the rate at which the currency of one economy can be traded for that of another: it's the relative prices of the two currencies. For example, an exchange rate of £1 = A$2 means that one British pound can be exchanged for two Australian dollars.

It's helpful to view an economy's currency in the same way we view any other product. This enables us to use the microeconomic tools we developed in Part 2. A nominal exchange rate is simply the price of one currency – let's call it currency A – in terms of another, currency B. As with all products, this is simply determined by the demand for, and supply of, currency A relative to that of currency B in the foreign exchange – or **forex** – market.

The demand for an economy's currency is influenced by a number of factors. For instance:

1 **The demand for the exports of that economy**. In order to purchase an economy's exports it's necessary to first purchase the relevant sum of currency of that economy. The trade can then take place. Thus an increase in export demand increases the demand for currency, whilst a reduction has the reverse effect.

2 **The attractiveness of investing in that economy**. As with the first factor, in order to invest in an economy it is necessary to first purchase the desired amount of that economy's currency. The purchased currency can then be invested. The attractiveness of investment is primarily determined by the rate of return from investing in that economy (the interest rate), but the perceived risk involved is also an important factor. An increase in the attractiveness of investing in a given economy thus leads to an increase in the demand for its currency, whereas a reduction has the reverse effect.

3 **Monetary authority holdings**. Monetary authorities, such as the Bank of England, hold stocks of a wide array of currencies. Action on their part to augment or diminish their stock of a particular currency inevitably changes the demand for it.

The supply of an economy's currency to the forex market, on the other hand, is simply the amount of that currency exchanged for other currencies in the forex market. One currency is supplied to the forex market only in exchange for another, so an increase in the demand of one currency is equivalent to an increase in the supply of another and vice versa. This is made clearer in the example below.

To simplify our examination of nominal exchange rate determination, consider the situation in which only two economies exist: the economies of Europe and the rest of the world. Let's assume the currency of Europe is the euro ($€$) and that of the world is the wor ($₩$, which is actually the symbol for the won used in North and South Korea). Figures 12.1a and 12.1b illustrate the forex market that exists for the trade of these two currencies. The initial supply of, and demand for, euros are represented by $S_{€1}$ and $D_{€1}$ in each case respectively. They're initially at equilibrium with a prevailing nominal exchange rate of e_1.

Now consider Figure 12.1a in particular. Suppose the demand for euros increases: perhaps because the interest rate in Europe has increased relative to that in the world economy or because the prices of European products have fallen relative to those of the world economy. Holders of wors supply their

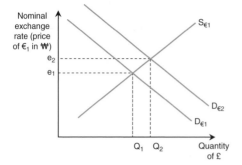

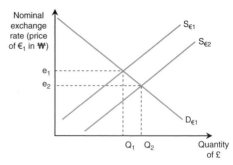

Figure 12.1a Increased demand for a currency and its nominal exchange rate

Figure 12.1b Increased supply of a currency and its nominal exchange rate

currency to the forex market in exchange for euros. The euro demand curve shifts to the right from $D_{\epsilon1}$ to $D_{\epsilon2}$, causing the price of the euro relative to the wor – and so the ₩/€ exchange rate – to increase. You can now get more wors for every euro you hold because the euro is now relatively more valuable. Conversely, if you're a holder of wors you can now get fewer euros in exchange for your wors because the wor is now relatively less valuable in comparison with the euro.

Now consider Figure 12.1b. Suppose the demand for wors increases, perhaps because of political instability making investment in Europe more risky or because the European Central Bank begins to expand its holding of wors. Holders of euros supply their currency to the forex market in exchange for wors. The supply curve of euros shifts to the right from $S_{\epsilon1}$ to $S_{\epsilon2}$ and the ₩/€ exchange rate declines. You can now get fewer wors for your euros because the euro is now relatively less valuable. Conversely, if you're a holder of wors you can now get more euros for your wors because the wor is now relatively more valuable in comparison to the euro.

12.4 the real exchange rate and the trade balance

In addition to the nominal exchange rate, there's also the **real exchange rate**, which we examine here.

Key term: the real exchange rate

The real exchange rate, usually denoted by ε, shows the relative prices of the actual products of two economies. It's also known as the **terms of trade** between two economies and is derived by multiplying the nominal exchange rate by the ratio of the domestic price level (P^d) to the price level prevailing in the foreign economy (P^f), as shown in Equation 12.4. If the real exchange rate is high, the products of the foreign economy are cheap relative to those of the domestic economy. If it's low, the products of the foreign economy are expensive relative to those of the domestic economy.

$$\varepsilon = e \cdot \frac{P^d}{P^f} \qquad\qquad \text{(Equation 12.4)}$$

Consider again the two economies of Europe and the rest of the world in the example above and the determinants of the nominal exchange rate between them.

1 It was demonstrated above that an increase in Europe's interest rate makes investment in Europe more attractive, ceteris paribus. As such, the demand for euros increases, causing its nominal exchange rate value to rise: see Figure 12.1a. Equation 12.4 shows the effect of this is to cause its real exchange rate to rise as well, making its exports relatively more expensive.

2 An increase in the European price level relative to that of the world economy – meaning inflation is higher in Europe than it is in the world economy – causes European products to become relatively more expensive than world products. Equation 12.4 reveals this exerts an upward pressure on Europe's real exchange rate. However, we see above that a relative increase in the price of European products causes the demand for European products to fall, which causes the supply of euros on the forex market to rise, pulling the nominal exchange rate of the euro down with it: see Figure 12.1b. This means it now costs fewer wors to buy a single euro, which according to Equation 12.4 puts downward pressure on the real exchange rate. How the real exchange rate changes overall depends upon which of these effects dominates. If the reduction in the nominal exchange rate outweighs the increase in the price ratio, then the real exchange rate falls, but if the reduction in the nominal exchange rate is outweighed by the increase in the price ratio, it rises.

From this analysis it's apparent that the trade balance is a function of the real exchange rate. If the real exchange rate is high, domestic exports are relatively more expensive than imports from abroad and so the trade balance is likely to be in deficit. If, on the other hand, the real exchange rate is low, domestic exports are cheap relative to imports from abroad and so the trade balance is likely to be in surplus.

We also see that the real exchange rate is determined by the nominal exchange rate and the ratio of the domestic price level to the price level abroad; and the nominal exchange rate is in turn determined by anything that affects the demand for, and supply of, the currency. We can now put all this together to analyse how various shocks to the economy and economic policies affect the trade balance. For example,

1 **A domestic negative supply shock**, such as an increase in the cost of the fuel upon which the domestic economy, but not the foreign economy, relies. This causes the domestic price level to increase relative to that of the foreign economy and so the demand for domestic products and currency to fall. If we assume that the increase in the price ratio outweighs the reduction in the nominal exchange rate from the reduced demand for the currency, the real exchange rate rises, domestic products become relatively more expensive compared to those of the foreign economy, and the trade balance declines. This corresponds to Equation 12.3.

2 **An increase in the rate of interest in the foreign economy alone**. This causes investment in that economy to rise, from actors in both economies. Holders of the domestic currency exchange their money for the foreign currency, causing the supply of the domestic currency on the forex market to rise. The nominal exchange rate falls, which leads to a reduction in the real exchange rate as well. Domestic products are now relatively cheaper than those from the foreign economy and so the trade balance increases. Again, this relates effectively to Equation 12.3.

3 **An increase in spending by the domestic government**. This has two effects. First, it leads to an expansion of domestic output, causing domestic expenditure on both domestic and foreign products to increase. The supply of the domestic currency on the forex market expands in order to finance the increased volume of imports, causing the nominal exchange rate to fall. Second, an increase in government spending causes the domestic interest rate to rise, leading to a partial crowding-out of the additional aggregate demand (see Section 9.5). This causes the demand for the domestic currency on the forex market to increase, causing the nominal exchange rate to rise. The overall effect on the nominal exchange rate is uncertain, depending on which of these affects dominates, and so the effect on the real exchange rate and the trade balance is also uncertain. This also agrees with the identity of Equation 12.3.

It has been assumed in the third example that the period being looked at is the short run, during which there can be changes in the level of output (see Section 10.3). In the long run output is determined by the fixed stocks of capital and labour, and so the fiscal stimulus fails to increase output. Consequently, the only effect it has is to increase the interest rate, thereby increasing foreign investment in the domestic economy. The nominal exchange rate increases, as does the real exchange rate, causing the trade balance to decline. This is exactly what Equation 12.3 implies in this situation: an increase in domestic expenditure whilst the level of output remains constant causes the trade balance to contract.

12.5 purchasing power parity

Key term: purchasing power parity (PPP)

PPP refers to the nominal exchange rate between two currencies that is necessary for the amount of products that can be bought with a sum of one currency to be exactly the same as the amount of products that can be bought when that sum is exchanged into the other currency. It's a long run theory of exchange rate determination, based on **international arbitrage**.

Purchasing power parity is a theory intended to help us understand how nominal exchange rates are determined in the long run. It's perhaps best understood through an example. Consider the nominal exchange rate between British pounds and American dollars, and suppose you hold £100. With that money you can buy a basket of products in the UK economy, or you can exchange it for dollars and buy a basket of goods in America. Now consider each of the following situations:

1 **You can buy a bigger basket of products in America than you can in the UK.** In this situation it makes sense for you to convert your pounds into dollars, which you then spend in America: you get more for your money that way. This is called **international arbitrage**: trading to take advantage of different prices in different economies. When this applies, the supply of pounds in the forex markets increases, causing the value of the pound to fall relative to that of the dollar: the nominal exchange rate value of the pound falls. As this happens the amount of dollars – and so the amount of products in America – you can buy with your £100 falls, and it continues to fall until you can buy precisely the same amount of products with your £100 in both the UK and America. At this point international arbitrage ceases, and the nominal exchange rate is in long run equilibrium.

2 **You can buy a bigger basket of products in the UK than you can in America.** In this situation you will naturally spend your money in the UK: but so will American consumers, who convert their dollars into pounds. This time international arbitrage causes the demand for pounds in the forex market to increase, thereby increasing the value of the pound relative to the dollar: the exchange rate value of the pound increases. As this happens the amount of dollars – and so the amount of products in America – you can buy with your £100 increases, and it continues to increase until you can buy precisely the same amount of products with your £100 in both economies. At this point international arbitrage stops, and the nominal exchange rate is in long run equilibrium.

In both cases, the nominal exchange rate adjusts until it's at the rate of purchasing power parity: the rate at which £1 can buy exactly the same amount of products in the UK as its equivalent amount of dollars can buy in America.

The Economist magazine calculates the **Big Mac Index**. This is an index of the nominal exchange rates needed so that if you had precisely the right amount of money to buy a McDonalds' Big Mac in one economy you could convert it into another currency and still have precisely the right amount to buy a Big Mac in that economy as well. The Big Mac is used as the base product for these calculations because of the high degree of similarity in the product across the world.

For example, at the end of January 2009 the price of a Big Mac in America was $3.54 and in the UK it was £2.29. For there to be PPP, then, the nominal exchange rate needed to be $1.55/£1: you needed to be able to get $1.55 for every pound you traded on the forex market. The actual exchange rate, though, was \$1.44/£1, meaning that the pound was undervalued against the dollar by 7 per cent: if you had converted £2.29 into dollars, you wouldn't have had enough to buy a Big Mac in America. At the same time, the price of a Big Mac in Australia was A\$3.45. For there to be PPP between the American and Australian dollars, the nominal exchange rate would have had to be A\$0.97/\$1. In reality, it was A\$1.57/\$1, meaning the Australian dollar was also undervalued relative to the American dollar, by 38 per cent. If you converted A\$3.45 into American dollars, you would have only received \$2.2, much less than you needed to buy a Big Mac in America.

The example above shows us nominal exchange rates are expressed in two ways. The first is to express it as the amount of the home currency needed to buy one unit of the foreign currency. For example, in the UK this would express the pound–dollar rate as £X = \$1. This is known as the **indirect nominal exchange rate** and is common in the UK and Europe. The second is to express it as the amount of the foreign currency needed to buy one unit of the home currency. For example, in the UK this would express the pound–dollar rate as £1 = \$X. This is known as the **direct nominal exchange rate** and is used in most other countries. In the Big Mac example above, if we assume that the home currency is the American dollar, the pound–dollar rate is expressed directly and the Australian dollar–American dollar rate is expressed indirectly. The pound–dollar and euro–dollar rates are usually expressed in terms of the number of dollars per pound or euro. How the nominal exchange rate is expressed determines which way round the price ratio is to convert it into the real exchange rate. In Equation 12.4 it's assumed that the exchange rate is expressed in the direct form. If a nominal exchange rate is expressed in the indirect form, converting it into a real exchange rate involves multiplying by the opposite price ratio.

The evidence from the Big Mac index regarding the ability of PPP to explain actual nominal exchange rates is mixed. The theory is roughly accurate in the long run, but there are significant short run disparities. There have been a number of explanations proposed for these significant short run, and less significant long run, disparities:

1. **Not all products are traded**. For this reason their relative prices don't have any effect on the nominal exchange rate. For example, if the price of a haircut in Australia is much lower than that in the UK, a UK citizen isn't able to take advantage of the price difference by getting his hair cut in Australia and so the nominal exchange rate isn't affected by this price differential. The economies – and so price levels – of developed countries tend to be dominated by services which aren't generally traded, and so large price differentials can exist and be immune to international arbitrage.

2. **There are significant transport costs**. This is related to the first point. Even if products are traded, significant transport costs drive a wedge between the

price levels in different economies meaning international arbitrage can't perfectly achieve PPP. For example, suppose a particular car in the UK costs £10,000 whereas in Japan it costs the equivalent of £7,000. It makes sense to buy it in Japan, but if the cost of shipping the car to the UK is £2,000, international arbitrage will cause the nominal exchange rate to adjust only to the point where £10,000 in the UK has an equivalent value of £8,000 in Japan.

❸ **Currencies in the modern global economy aren't primarily traded for consumption purposes, but for investment.** Currency traders aren't very concerned with the relative prices of products within different economies, but with what returns they can get from holding different currencies as investments and the security that different currencies provide them: they want to hold the currencies of economies with relatively high interest rates and where the economy is expected to grow, meaning their investments are safe. The international arbitrage process isn't the dominant force in determining nominal exchange rates.

12.6 summary

> David Ricardo demonstrated the benefits of specialisation according to comparative advantage and international trade.
> The nominal exchange rate represents the rate at which the currency of one economy is traded for that of another. The real exchange rate (also known as the terms of trade) shows the relative prices of the actual products of the two economies.
> Purchasing power parity refers to the nominal exchange rate between two currencies necessary for one currency to be of exactly the same value in terms of what it can buy as to that when it is exchanged into the other currency.

how it has all come about

In this Part we briefly explore how economics as a subject
has evolved and where the theories and ideas of Parts 2
and 3 have come from – we explore the history of economic
thought, looking in particular at:

1   How economics has developed (Chapter 13).

2   Who the key contributors to this development have
     been: the masters of the subject (Chapter 14). This
     is inevitably a subjective list – others would present
     different lists of economists – but the focus here is
     on those who have shaped the material examined in
     Parts 2 and 3, together with other economists to look
     out for.

The history of economic thought isn't often taught during economics degree courses: at most it's an optional module
in the final year, as at the University of Bath. This is a shame
because understanding how economic ideas have

4

developed – the people behind the thinking and the factors that motivated it – is crucial if we're to truly understand the ideas themselves. For example, Alfred Marshall (see Section 14.5) was the one to synthesise the neoclassical view of economics, emphasising among other things comparative statics (see Section 1.4) rather than the processes by which equilibrium points are reached. However, he himself saw this as a huge weakness of this approach to the subject, but this criticism has largely been forgotten by all apart from post-Keynesian and computable economists, and so economists largely continue in the neoclassical vein without thinking of the possibly better approaches that could be adopted instead. It's crucial we know the arguments involved in the evolution of economic ideas – the paths that weren't taken but that could prove fruitful if taken now – if the subject is to move forward.

It's also important for us to remember the policy lessons that have been learned in the past. For example, the lesson about stimulating aggregate demand learned during the Great Depression of the 1930s (see Section 13.4) has helped to shorten the most recent financial crisis.

It's these issues that are explored in the two chapters that follow.

13 the evolution of economics

13.1 the development of economic thought

Writing a chapter about the development of economic thought is far from easy. Primarily this is because to do so means we have to assume the existence, at any one point in time, of a single set of ideas and theories that comprise 'economic thought' at that moment. This clearly isn't the case in economics. At any one time there are competing schools of thought, with some economists promoting ideas and theories very different to those of others. This wouldn't be so bad if those different ideas and theories changed in the same direction and at the same speed, but that also isn't the case. Some of the proponents of different ideas converge to one another, whilst others move further away. These observations make a thoroughly comprehensive discussion of the development of economic thought almost impossible. However, the cause is not completely hopeless. At any one time there's what Thomas Kuhn labelled a **paradigm**: the ideas and theories of those in the mainstream of the subject. Despite the continual presence of different schools of thought, economics has never been in total disarray. A mainstream of thought has always existed, being identifiable by three elements:

1. The ideas widely taught to undergraduates in the subject.
2. The content of widely used textbooks.
3. The focus of criticism from dissenting points of view.

It's the development and evolution of this mainstream and the ruling paradigms that we focus on in this chapter.

A brief timeline of the history of economic thought, which is explored throughout this chapter, is presented in Figure 13.1.

13.2 classical economics

Until the onset of the industrial revolution in Britain in the eighteenth century there was little need for economics as we conceive it today because the questions the subject seeks to address simply didn't arise. For example, in the ancient civilisations of Egypt, Greece and Rome the labour force predominantly comprised slave labour, so there was no need for an analysis of wage rates; borrowing and lending was effected purely for private purposes, so there was no call

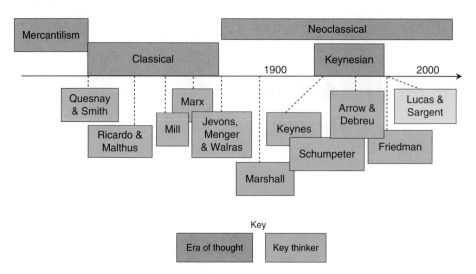

Figure 13.1 Very brief timeline of economic thought

for an analysis of interest rates; and trade, although clearly in existence, was minimal compared with the level of activity today, so there wasn't a need for an analysis of prices. Much the same can be said of the medieval period. Although trade certainly expanded during the Middle Ages, it was still a tiny part of life, and labour consisted primarily of serfs working to provide their feudal lords with commodities in exchange for parcels of land they could live on. Thinkers about 'economic' issues, such as Aristotle in ancient Greece and the **medieval scholars** in Europe, focused on ethical matters such as the wisdom of using slave labour, the appropriate supply of coins, and the fair prices – or value – of products. The very notion of using trade for financial gain was shunned.

In the subsequent age of empire building, great voyages of discovery and the expansion of merchant cities, the **mercantilists** – so called because they were the thinkers during the period in which merchants expanded trade across the world – emphasised the importance of trade on terms most beneficial to the domestic country, economic expansion through conquest and trade, and companies possessing and taking advantage of market power. The ethical standpoint that trade for financial gain was morally reprehensible had certainly been superseded!

However, the birth of modern economics came with Adam Smith (see Section 14.1) and the French **physiocrats** – 'physiocracy' effectively meaning 'law of nature' – such as François Quesnay. These writers were arguably the first to view the economy as a single entity, to be studied in much the same way as the physical world in the natural sciences. They emphasised economic growth as the main challenge, and the development of the domestic market along with domestic investment as the solution, in contrast to the mercantilist emphasis on conquest, overseas expansion and exploitation of less developed countries.

Smith showed that the market system results in the overall maximisation of social welfare (see Section 7.2) and any government interference in the economy should be minimised. He also showed that an effective approach to studying the economy is to start with a set of pre-defined assumptions and to then analyse their logical implications – an economic model against which observations from reality can be compared (see Section 4.2). However, this final point shouldn't be taken too far. Smith didn't use data to test his conclusions in anything like a formal sense. Instead he used anecdotes from the real world and history to illustrate his ideas. This was the first economic paradigm.

Drawing on Smith's work and responding to the inflation that Britain was experiencing during the Napoleonic Wars, by the middle of the nineteenth century the classical theory of money (see Section 11.2), which says the supply of money is crucial to its value, had started to emerge. It was also believed there was a clear separation between real and monetary variables: the classical dichotomy (see the introduction to Chapter 10). The possibility that monetary policy (see Section 9.5) could influence the real side of the economy – meaning the level of output and employment – was completely overlooked. Changes in the money supply couldn't have real effects: money was neutral.

David Ricardo (see Section 14.2), having been involved in the development of the classical theory of money, soon turned his attention to what he considered to be a significant omission from Smith's work: a theory of the distribution of output between land (rent), labour (wages) and entrepreneurs (profit), and the effects of price changes on the investment that Smith had identified as being the key to economic growth. Not only did he succeed in developing such a theory, which was widely accepted and welcomed – and also the theory of comparative advantage that demonstrated the benefits of international trade (see Section 12.1) – Ricardo also established the approach to studying the economy that has dominated ever since. It was about this approach that he entered into a prolonged and public debate with another important economist at the time – who also happened to be his best friend – Thomas Malthus (see Section 14.3). Ricardo favoured the **deductive approach** to analysis: starting with a set of assumptions that only abstractly resemble reality and then logically deriving their implications through the development of a theoretical model. He saw economic analysis as being purely logical and mathematical, necessitating only a minimum of observations about reality. To Malthus, on the other hand, economic analysis was an extension of philosophy, which needed to be based concretely on reality and observation. He argued the **inductive approach** was necessary, drawing out economic conclusions from real-life data and evidence. Ricardo triumphed in this debate, and the nature of economic analysis ever since was set.

By the 1830s political economy (as economics was then known) had been established as a science in its own right, and child protégé John Stuart Mill (his father James, a friend of Ricardo, started teaching him Greek at the age of three; by the age of eleven he was tackling calculus; and at the age of thirteen he was being taught political economy by Ricardo) formalised the Ricardian approach to the subject in his widely adopted textbook. Mill characterised political economy as an abstract science, arguing it should draw on empirical evidence only as a means to test theories, certainly not to derive them.

13.3 neoclassical economics

By the 1870s there was dissatisfaction with the classical economic analysis that had gone before and a widely felt need amongst economists for the subject to be even more scientifically rigorous. This need was satisfied by what has become known as the **marginal revolution** – the introduction of calculus and the analysis of marginal figures (see Section 5.1) – which ushered in the second paradigm in the development of economic thought, that of **neoclassical economics**. This revolution was initiated independently by three separate writers: English economist William Stanley Jevons, Austrian economist Carl Menger, and French economist Leon Walras.

None of these three fully supplanted the existing classical analysis with marginal analysis, though. That accolade was claimed by the English economist Alfred Marshall (see Section 14.5), who outlined the new approach to political economy in 1890. This work was strengthened by that of John Neville Keynes in the same year. J. N. Keynes – the father of John Maynard – was one of Marshall's earliest students and a colleague of his at Cambridge. He argued economics should be seen as a **positive science** (the study of what actually is and the laws that govern it) rather than a **normative science** (the study of what it should be) or **an art** (the study of what rules should be used to make it what it should be). He also addressed the issue of induction versus deduction, which had began to surface again during the middle of the nineteenth century, arguing there was a need for both: economic theories should be derived from theory and logic, and then tested against empirical evidence.

Marginal analysis, leading to market equilibrium, continues to dominate economics today: most of the theories and models in this book are based on this concept. The marginal revolution of neoclassical economics brought with it four significant benefits:

① It enabled economists to neatly identify points of optimality. For example, the amount of output a producer supplies in order to maximise its profit (see Section 6.3) and the consumption bundle consumers buy to maximise their utility (see Section 5.3).

② It answered the question as to what determines the price and value of a product. Marshall demonstrated that the price of a commodity is determined by both its cost of production and its desirability, by its supply and demand (see Section 7.1).

③ It opened up the possibility of a range of useful analytical tools, such as that of elasticity (see Section 5.6) and the different periods of time: Marshall suggested there were four time periods, which today are merged into the more general short and long runs (see Section 6.1).

❹ It gave the subject an air of sophistication that had been lacking up until that point. This sophistication further set the discipline apart as a science.

It isn't surprising that marginal analysis was readily adopted into economics. However, these benefits came at a cost:

❶ Marginal analysis further narrowed the appropriate field of study for economists. The focus fell very much on the behaviour of individual actors and their interaction within markets, which on the whole were assumed to be perfectly competitive (see Section 7.3). Issues of distribution, growth and development – the macroeconomic issues generally – were largely sidelined in favour of marginal-based microeconomic analysis.

❷ It also led to a further narrowing of the methodological approach deemed appropriate for economists. Mathematical analysis became the way to do economics, meaning philosophical and historical arguments were neglected.

❸ It established the comparative static approach to economic analysis (see Section 1.4), removing the effects of time – the focus of analysis was fixed on equilibrium points and the comparison of them across different situations. The actual processes by which the equilibrium points were to be attained was neglected, a development that Marshall himself was unhappy with. Joan Robinson (see Section 14.7) referred to this as the greatest 'fudge' of economic analysis. Consider the market analysis of Section 7.1: we can say what the equilibrium will be, but we can't explain how the market actually gets to it.

A notable alternative to the neoclassical economic paradigm was developed by Karl Marx (see Section 14.4), the first part of which he published in 1867. As with Ricardo, Marx developed a theory about how output is distributed between the factors of production and the effects of changes in prices on the investment necessary for economic growth. Very briefly, in Marx's theory those who own capital – whom he called capitalists – exploit workers in order to extract all the surplus value generated from production (see Section 7.2). This exploitation gradually escalates to a degree that's unbearable for workers, leading to class conflict and, ultimately, revolution. Marx, and his co-worker Engels, didn't intend to provide the economy with a solution to this inevitability. Rather, publishing their work in German, they targeted the working class on the continent, encouraging them in their struggle.

Marshall's work was widely accepted as the Bible of political economy for the best part of forty years after its publication. Towards the end of the 1920s, though, dissatisfaction with its analysis started to emerge. Pierro Sraffa (see Section 14.7) criticised the neoclassical assumption of perfect competition, suggesting instead that individual firms should be analysed – effectively the pure monopoly model (see Section 7.4) – rather than entire markets. Seven years after Sraffa published his work in this area, Joan Robinson and Edward Chamberlain independently published their works along similar lines, in which they introduced monopolistic competition (see Section 7.5) and essentially devised the spectrum of competition. These works weren't an attack on the Marshallian paradigm as they were themselves firmly rooted in Marshallian marginal analysis. Instead, they should be viewed as refinements of neoclassical theory.

With the neoclassical economists came dissatisfaction with the classical theory of money. This was first seen in the 1890s in the writings of Swedish economist Knut Wicksell. Unfortunately, Wicksell's work was published in German and so was largely overlooked by other economists. However, in the run-up to the First World War the same issue was being discussed in Cambridge under the leadership of Marshall, with thinkers such as Arthur Pigou, Dennis Robertson and John Maynard Keynes playing active and influential roles. The simple quantity theory of money was re-examined, with new emphasis being placed on the reasons why individuals demand money. The heretical possibility that money isn't neutral – a notion that, unbeknownst to the Cambridge economists, was being modelled by Wicksell – also featured in the Cambridge discussions (see Section 11.2).

13.4 keynes's revolution

The world in the 1930s failed to resemble neoclassical theory. Far from the labour market continually clearing at full employment, there were multitudes of people in long-term unemployment and absolute desolation. The mainstream argument that this was caused by an over-inflated nominal wage rate, and that by accepting lower wages workers would be offered jobs, simply wasn't realistic (see Section 11.1). There was clearly a need to re-examine the existing economic paradigm, a need which John Maynard Keynes (see Section 14.6) sought to satisfy with the publication of *The General Theory of Employment, Interest and Money* in 1936.

Keynes presented a thorough re-examination of the existing framework, demonstrating that:

1. There's a direct causal relationship between money and real variables: money isn't neutral.
2. The level of output and employment is dependent on the level of aggregate demand (see Section 10.1).
3. There's no reason why the economy as a whole should tend towards a position of full employment: it can be stuck in a depressed state for a prolonged period of time.
4. The standard solution to unemployment of forcing workers to accept lower wage rates actually worsens the situation through its suppression of aggregate demand.

⑤ It's the responsibility of the government to employ monetary and fiscal policies to stimulate aggregate demand and economic activity, taking advantage of the multiplier effect (see Section 9.1).

⑥ The economy should be studied at an aggregate level rather than solely at the level of individual consumers and producers (which had been the focus of the neoclassical writers).

⑦ The whole notion that the economy can be studied along the same lines as study in the natural sciences is mistaken.

Many of these ideas weren't new. For example, the multiplier effect had been suggested by Richard Kahn (see Section 14.7) in 1931. What was new was their synthesis into a coherent model of the whole economy, which was quickly adopted by economists across the world. Perhaps this was because it came at precisely the right time, reflecting the real world far more accurately than that of neoclassical economics. Perhaps it was because it opened up new avenues of research, such as that of macroeconomics as a separate branch of economics and econometrics as a way of measuring and evaluating the new concepts of aggregate demand and the like. Either way, Keynes successfully ushered in an age of demand management policies, aggregate macroeconomic analysis and econometrics. The third paradigm had arrived.

The General Theory, perhaps because of its complexity in parts, never became a Bible of economics in the same way that Marshall's work had done. Instead, it was studied through other textbooks, such as that of Paul Samuelson. As a consequence of this, Keynes's true message – which it must be admitted isn't always entirely clear – has arguably been distorted. Sir John Hicks's (see Section 14.8) interpretation of *The General Theory* – the IS-LM model – became the basis of Keynesian analysis in textbooks, a development many Keynesian economists today lament (see Box 9.4). The relationship between the levels of employment and inflation, which emerged from the textbook interpretation of Keynes's theory and was empirically demonstrated by William Phillips in 1952 (see Section 11.4), wasn't part of what Keynes had intended either.

13.5 neoclassical economics – but with serious maths

The Keynesian revolution successfully created in the form of macroeconomics a new branch of the subject that was valued at least as much as the analysis that was already in existence. The Second World War caused leading academic economists – particularly in Britain – to take up positions in government, which meant Keynesian macroeconomics quickly influenced policy-makers. It also led to the creation of macroeconomic datasets specifically intended for Keynesian analysis: it isn't too much of an exaggeration to say the only data that existed in the middle of the twentieth century was specifically designed for Keynesian use. As such, until the 1970s Keynesian macroeconomics largely dominated economic research and the policies of governments.

However, it failed to remove neoclassical microeconomics, which is still practised today. In fact, since the last quarter of the twentieth century there has been an explosion in the areas of analysis to which neoclassical micro-economics is applied: public choice (see Box 9.1), public economics (see Box 8.1), labour economics (see Box 11.1), environmental economics (see Box 8.2); money, banking and finance (see Box 11.4) – the list goes on. This ever-widening application of neoclassical economics has simply re-established the neoclassical approach at the heart of mainstream economics: it's by far the approach most widely applied and so the most useful set of tools to learn.

The only real attempt to bridge the gap between microeconomics and macroeconomics has been through the revival of **general equilibrium** analy-sis, which had been initially developed by Leon Walras and which attempts to base macroeconomic analysis solidly on microeconomic foundations, foun-dations that are undisputedly neoclassical. The pioneering work in this field was undertaken by Kenneth Arrow (see Section 14.11), Gerard Debreu, Frank Hahn and Lionel McKenzie who recast the Walrasian model in mathemati-cal terms. The significance of this modern general equilibrium framework can scarcely be overexaggerated, being used to inform policy-making across the world, and today being used as a primary analytical tool by the central banks of Canada, England, Norway and Sweden, and peripherally by those of Peru, Europe and the USA.

Not only did the Keynesian revolution fail to replace neoclassical micro-economics, its macroeconomic effects have also been largely reversed. With the onset of **stagflation** – inflation coupled with unemployment – in the 1970s, the **monetarist school** under the leadership of Milton Friedman (see Section 14.9) successfully reinstated the quantity theory of money as the dominant monetary theory. Alongside the emergence of monetarism, Rob-ert Lucas (see Section 14.12) and Thomas Sargent initiated the start of **new classical economics**, based firmly on the notion of rational expectations that means government policy is impotent (see Section 11.4). Others have also tried to develop macroeconomic theories based on standard neoclassical microeconomic foundations, thereby creating a synthesis between some of Keynes's ideas and the assumptions of neoclassical economics: the **new Key-nesian school**.

There are now a number of different schools of thought within economics, some of which are identified in Figure 1.2. The mainstream, though, remains one of neoclassical economics.

13.6 a new chapter?

With the continued dominance of neoclassical economics in microeconom-ics and the dominance of neoclassical, monetarist and new classical ideas in macroeconomics, the economics mainstream since the 1970s has been based largely on:

1. Marginal analysis.
2. Comparative statics: the focus being on equilibrium positions rather than on the movement to equilibrium.
3. Market clearing.
4. Rational expectations.

This has led to policy recommendations focused on removing market rigidities, allowing them to function freely without interference. However, the recent global financial crisis has shaken this paradigm – indeed, the tremors continue to be felt by academics and policy-makers – and an increasing number of eminent economists are calling for a reappraisal of these foundations and recommendations. Will this dissatisfaction lead to an overhauling of the discipline? Only time will tell; but looking back through the history of the subject it's certainly possible that we're on the brink of the next revolution in economic thought.

13.7 summary

> The classical economists focused on economic growth and emphasised the importance of free markets, both domestic and global. They also established deduction as the appropriate methodology for studying economics.
> The neoclassical economists emphasised microeconomic study based on marginal analysis and comparative statics.
> The Keynesian revolution established macroeconomics as a separate branch of study and demonstrated the importance and effectiveness of government intervention in the economy.
> More recently, neoclassical economics has come to dominate again but this is being increasingly challenged because of the recent financial crisis.

14 **the masters of the subject**

In this chapter we explore in more detail the works and lives of the economic thinkers who have significantly shaped the material covered in Parts 2 and 3. At the end of the chapter selected economists you should look out for are discussed.

14.1 Smith (1723–1790)

Adam Smith was born in Scotland in 1723, kidnapped by gypsies at the age of four, educated at Oxford University, and prone to going into trance-like states and other odd behaviour, sometimes walking for miles talking to himself before realising what he was doing. He was an academic philosopher, who studied political economy as a constituent part of society. Greatly influenced by the physical laws of Newton, he sought to identify the corresponding laws governing society. The starting point of his work was a deep-seated conviction that human society, having been designed by a benevolent God, was a machine-like system working towards the maximisation of human welfare. He argued that humans are endowed with moral sentiments that govern their behaviour, and that whenever they strive to better their lives in a way that conforms to these sentiments they inadvertently maximise the total welfare of society as a whole. This is perhaps the most famous of his ideas, which he outlined in his first major work, *The Theory of Moral Sentiments*, which was published in 1759 whilst he was Professor of Moral Philosophy at the University of Glasgow.

In 1764 he accompanied the stepson of the British Chancellor of the Exchequer on an educational trip around Europe – the **Grand Tour** – during which he was able to discuss political economy with the Physiocrats (see Section 13.2). The tour was invaluable to Smith as it was largely while he was abroad that he developed his most famous work, the *Wealth of Nations*. Clearly applying the ideas from *The Theory of Moral Sentiments*, he writes in perhaps the most famous of his passages, that,

By pursuing his own interest [each individual] frequently promotes that of the society more effectually than when he really intends to promote it. (*Wealth of Nations*, Vol. 1, p. 421)

There are three points of particular note in the *Wealth of Nations*:

❶ Smith suggests that the value of commodities can be looked at in both real and monetary terms; that they're determined by their demand and supply (although it must be stressed he was certainly not the first to think along these lines); and that such values can be artificially distorted from their true values.

❷ The divine market system doesn't always work perfectly. In particular, government and church intervention in the economy is usually harmful as it distorts the workings of the system and so should be reined in; and entrepreneurs are able to manipulate the market and the prices of commodities through collusion, to the detriment of society.

❸ Writing on the eve of the industrial revolution and the explosion of technological progress it would bring, Smith emphasised specialisation (see Section 12.1) and investment as being central to economic growth, features that would make industry more important than agriculture.

Smith died in Kirkcaldy in 1790, leaving behind him the seeds of a new discipline: political economy, which would later become economics. It's unsurprising that he has become known as the father of modern economics.

14.2 Ricardo (1772–1823)

It isn't possible to unduly exaggerate the influence that David Ricardo had on the new discipline of political economy. This is all the more remarkable in that Ricardo, who became a wealthy and landed stockbroker, was only educated to the age of fourteen. This influence can be seen to have three elements:

❶ The extension of Smith's analytical method. Unlike any author before him, Ricardo reduced the use of evidence to a minimum, relying almost entirely on the logical development of theoretical implications from a set of pre-specified assumptions. He drew upon evidence solely for illustrative purposes, establishing modern economic modelling and analysis as the central approach of the new subject.

❷ The discussion of economics as a subject in its own right. All previous writers had discussed philosophy, politics and history in their work, whereas Ricardo focused solely and concretely on the economic problems at hand.

❸ Addressing the shortcomings of Smith's analysis, particularly regarding the distribution of income and the effects that changes in the distribution of income had on profits.

Ricardo's major work was his *Principles of Political Economy and Taxation*, in which he primarily developed his theory of value and distribution, and their effects on growth. He presented what was arguably the first coherent model of the economy, in which there are three actors: the worker, the landowner and the capitalist. He agreed with Smith that economic growth is caused by the capitalist investing in technology that expands the productive capacity of the economy, but was less optimistic than Smith about the future of this growth since he saw the role of land being an ultimate constraint. His model went as follows. Industrial expansion causes incomes to rise and the demand for food and other agricultural produce to increase, necessitating the cultivation of less fertile and productive land. However, landowners will only cultivate additional land if their return makes it profitable to do so. As the marginal productivity of land falls, then, rents and food prices must rise for the additional land to be cultivated. The profits of industrialists are squeezed between the rising rental rates of land they have to pay and the demand for higher wages from workers who need higher incomes to afford food. As the economy grows, these forces become ever stronger, with the result that profits continually fall, reducing investment expenditure, capital accumulation and ultimately growth. The economy eventually reaches a plateau as the constraints to its size take effect.

14.3 Malthus (1766–1834)

Thomas Malthus, a parson who was formally educated at Jesus College at the University of Cambridge, was the first professional economist: he taught at a college founded by the East India Company to train its administrators. He's largely remembered for two things.

The first is for being defeated in the debate with his best friend Ricardo over the appropriate approach to economic study. Whilst Ricardo favoured an abstract deductive and mathematical approach to economic analysis, Malthus argued it should be based on an examination of reality:

The tendency to premature generalization among political economists occasions also an unwillingness to bring their theories to the test of experience. The first business of philosophy is to account for things as they are. A comprehensive attention to facts is necessary, both to prevent the multiplication of theories, and to confirm those which are just, (Malthus, *Principles of Political Economy*, reprinted in volume 2 of *The Works and Correspondence of David Ricardo*, edited by Pierro Sraffa and Maurice Dobb).

Numerous reasons have been suggested as to why Ricardo won the day, ranging from his greater success at anticipating the seismic changes – in the form of the industrial revolution – that society was on the brink of, to his being able to enlist the more aggressive supporters. Whatever the reason, Malthus's inductive approach was rejected and the nature of economic analysis was thereby determined, a fact that was greatly lamented by Keynes, who argued the subject would have been far better had Malthus been accepted as its father.

The second reason why Malthus is remembered, and perhaps the greater of the two, is for *An Essay on the Principle of Population as it Affects the Future Improvement of Society*, which emerged from a discussion with his father. Like Ricardo, Malthus agreed with Smith's assertion that growth is generated by investment, but, also like his friend, he was less optimistic than Smith about the future prospects for growth. The problem for Malthus was that agricultural production was unable to expand at a rate sufficient to support the growth of the population, and this would ultimately constrain the economy, consigning it to poverty. The *Essay* was published in 1798 and went against the commonly held belief that rapid population growth was beneficial to society. Malthus demonstrated that as output expands and the incomes of workers increases, population growth also increases, eroding the initial increase in income per worker. Furthermore, he argued the population would grow geometrically (2, 4, 8, 16...), but that agriculture would be able to grow only arithmetically (2, 3, 4, 5...) due to diminishing returns (see Section 6.1). The inevitable consequences of these processes are famine, disease and destitution – natural checks on the growth of population. The population would be decimated and the processes would begin again. The economy would simply fluctuate around the subsistence level of income per worker.

> BOX 14.1: **The first female economist**
>
> Daughter of a politician and aunt of Francis Ysidro – of indifference curve (see Section 5.1) and Edgeworth box (see Section 8.3) fame – Maria Edgeworth (1767–1849) was possibly the first woman in economics. As a novelist, her interest in economics was initially shown in the writing of moral tales for children. Then in 1800 she published *Castle Rackrent*, a novel in which she dealt with the issues of rent-setting and spending, based around a family-owned estate and its tenants. She was a good friend of Ricardo, spending much time in discussion with him about the issues of the day.

14.4 Marx (1818–1883)

Amongst all the key thinkers in this chapter, and the other contributors to the development of economic thought in the previous chapter, Karl Marx was the revolutionary. Born in Germany in 1818 he went on to study philosophy at the Universities of Bonn and Berlin, before becoming the editor of a number of radical newspapers in France and Germany. After being expelled from Paris in 1848 and having his newspaper in Germany closed down by the authorities, he and his wife moved to London where he began to study the political economy literature in the Reading Room of the British Museum. This study would eventually lead to the publication of the first volume of *Das Kapital* in 1867, his major contribution to economic thought.

He was a follower of Ricardo, but one that sought to completely replace the Ricardian framework with one of his own design. Like Smith, he was interested in studying the development of modern societies and in the laws that govern such development; studying them in what can be called a hypothetical-historical way. Also like Smith, his study was driven largely by his wider philosophical beliefs. Those beliefs, though, were almost antithetical to those of

Smith. Instead of believing that human society develops harmoniously, Marx believed progress came from conflict.

His starting point was the same as Ricardo's, a belief that value and distribution were central to growth and that the key players were the workers, capitalists and landowners. His model is starkly different to that of Ricardo, though, largely because of the philosophical beliefs that guided its development. His model particularly focuses on the relationship between capitalists and workers, labour being the sole source of profit and capitalists the monopoly owners of the production processes. The monopoly power over capital that capitalists enjoy enables them to coerce workers to work for a minimal wage rate but for longer hours than they would like to work. In this way, the capitalists are able to create a surplus value that isn't paid for, which they seize for themselves as profit. This profit enables them to invest in the production process, expanding the economy as they do. However, the expansion of production causes the demand for labour to increase, in turn causing the wage rate to rise. Capitalists see their profit margins being squeezed and so employ labour-saving technology, allowing them to reduce their workforce. This fails to increase their profit margins, though, because labour is the only source of profit: they have to pay the full value for the equipment they replace labour with and so receive no surplus from its employment. The process continues – with wages rising and profits and employment falling – until the profit level hits zero, causing widespread bankruptcies. The larger capitalists purchase their smaller rivals, further intensifying the monopoly power of the production process and of employment, and the process starts again but with the initial exploitation of labour worsened by the increased disparity between the powers of capitalist and worker. With each subsequent crisis the situation becomes worse, eventually leading to the complete breakdown of capitalism. Marx said remarkably little about what capitalism would be replaced with, apart from asserting there would be a time of socialism, which is a dictatorship of the workers, and then pure communism.

Marx and his work have been treated harshly by the West. Indeed, wars have been waged on the basis of them. However, his perceptive and analytical ability are beyond doubt. His model predicts business cycles, which there are; the decline of profit margins, which is observed; and the monopolisation of production, which has also been realised. His failing was that he didn't appreciate that society would find a way of dealing with these phenomena.

14.5 Marshall (1842–1924)

Alfred Marshall was born and brought up in London. He studied mathematics at St. John's College at the University of Cambridge, where he achieved the rank of Second Wrangler in 1865: in other words, he scored the second highest first in the Mathematics tripos. Having demonstrated such an aptitude for academia, he became a professor in 1868, specialising in political economy. In 1877 he married one of his students, Mary Paley, after which they moved to Bristol where he became the first principal at what would later become the University of Bristol. After a brief spell at Balliol College at the University of Oxford, he returned to Cambridge where he subsequently established the Political Economy tripos. The library of the Economics Department there still bears his name, a fitting memorial for someone who had such a permanent impact upon the discipline, both there and across the world.

Being such an accomplished mathematician, Marshall re-founded political economy on a mathematically rigorous basis. Synthesising the developments in marginal analysis by Jevons, Menger and Walras (see Section 13.3), he published his *Principles of Economics* in 1890. It was an immediate bestseller and created a whole new paradigm in the subject, a paradigm securely based on marginal analysis and focused solely on economic investigation rather than politics and philosophy. The effect of this wasn't only a new approach to economic study, but also a restriction of the fields that were appropriate for economists to examine: economists were to focus on individual decision-making to which marginal analysis was well suited, and so phenomena such as economic growth were neglected. Political economy became economics.

Not only did Marshall reformulate existing models and approaches into a new coherent whole, he also made significant contributions to the analysis himself. He established modern demand and supply analysis (see Section 7.1), contributed the analysis of consumer and producer surplus as a measure of welfare (see Section 7.2), proposed the concept of price elasticity of demand (see Section 5.6), and established the analytical technique of focusing on and comparing different equilibrium points, although he acknowledged that ignoring the processes by which markets actually reach equilibrium was unsatisfactory. He also introduced the concept of different time periods: in his analysis there were actually four periods, but these have since been condensed into the short and long runs (see Section 6.1). He was also a part of the group of Cambridge economists who reformulated the quantity theory of money in terms of the demand for money rather than its supply, thereby devising the Cambridge equation (see Section 11.2).

There is perhaps no other economist since Smith who has single-handedly shaped the subsequent course of the discipline as much as Alfred Marshall. It's not surprising, then, that his *Principles* went through eight editions in his lifetime. He died at his home in Cambridge at the age of eighty-one.

14.6 Keynes (1883–1946)

John Maynard Keynes was born in the year Marx died, into an affluent family in Cambridge, where his father, John Neville, was an eminent professor. He demonstrated his intelligence and curiosity at a very early age – at four and a half he was concerned with the meaning of interest – which he developed further during his studies at Eton and Cambridge. His life was hugely varied: he worked as a civil servant, as a professor at Cambridge, as an advisor to the prime minister, as a foreign envoy to America with the task of securing financial aid for the devastated UK after the Second World War, as a founder of a theatre in Cambridge and as chairman of a governmental arts committee (amongst other things).

His publications and contributions to economics were abundant. Some of particular note include:

❶ His *Tract on Monetary Reform* of 1923, in which he argued that countries should actively control their currencies rather than leaving them to the Gold Standard (see Section 11.2).

❷ His *Treatise on Money* of 1930, in which he examined the business cycle by resurrecting the idea from Malthus that a lack of aggregate demand in the economy can lead to unemployment. However, he accepted there was a natural correction mechanism in the economy for this: surplus saving would depress the interest rate, which would stimulate investment expenditure (see Box 10.1).

❸ In *The General Theory of Employment, Interest and Money* of 1936, his most famous work, he effectively extended his analysis from the *Treatise on Money*. He argued that there's no natural correction mechanism for an economy in recession. Far from the economy being able to correct itself, as the classical and neoclassical economists maintained, it finds itself condemned to a depressed state, requiring active policy to correct it and to take advantage of the multiplier effect (see Section 9.1).

Keynes's contribution cannot be overstated. His ideas ushered in an age of government intervention in the economy that lasted until the 1970s. They also changed economics, establishing macroeconomics as a separate field from microeconomics, providing the stimulus needed for econometrics to develop in its own right (an ironic effect as Keynes wasn't wholly convinced of the merits of econometrics) and leading to an alternative view of, and approach to, the subject. He also questioned the ability to conduct economic study along the lines of those in the natural sciences because of the hugely significant influences of psychology, expectations and uncertainty,

I might have added that [economics] deals with motives, expectations, psychological uncertainties... It is as though the fall of the apple to the ground depended on the apple's motives on whether it is worthwhile falling to the ground, and whether the ground wanted the apple to fall, and on mistaken calculations on the part of the apple as to how far it was from the centre of the earth. (Keynes, *Collected Writings*, Vol. 14, pp. 297–300)

14.7 The Cambridge Circus

Knowing that Keynes was to publish his *Treatise on Money* in 1930 led five young economists – the oldest, Austin Robinson, was in his early thirties – at the University of Cambridge to start meeting together in order to discuss the ideas he was developing. The group, which became known as the **Cambridge Circus**, comprised Richard Kahn, Joan and Austin Robinson, Pierro Sraffa and James Meade, whose discussions about Keynes's work ran from October 1930 to March 1931, a brief but undoubtedly fruitful period of time. Kahn acted as the link between the Circus and Keynes, meeting with Keynes weekly to exchange ideas. Keynes always listened intently, exploring with Kahn how the *Treatise* could be improved. Even when the Circus officially disbanded, discussions continued between Keynes, Kahn and Joan Robinson until the publishing of *The General Theory*. There's no doubt that the discussions of the Circus helped Keynes greatly as he developed his ideas. The Circus was immeasurably more than just a discussion group: it played an active role in the Keynesian revolution.

Each member of the Circus went on to make their own individual contributions to economics, many of which were significant. It's worthwhile looking at two of them in more detail as their works are referred to in Parts 2 and 3.

Kahn (1905–1989)

Richard Ferdinand Kahn was born in London, the son of an inspector of schools. He studied for a degree at King's College at the University of Cambridge, during which he studied mathematics for one year (achieving a first in part one of the tripos), for the next two he studied physics (obtaining a second in part two of the natural sciences tripos) and then for a further year he studied economics (attaining a first in part two of that tripos): he was certainly an all-rounder. He chose to pursue the third of these subjects, becoming a fellow of the subject at King's in 1930.

Kahn's dissertation, *The Economics of the Short Period*, was a remarkable contribution to the development of imperfect competition (see Section 7.5), containing many of the elements of Joan Robinson's *The Economics of Imperfect Competition* (1933) and Edward Chamberlain's *The Theory of Monopolistic Competition* (1933). He also developed the multiplier effect (see Section 9.1) in his article *The Relation of Home Investment to Unemployment* (1931) – a fundamental component of Keynes's *General Theory* – and made other important contributions to welfare economics (see Section 7.2) and international trade (see Chapter 12).

As with most economists at the time, Kahn spent the Second World War working at Whitehall as a civil servant. After the war he returned to Cambridge – although he spent periods working at the United Nations – where he lived a quiet life. He was created a life peer in 1965 and died in Cambridge in 1989.

Robinson (1903–1983)

Joan Robinson (née Maurice) started her degree studies of economics at Girton College at the University of Cambridge in 1922 because she wanted to understand the causes of unemployment and poverty. She graduated in 1925, after which she married Austin Robinson, with whom she went to India for two years, a country where she spent a considerable amount of her life. She obtained her first academic post at the University of Cambridge in 1934, where she remained until her retirement in 1971.

Robinson didn't like Marshall, although she respected his abilities. Nor did she like the neoclassical approach to economics, arguing that there must inevitably be a trade-off between realism and model tractability (see Section 4.4). Her major contribution was with the development of monopolistic competition, published as *The Economics of Imperfect Competition* in 1933, which was the result of initial suggestions by Pierro Sraffa. However, despite its importance in the subsequent development of economic thought, she became increasingly dissatisfied that the book maintained Marshall's focus on equilibrium points rather than allowing the process by which markets reach those points to be analysed: she called this a 'shameless fudge'.

This was certainly far from her only contribution, though. She played an active role in the development of Keynes's ideas as he worked on *The General Theory*, publishing a number of articles alongside it, one of which demonstrated how the conclusions of *The General Theory* can be generalised to the long run. She became ever more convinced that the framework of Marx (see Section 14.4) was the appropriate way of examining the economy, rather than the demand and supply framework of neoclassical economics (see Section 7.1). She also contributed to the field of development economics (see Box 9.2) in which she demonstrated her continued concern about unemployment and poverty.

Throughout her life she emphasised the importance of taking into account the past histories, institutions and social characteristics of economies when analysing specific situations, and of analysing how economies move rather than simply comparing possible equilibrium states. She felt economics failed to do this, leading her towards the end of her life to become increasingly nihilistic about economic theory and even about her own work.

14.8 Hicks (1904–1989)

There was perhaps no other economist in the twentieth century who made as many highly significant contributions to such a wide array of economic fields as Sir John Hicks. His input into academic economics was truly astonishing.

Hicks was born in England in 1904 and graduated from Oxford University in 1925. His first academic position was at the London School of Economics, which he held for nine years before moving to Manchester University. After eleven years in Manchester he returned to Oxford, to Nuffield College, where he remained until his retirement in 1965.

He's best known for the creation of the IS-LM model as an interpretation of Keynes's *General Theory*, which he published as an article in the journal *Econometrica* in 1937 (see Section 9.5). In the IS-LM he synthesised his understanding of *The General Theory* into a single diagram, composed of two curves: the IS curve representing points of equilibrium in the product market, and the LM curve representing points of equilibrium in the money market. Only when the IS and LM curves intersect does the economy have a level of output and a rate of interest at which both the product and money markets clear and where the economy is in overall equilibrium. It's a remarkable model, useful for understanding equilibrium in the economy and also for analysing the effects of different policies and external shocks, and continues to be at the heart of degree courses in macroeconomics across the world.

The IS-LM model was certainly not his only significant contribution, though. Another equally important model, which he developed with Sir Roy Allen and published in 1934, was that of modern indifference curve analysis as the basis of consumer theory (see Chapter 5). There was dissatisfaction with the Marshallian theory of consumer behaviour, which had existed beforehand, because of its assumption that consumers are able to exactly quantify how much they value each consumption bundle. In the model of Hicks and Allen consumers need only be able to rank them – a change that dramatically weakened the cognitive ability assumed of consumers. Indifference curve analysis continues to be the foundation of consumer theory.

That still isn't the extent of his groundbreaking work, though. Hicks also made important contributions to the analysis of economic dynamics (how an economy changes over time), to the economics of general equilibrium and welfare, to the understanding of economic history, and to monetary economics, particularly to the issues surrounding local taxation, which he worked on with his wife. It's no wonder he was knighted in 1964 and was awarded the Nobel Prize for Economics with Kenneth Arrow (see Section 14.11) in 1972.

14.9 Friedman (1912–2006)

Starting from somewhat humble beginnings – he was born to poor Hungarian immigrants in New York City in 1912 – Milton Friedman went on to become arguably the most widely known economist in the world. He received his Ph.D. from the then hotbed of outstanding economists – Columbia University – in 1946: Kenneth Arrow was also finishing his doctoral studies there at this time. After remaining at Columbia for a time he returned to the University of Chicago, from where he had graduated with an M.A. and where he remained until his retirement in 1979. His fame came from his regular contributions to *Newsweek*, his TV documentary series *Free to Choose* and from being adviser to Presidents Nixon and Reagan.

Friedman made his academic name with his statistical doctoral thesis, *Income of Independent Professional Practice*. He followed this with a series of noteworthy papers and books, covering issues including economic methodology, the Marshallian demand curve, the marginal utility of income, a reformulation of the Keynesian consumption function in terms of lifetime rather than current income (see Box 9.3), and the effectiveness of the free market. He demonstrated a flair for not only writing groundbreaking academic pieces but also highly popular pieces on economics for the wider public.

However, it's perhaps for his work on monetary economics that he's best known. In 1956 he published *Studies in the Quantity Theory of Money*, reviving the discredited quantity theory of money and launching an attack on Keynesian economics (see Section 11.2). He argued that dramatic changes in the price level are always preceded by substantial changes in the rate of growth of the money supply. The implication of this was that governments should leave the free market to itself, linking the rate of growth of the money supply to that of real GNP (see Section 9.1). This so called **monetarism** was given further support by the publication in 1963 of his most famous work, *Monetary History of the United States, 1867-1960*, which was written in collaboration with Anna Schwartz, and led to the subsequent introduction of the **non-accelerating inflation rate of unemployment (NAIRU)**, although he referred to it as the natural rate of unemployment, which is a term that's now used for something subtly different (see Sections 11.1 and 11.4).

Friedman was made President of the American Economic Association in 1967 and was awarded the Nobel Prize for Economics in 1976. In his obituary in 2006, *The Economist* suggested he was the most influential economist in the second half of the twentieth century, perhaps even in the whole of the century.

14.10 Simon (1916–2001)

Herbert Simon was born in 1916 in Milwaukee, Minnesota. He graduated with a B.A. and a Ph.D. from the University of Chicago, where he obtained his first academic position. He subsequently held a number of roles at various institutions before becoming a professor of political science in 1947 at the Illinois Institute of Technology. In 1949 he moved to Carnegie-Mellon University, first as Professor of Administration and Psychology and then as Professor of Computing Science and Psychology.

As his posts suggest, Simon wasn't purely an economist. His interest, and the focus of much of his work, was how individuals and businesses make their decisions. His major contribution was that of **bounded rationality** and **satisficing** (see Section 5.7), which emerged from his work at Carnegie-Mellon (now the Carnegie Institute of Technology). For a number of years there he worked in collaboration with John Muth, Charles Holt and Franco Modgliani on a project looking at business decision-making. It was from this single project that the two opposing views of rational expectations and bounded rationality were devised. The former, by Muth, suggests that individuals are able to make optimal decisions with the same degree of accuracy and with the same speed as policy-makers. In the starkest of contrasts, Simon's notion of bounded rationality is that individuals simply don't possess the cognitive ability to make optimal decisions, requiring them to satisfice instead – to make decisions that are good enough – and to employ **heuristics**, or rules of thumb, to help with the decision-making process. Giving birth to two such different views eventually led to tensions amongst the economists at the Carnegie Institute of Technology (the culmination of which was Simon's relocation to the Psychology

Department) and within the economics profession as a whole. Rational expectations has been the more successful of the two theories in terms of being used for economic analysis, although economists in all sub-disciplines are now increasingly incorporating the more realistic view of human cognition into their economic models in one guise or another. Simon's work was the starting point of the rapidly expanding field of behavioural economics (see Box 5.5).

Simon also took an interest in management science – the study of decision-making in hierarchically organised institutions with multiple objectives – and in the ways that computers can be used to model decision-making in a realistic manner. His contributions are so widely spread that he can be considered to have been an economist, a psychologist and a computer scientist. He was also extremely active in research and advisory committees.

To mark his innovative and influential contributions, Simon received a whole array of awards and honorary degrees. In 1969 he received the Award for Distinguished Scientific Contributions of the American Psychological Association, in 1976 he was elected to be a Distinguished Fellow of the American Economic Association, and in 1978 he received the Nobel Prize in Economics for his lifetime's study of administrative behaviour and decision-making.

14.11 Arrow (1921–)

Born in New York City in 1921, Kenneth Arrow demonstrated an exceptionally high ability in both mathematics and economics at an early age. He graduated from City College in New York in 1940 at the age of only nineteen. He pursued his postgraduate studies at Columbia University, the result of which was a thesis that stunned the economics community. Published as *Social Choice and Individual Values*, it demonstrated, using symbolic logic (which it introduced to economics), that if all members of society are able to rank all possible states of the world in order of preference, there's no voting rule that will always ensure one of the most preferred states is chosen. This is known as **Arrow's impossibility theorem** and it has spawned a vast literature in both public choice and welfare economics, much of which has attempted unsuccessfully to refute it.

This contribution was certainly not his only one, though. After establishing himself with *Social Choice and Individual Values* he collaborated with Gerard Debreu to correct Walras's proofs of the existence of general equilibrium. Taking economics to a whole new level of technical mathematics and pioneering modern general equilibrium analysis, they demonstrated how general equilibrium models can be built up from basic preferences and that for general equilibrium to exist under conditions of perfect competition requires forward markets for all products: forward markets are those in which the payment for a product is made today for its delivery in the future. Since their first contributions, modern general equilibrium modelling has taken a central role in macroeconomics and increasingly in the analysis of the economy-wide effects of microeconomic policies. Arrow also made significant contributions to the economics of risk and uncertainty, optimal social investment, growth theory in the form of learning-by-doing models, and production.

During a truly remarkable career, Arrow held posts at Stanford and Harvard, and the presidencies of the Econometric Society and the American Economic Association. He received the American Economic Association's John Bates Clark medal for the most distinguished work by an economist under the age of forty, and then in 1972 the Nobel Prize for Economics, which he shared with Sir John Hicks.

14.12 Lucas (1937–)

Since obtaining his Ph.D. from the University of Chicago in 1964, Robert Lucas Junior – along with Thomas Sargent – has had a profound influence on economics. Neither of them came up with the notion of rational expectations, but they applied it to macroeconomic analysis, founding the school of thought known as **new classical economics** (see Section 11.4).

The idea of rational expectations is that individuals are able to make precisely the same decisions as policy-makers, that they possess all the relevant information and are able to process it in the optimal manner. Policy-makers, then, have no informational advantage over private individuals. Lucas and Sargent developed the macroeconomic implications of this idea to their logical conclusions. If individuals are characterised by rational expectations, they quickly respond to any policy the government implements. The stark implication of this is that policy has no real effects – meaning on output and employment – apart from perhaps in the very short run. Consider, for example, an aggregate demand and supply diagram (see Chapter 10). If the government attempts to increase output and reduce unemployment by expanding the money supply, thereby shifting the aggregate demand curve to the right, producers soon expect the price level to rise, making their input costs higher. They quickly take this impact into account, thereby causing the short run aggregate supply curve to quickly shift inwards. Effectively, the policy only increases the price level. This idea is represented by the vertical long run Phillips curve.

Not only has Lucas attacked the fundamental basis of Keynesian economics – that economic policy is effective at influencing real variables such as output and unemployment – he has also attacked the premise upon which applied Keynesian macroeconomic models were based. Throughout the 1960s and 1970s such models were fashionable with policy-makers, models structured around empirically observed relationships between variables, which could be used to examine the wider, knock-on effects of policies that directly influence only a single variable. Such models are, of course, essentially founded on the premise that the relationships between variables remain stable and so when a single variable is changed it's possible to ascertain the effects on related variables. In his famous **Lucas critique**, he argued this simply isn't the case and that policy changes cause the underlying relationships between variables to change as well. This led to the development of the new Keynesian school of economics, which emphasises the importance of building macroeconomic theories up from microeconomic foundations.

Lucas has held posts at Carnegie-Mellon University and at the University of Chicago, and was awarded the Nobel Prize for Economics in 1995.

14.13 Acemoğlu (1967–)

Daron Acemoğlu was born on 3 September 1967 in Istanbul, Turkey. He graduated with a B.A. from the University of York, and then with an M.Sc. in econometrics and mathematical economics and a Ph.D. in 1992 from the London School of Economics. He remained at the LSE for a year as a lecturer in economics, after which he moved to the Massachusetts Institute of Technology. He was promoted to full professor in 2000.

Since writing his exceptional doctoral thesis, entitled 'Essays in Microfoundations of Macroeconomics: Contracts and Economic Performance', he has written and published a vast number of articles and books: many of which present highly important contributions to fields including public choice (see Box 9.1), economic development (see Box 9.2) and growth and economic theory. Of particular note is his *Introduction to Modern Growth Theory* published in 2009, which is a remarkable overview of growth theory, brimming with his own valuable insights and contributions; and his recent work on the economics of technology and non-democracies. His paper in collaboration with Simon Johnson and James Robinson, 'The Colonial Origins of Comparative Development: An Empirical Investigation', published in 2001 is an excellent example of his work: an influential paper that has led to much debate (see Box 4.4).

Acemoğlu has received an array of awards, including the John Bates Clark Medal of the American Economic Association in 2005, acknowledging his work as the most outstanding work of an economist under the age of forty. Considering that previous winners of the medal include Milton Friedman, Kenneth Arrow and Sir John Hicks, it's clear his status is likely to become ever greater.

14.14 Saez (1972–)

Another recent winner of the John Bates Clark Medal is Professor Emmanuel Saez from Berkeley, University of California. Saez was born in France in 1972, where he graduated with a B.A. in mathematics and an M.A. in economics in 1996. He studied for his Ph.D. at the Massachusetts Institute of Technology, which he was awarded in 1999. He began teaching at Berkeley in 2002, where he's now a professor.

He has made particularly important contributions to the fields of tax policy, specifically to the understanding of the personal and corporate behavioural responses to taxation and the links between consumer behaviour and retirement savings, and the distribution of income and wealth in the United States and other countries.

Saez is the editor for the *Journal of Public Economics* and the co-director of the public policy programme at the London-based Centre for Economic and

Policy Research. In addition to the American Economic Association medal, he has received numerous other awards and honours, including being nominated for the Best Young French Economist Prize in 2006 and being included in the 1999 *Review of Economic Studies* tour of the leading four graduating Ph.D. students in the world. As with the earlier recipients of the John Bates Clark Medal, Saez is on course to achieving still greater accolades during his career.

where else to look

Chapter 15 presents a range of resources you might find helpful in your study of economics. I think they're all useful but I have rated them according to a number of criteria to help you select those most suited to you.

5

15 recommended resources

15.1 books

Title	Author(s)	Introductory coverage	Ease of reading	Level of maths	A must read?
Study Guides					
❯ The Study Skills Handbook	S. Cottrell	Excellent	Easy	None	Yes
❯ Critical Thinking Skills: Developing Effective Analysis and Argument	S. Cottrell	Excellent	Easy	None	
❯ How to Write Better Essays	B. Greetham	Excellent	Easy	None	
❯ The Exam Skills Handbook	S. Cottrell	Excellent	Easy	None	Yes
❯ Write it Right: a Handbook for Students	M. Coyle & J. Peck	Excellent	Easy	None	
❯ Cite Them Right: the Essential Referencing Guide	R. Pears & G. Shields	Excellent	Easy	None	
❯ Economical Writing	D. McCloskey	Excellent	Easy	None	Yes
General Economics					
❯ Economics: a Very Short Introduction	P. Dasgupta	Brief	Easy	Light	Yes
❯ Economics	D. Begg, S. Fischer & R. Dornbusch	Good	Easy	Light	
❯ Economics	R. Lipsey & A. Chrystal	Good	Easy	Light	
❯ Economics	J. Sloman	Good	Easy	Light	
❯ Economics	N. G. Mankiw & M. Taylor	Excellent	Easy	Light	
❯ Applied Economics	A. Griffiths & S. Wall	Excellent	Easy	Light	

Title	Author(s)	Introductory coverage	Ease of reading	Level of maths	A must read?
Microeconomics					
❭ Intermediate Microeconomics: a Modern Approach	H. Varian	Excellent	Moderate	Moderate	Yes
❭ Transport Economics: Theory, Application and Policy	G. Mallard & S. Glaister	Selective	Easy	Light	
Macroeconomics					
❭ Macroeconomics	N. G. Mankiw	Excellent	Easy	Moderate	Yes
❭ Macroeconomics	O. Blanchard	Excellent	Moderate	Heavy	
❭ Macroeconomics	R. J. Gordon	Excellent	Moderate	Light	
Maths for economics					
❭ Fundamental Methods of Mathematical Economics	A. C. Chiang & K. Wainwright	Excellent	Difficult	Heavy	
❭ Mathematics for Economists: an Introductory Textbook	M. Pemberton & N. Rau	Excellent	Moderate	Heavy	
❭ Essential Mathematics for Economics and Business	T. Bradley & P. Patton	Excellent	Easy	Moderate	Yes
Statistics for economics					
❭ Basic Statistics for Business and Economics	D. A. Lind, W. G. Marchal & S. Wathen	Excellent	Easy	Moderate	
Selected economic schools of thought					
❭ An Introduction to Behavioral Economics	N. Wilkinson	Excellent	Easy	Light	
❭ An Introduction to Post-Keynesian Economics	M. Lavoie	Excellent	Easy	Light	
❭ Institutional Economics: an Introduction	J. Groenewegen, A. Spithoven & A. Van den Berg	Excellent	Easy	Light	
Selected fields of application					
❭ Game Theory: a Very Short Introduction	K. Binmore	Excellent	Easy	Light	
❭ Introduction to Industrial Organization	L.M.B. Cabral	Excellent	Moderate	Moderate	
❭ The Unemployment Crisis	R. Layard, S. Nickell & R. Jackman	Excellent	Moderate	Moderate	

Title	Author(s)	Introductory coverage	Ease of reading	Level of maths	A must read?
❯ Introduction to Economic Growth	C. I. Jones	Excellent	Moderate	Moderate	
❯ Happiness: Lessons from a New Science	R. Layard	Excellent	Easy	Light	
History of economic thought					
❯ The Worldly Philosophers: the Lives, Times and Ideas of the Great Economic Thinkers	R. Heilbroner	Selective	Easy	None	Yes
❯ A History of Economics: the Past as the Present	J. K. Galbraith	Excellent	Easy	None	
❯ The Evolution of Economic Ideas	P. Deane	Excellent	Difficult	None	
❯ Great Economists Before Keynes: an Introduction to the Lives and Works of One Hundred Great Economists of the Past	M. Blaug	Excellent	Easy	None	
❯ Great Economists After Keynes: an Introduction to the Lives and Works of One Hundred Modern Economists	M. Blaug	Excellent	Easy	None	
Methodology					
❯ Economic Methodology: Understanding Economics as a Science	M. Boumans & J. B. Davis	Excellent	Difficult	None	

15.2 useful websites

Website	Use
❯**The Institute for New Economic Thinking**: http://ineteconomics.org/	Videos of eminent economists discussing various interesting issues
❯ **The Library of Economics and Liberty:** http://www.econlib.org/	A range of learning resources, including articles, books, guides and podcasts
❯ **Studying Economics:** http:// studyingeconomics.ac.uk/	A guide for studying economics, including study tips and overviews of further module options
❯ **Tutor 2u:** http://tutor2u.net/blog/index.php/ economics/	A range of introductory resources for economics

15.3 interesting journal articles

Listed below are a number of journal articles that you might find interesting. They are all taken from the *Journal of Economic Perspectives* – a journal that publishes articles that are usually of a more general-interest nature – and each presents an excellent discussion of a topic mentioned in this book in a non-mathematical and moderately easy-to-read way. You should be able to access them through your university.

Title	Author(s)	Year, volume, number & pages	Topic
〉Retrospectives: on the definition of economics	R. E. Backhouse & S. G. Medena	2009, volume 23, number 1, pp. 221-231	What is economics? (Chapter 1)
〉The American family and family economics	S. Lundberg & R. A. Pollak	2007, volume 21, number 2, pp. 3-26	Family economics as a field of application (Section 1.4)
〉The purchasing power parity debate	A. M. Taylor & M. P. Taylor	2004, volume 18, number 4, pp. 135-158	Purchasing power parity (Sections 9.2 & 12.5)
〉Some uses of happiness data in economics	R. Di Tella & R. MacCulloch	2006, volume 20, number 1, pp. 25-46	Happiness as a field of application (Section 1.4)
〉The consumer price index: conceptual issues and practical suggestions	C. L. Schultze	2003, volume 17, number 1, pp. 3-22	Measuring inflation (Section 11.3)
〉Evolutionary theorizing in economics	R. R. Nelson & S. G. Winter	2002, volume 16, number 2, pp. 23-46	Evolutionary economics as an economic school of thought (Section 1.4)
〉Institutional economics: then and now	M. Rutherford	2001, volume 15, number 3, pp. 173-194	Institutional economics as an economic school of thought (Section 1.4)
〉Feminism and economics	J. A. Nelson	1995, volume 9, number 2, pp. 131-148	Feminist economics as an economic school of thought (Section 1.4)

index

Acemoğlu, D. 265
advantage
    absolute 230–1
    comparative 230–1, 239, 245
analysis:
    diagrammatical 37–43, 54
    mathematical 37, 40–9, 54
anti–competitive behaviour 122, 135
Arrow, K. 250, 261, 263–4
asymmetric information 133, 150
average propensity 155, 168–9

balance of payments 35
barriers to entry/exit 118, 121–2, 124,
    127, 129
barter 210
basic economic problem 3, 6
behavioural economics 6, 9–10, 14–15,
    84–5, 143, 263, 265
Big Mac index 237–9
black economy 165
booms 198
bounded rationality 83, 262–3
brand loyalty 121
Bretton Woods financial system 212
budget
    balanced 170
    constraint 64–73, 85, 142
    deficit 170
    surplus 170, 173
business cycle 9, 35, 197–9, 256, 258
busts 198

Cambridge
    Circus 176, 258–60
    equation 215, 257

capital
    in the classical model of output
        determination 171–4
    in the sticky wage model 191
    defined 3
    investment 166
    symbol 35
central planning 5
circular flow of income and expenditure
    153–9, 171, 180, 213, 232
classical
    dichotomy 187, 214–15, 245
    economics 165–75, 243–6, 251, 258
    model of output determination 165–75,
        186, 190, 201
command and control policy 140–2,
    148, 204
Common Agricultural Policy 142
comparative statics 9, 14–16, 247, 251,
    257, 260
competition policy 123, 135–6
complementary goods 75, 80, 83
computable economics 10, 15, 242
constant returns to scale 229
constrained optimisation 69–71
consumer
    price index 216
    surplus 42–43, 112–15, 117–42, 257
    theory 25, 37–40, 55–86, 108–50,
        246, 261
consumption
    and aggregate demand 190
    and inflation 215–18
    and the size of the economy 154–19,
        165–74, 177–86,
    bundle 58–66, 73, 80, 85

function 166–9, 261
symbol 35
cost
average 4, 88–94, 97–100, 117–30
fixed 88–91, 99
marginal 89, 93–101, 106–7, 111–12, 117–30
menu 217
semi-variable (or semi-fixed) 88–9
shoe-leather 217
total 89, 97
variable 88–91, 99–100, 104, 125
crowding-out 174, 186, 236
currency 180, 212, 232–9, 258

dead-weight welfare loss 42, 123, 128, 130, 137
deductive methodology 10–11, 14–16, 37–40, 245–6, 251, 254
deflation 187, 216, 223
deindustrialisation 207
demand
and average revenue 95, 97
and market structure 108–32
and merit and demerit goods 136–42
aggregate 25, 187–205, 216, 219–28, 248–9, 258, 264
consumer theory 40–7, 57–86, 246, 260
foreign exchange 233–7
labour 201–5, 208–9
the law of demand 71, 141
demerit goods 133, 136–42, 149
depreciation 35
deregulation 134–6
development 9, 26–9, 149, 163–4, 260, 265
differentiation 63–4, 89, 94–6, 167–9
diminishing marginal returns 90, 200, 229
diminishing marginal utility 60, 62, 144
diseconomies of scale 93

econometrics 11, 15, 23, 29, 49–51, 52–3
economic bad 63
economies of scale 92–93, 121
Edgeworth, M. 255
efficiency
allocative 4–5, 120–33

productive 4–5, 91–2, 120–33, 200
Pareto 5, 121–33, 146–9
efficient market hypothesis 227
elasticity
cross-price elasticity of demand 77–80, 86
income elasticity of demand 77–9, 86
own-price elasticity of demand 41–7, 77–9, 86, 125–6, 139–40, 246, 257
own-price elasticity of supply 101–3, 107, 129
employment opportunities 17–23
Engel curve 69, 79, 86
entrepreneurship 3, 98, 101
environmental economics 6, 9, 22, 26–8, 148–9, 162, 250
equation of exchange 213–14
exchange rate 229–31
real 35, 234–9
nominal 232–9
expectations 25, 190–97, 217–18, 222–7, 258
adaptive 225–7
rational 225–7, 250–1, 262–4
expenditure
and aggregate demand 187–90, 194–6
the classical model of output determination 165–74
the Keynesian model of output determination 177–9, 184–6
exports 35, 154–9, 166, 190, 232–9
externality 8, 133, 143–50
evaluation 18, 30, 35, 51–4
evolutionary economics 10, 15

factors of production 3, 154, 172, 190, 200–2; see also land, labour, capital and entrepreneurship
fallacy of composition 187
feminist economics 10, 14
fiscal policy 34–5, 156–9, 172–4, 186, 193, 198, 249
Fisher, I. 213–14
Fisher
effect 216
equation 216

free market 5, 12
Friedman, M. 168, 222, 250, 261–2

game theory 9, 149
general equilibrium 250, 261, 263
Giffen good 74
Gini coefficient 162
Gold Standard 212, 258
growth 9, 156, 163–4, 197–8, 214–15,
    245, 265
  maximisation 105
gross domestic product (GDP) 35,
    156–65, 186, 197
gross national product (GNP) 35, 157, 262
government spending 34–5, 154–60,
    170–9, 185–6, 190–196, 236

heuristics 82–4, 262
Hicks, Sir John 59, 72, 175–6, 249, 260–1
hidden economy 164
history of economic thought 26, 241–66
Hotelling model 130–2

immobility
  geographical 207
  occupational 207
imports 35, 154–9, 190, 232–9
income
  and the consumption function 166–9
  and demand 68–9, 75, 86
  and development 50–1
  effect 71–4, 86, 140
  elasticity of demand 79
  inequality 161–2
  natural level 190–9, 201–6, 219–21, 225
  offer curve 69
  symbol 35
  the circular flow 153–9
indifference curves 58–63, 66–9, 72, 85,
    146–8, 261
inductive methodology 245–6
inferior good 74, 79
inflation
  and demand 66
  and development 164
  and the money supply 213–15

and unemployment 222–8, 249
  causes 219–22, 228, 250
  costs 216–19
  defined 216
  hyperinflation 219
  symbol 34–5
inflationary gap 193, 221–6
institutional economics 10
integration 114–17
interest rate
  and inflation 216–18
  and exchange rates 233–6, 239
  determination 170–89, 194–7, 258
  effects 170–89, 194–7
  ex ante 218
  ex post 218
  nominal 170, 216–18
  real 170, 216–18
  symbol 34–5
international trade 9, 35, 156–9, 229–39,
    244–5, 259
investment
  and aggregate demand 187–90, 194–6
  and the circular flow of income 154, 156
  in the classical model of output
    determination 166–74
  in the Keynesian model of output
    determination 177–86, 194–6, 258
  international 233–6, 239
IS–LM 175–86, 188–99, 249, 260; *see also*
    Keynesian model of output determi-
    nation

Kahn, R. 176, 249, 258–9
Keynes, J.M. 5, 167, 175–6, 187, 213–16,
    246–9, 257–8
Keynesian
  cross 176–9, 184–6, 189
  model of output determination 175–87
  Revolution 175–6, 248–9, 259–60
kinked demand curve 129–30

labour
  and aggregate demand and supply 193–5
  and unemployment 201–9
  defined 3

economics 209, 250
in the classical model of output determination 171–4
in the sticky wage model 190–3
symbol 35
land 3, 87, 90, 98, 101, 209
licences *see* patents
life cycle hypothesis 168
liquidity preference 180–6, 189
long run
defined 87–8
Lorenz curve 161–2
Lucas, R. 225, 250, 264

Malthus, T. 6, 245, 254–5, 258
managerial utility maximisation 105
marginal
benefit 144–6
propensity 154–9, 166–9
rate of substitution 62, 66, 85
market
defined 108
failure 13, 32, 133–50
structure 8, 25, 108–32
power 133–6, 149, 244, 256
welfare *see* consumer and producer surplus
Marshall, A. 68, 215, 242–9, 256–7, 260
Marx, K. 213, 247, 255–6, 260
mathematical symbols 48–9
medieval scholars 244
mental accounting 84
mercantilism 244
merit goods 133, 136–42, 149
Mill, J.S. 245–6
minimum efficient scale 91
money
as economics 8–9
banking and finance 227, 250
classical theory 213, 245, 248
commodity theory 213
definition 210
demand 180–6, 188–9, 215, 248
functions 227–8
history 210–12
neutrality 213–17, 245, 248

quantity theory 214–17, 222, 228, 248, 250, 257, 261
supply 179–86, 213–17, 220–2, 227–8, 262–4
nominal 180–6, 188, 197
real 180–6, 188, 194, 197
monetarism 250, 262
monetary
accommodation 220–1, 228
policy 22, 34–5, 185–6, 194–5, 227, 245, 249
validation 221–2, 228
monopolistic competition 108, 126–8, 132–6, 248, 260
monopoly 17, 108, 121–6, 132–6, 248
natural 135–6
multiplier effect 158–9, 249, 258–9

nationalisation 136
net national product (NNP) 35, 157
neoclassical economics
defined 8–10, 14–16
history 246–51, 258, 260
theory of money 213–15
new classical economics 10, 225–7, 250, 264
new Keynesian economics 10, 250, 264
normal good 74, 79
normative economics 6–7, 142–3, 160
note-taking *see* reading

oligopoly 108, 128–34
open market operations 213
output
determination 25, 165–86
maximisation 105; *see also* classical and Keynesian models

paradigm 8, 243–51
patents 121
perfect competition 108, 117–33, 146, 247, 263
permanent income hypothesis 168–9
Phillips curve 153, 176, 222–8, 264
Phillips, W. 222, 249
physiocrats 244, 252
Pigou, A. 215, 248

political economics *see* public choice
positive economics 6–7, 142–3, 160
post-Keynesian economics 5, 9–10, 242
preference ordering 58–61, 80–4, 146
price
    ceiling *see* command and control policy
    determination 40–9, 108–32, 181
    discrimination 124–6, 132
    floor *see* command and control policy
    offer curve 67
    war 129
privatisation 134
producer
    surplus 42–3, 112–17, 121–42, 257
    theory 25, 38–40, 55–6, 87–150, 246
production
    function 171–4, 187, 190, 201, 215
    possibility frontier 200
profit
    abnormal 96–8, 119, 121–7, 136
    marginal 97, 102
    maximisation 104–7, 119, 124–6,
        129, 246
    maximising condition 97
    normal 96–8, 101, 128, 136
    operating 113
    subnormal 98
public
    choice 8–9, 14, 159–60, 170, 199,
        250, 265
    economics 26, 142–3, 250
    good 133, 149–50
purchasing power parity 165, 236–9

reading 30–7, 54
recessionary gap 195, 204, 220–5
regulation 136
reservation ratio 212
reserve earnings 117
resources 267–72
retail price index 216
revenue
    average 94–8, 100, 105, 107, 117–30
    marginal 94–8, 106–7, 117–30, 145–6
    maximisation 104–105
    total 94–7

Ricardo, D. 213, 229–31, 239, 245–6, 253–6
Robinson, J. 126, 176, 247–8, 258–60

Saez, E. 265–6
Samuelson, P. 176–7, 222, 249
satisficing 83, 262
saving 35, 154–9, 163, 179, 217
    national 173–4
    private 173
    public 173
seigniorage 219
short run
    defined 87–88
shut-down point 100
Simon, H. 83, 105–6, 262–3
skill atrophy 208
Smith, A. 231, 244–5, 252, 255
specialisation 230–1, 239, 253
stabilisers 197–8
standard of living 160–4, 186
Solow, R. 222
subsidisation 35, 78, 83, 136–43
substitute goods 75, 79–80, 83
substitution effect 71–4, 86, 140
supply
    and market failure 136–42
    and market structure 108–32
    aggregate 25, 187–205, 219–28, 264
    foreign exchange 233–7
    labour 201–5, 208–9
    producer theory 40–7, 98–104, 107,
        246, 260
    side policy 209

Tarshis, L. 175–6
taxation
    and elasticity 78
    and market failure 40–7, 138–43
    and output determination 170–3, 177–8
    and the circular flow of income 154–9
    and the consumption function 166
    symbol 34–5
technological progress 172, 215
terms of trade 234
time lags 198
trade balance 231, 234–6, 239

trade unions 203–4, 209
transferable skills 17–23,
treasury view 174, 186

underground economy 164
unemployment
    and business cycles 197–8
    and development 163
    and inflation 222–8
    classical view 201–5, 208, 228
    frictional 205–7, 225
    hysteresis 207–9, 228
    involuntary 201–8, 228
    Keynesian view 201, 228, 248, 258
    NAIRU 224–6, 262
    natural rate 205–9, 228, 262
    structural 207–8
    symbol 35
    voluntary 201–2, 205
utility
    defined 4–5

maximisation 57–85, 147, 246; *see also*
    welfare and consumer and pro-
    ducer surplus

value judgements 7
variables
    endogenous 11
    exogenous 10–11
Veblen good 74

wage
    efficiency 203–4
    minimum 17, 204, 209
    nominal 191–5, 201–5, 208, 220, 248
    real 191, 195
    sticky 191–3, 199, 203–4, 208–9
welfare 13, 112–30, 133–50, 159–60,
    163–4, 252; *see also* utility

X–inefficiency 105–6